PRAXIS

CORE ACADEMIC SKILLS
FOR EDUCATORS
5712, 5722, 5732

By: Sharon A. Wynne, M.S.

XAMonline, INC.
Boston

To obtain permission(s) to use the material from this work for any purpose including workshops or seminars, please submit a written request to:

XAMonline, Inc.
21 Orient Avenue
Melrose, MA 02176
Toll Free 1-800-301-4647
Email: info@xamonline.com
Web: www.xamonline.com
Fax: 1-617-583-5552

Library of Congress Cataloging-in-Publication Data

Wynne, Sharon A.
    PRAXIS Core Academic Skills for Educators 5712, 5722, 5732 / Sharon A. Wynne.
    ISBN 978-1-60787-458-4
    1. Core Academic Skills for Educators 5712, 5722, 5732
    2. Study Guides
    3. PRAXIS
    4. Teachers' Certification & Licensure
    5. Careers

Disclaimer:

The opinions expressed in this publication are the sole works of XAMonline and were created independently from the National Education Association, Educational Testing Service, or any State Department of Education, National Evaluation Systems or other testing affiliates.

Between the time of publication and printing, state specific standards as well as testing formats and Web site information may change and therefore would not be included in part or in whole within this product. Sample test questions are developed by XAMonline and reflect content similar to that on real tests; however, they are not former test questions. XAMonline assembles content that aligns with state standards but makes no claims nor guarantees teacher candidates a passing score. Numerical scores are determined by testing companies such as NES or ETS and then are compared with individual state standards. A passing score varies from state to state.

Printed in the United States of America   œ-1

PRAXIS Core Academic Skills for Educators 5712, 5722, 5732
ISBN: 978-1-60787-458-4

Table of Contents

DOMAIN I
READING 1

COMPETENCY 1
KEY IDEAS AND DETAILS 3

Skill 1.1: Draw inferences from and understand implications of the directly stated content of a reading selection 3

Skill 1.2: Identify summaries or paraphrases of the main idea or primary purpose of a reading selection.....................................5

Skill 1.3: Identify summaries or paraphrases of supporting ideas...6

Skill 1.4: Identify how and why ideas, people, occurrences, and details interact within and inform a text.....................................7

COMPETENCY 2
CRAFT, STRUCTURE, AND LANGUAGE SKILLS.. 10

Skill 2.1: Determine the author's attitude toward material in a reading selection through word choices that reflect meaning and tone 10

Skill 2.2: Identify the key transition words and phrases and how they are used to denote meaning 11

Skill 2.3: Identify how a reading selection is organized in terms of cause/effect, compare/contrast, problem/solution, etc. 13

Skill 2.4: Assess how point of view or purpose shapes the content and style of a text 13

Skill 2.5: Determine the role than an idea, reference, or piece of information plays in an author's discussion or argument 13

Skill 2.6: Determine whether an idea, reference, or piece of information in an author's discussion or argument is valid or relevant.... 13

Skill 2.7: Identify the meanings of words as they are used in the context of a reading selection... 14

Skill 2.8: Determine the meaning of unknown and multiple-meaning words and phrases by using context clues........................... 15

Skill 2.9: Understand figurative language and nuances in word meanings.. 19

Skill 2.10: Understand a range of words and phrases sufficient for reading at the college and career readiness level 21

COMPETENCY 3
INTEGRATION OF KNOWLEDGE AND IDEAS 22

Skill 3.1: Analyze content presented in diverse media and formats, including visually and quantitatively, as well as in words 22

Skill 3.2: Identify and evaluate the argument and specific claims in a text, including the validity of reasoning as well as the relevance and sufficiency of the evidence 23

Skill 3.3: Determine whether evidence strengthens, weakens, or is relevant to the arguments in a reading selection 26

Skill 3.4: Determine the logical assumptions upon which an argument or conclusion is based 26

Skill 3.5: Draw conclusions from material presented in a reading selection 26

Skill 3.6: Analyze how two or more texts address similar themes or topics in order to build knowledge and/or compare approaches the authors take 27

SAMPLE TEST

READING 32

Answer Key 56

DOMAIN II
WRITING 57

COMPETENCY 4
TEXT TYPES, PURPOSES AND PRODUCTION 59

Skill 4.1: Producing an Argumentative Essay 59

Skill 4.2: Producing Informative or Explanatory Texts 64

Skill 4.3: The Revision and Editing Process in Text Production 69

Skill 4.4: Apply Knowledge of Language and its Functions to Enhance Meaning and Style when Revising 72

Skill 4.5: Revising to Maintain Consistency in Style and Tone 73

COMPETENCY 5
LANGUAGE SKILLS FOR WRITING GRAMMATICAL RELATIONSHIPS 75

Skill 5.1: Identify errors in the use of adjectives and adverbs 75

Skill 5.2: Identify errors in noun-noun agreement 81

Skill 5.3: Identify errors in pronoun-antecedent agreement 84

Skill 5.4: Identify errors in pronoun case 88

Skill 5.5: Identify errors in the use of intensive pronouns 89

Skill 5.6: Identify errors in pronoun number and person 89

Skill 5.7: Identify errors in the use of vague pronouns 89

Skill 5.8: Recognize and correct errors in subject-verb agreement 90

Skill 5.9: Recognize and correct inappropriate shifts in verb tense 95

COMPETENCY 6
LANGUAGE AND RESEARCH SKILLS FOR WRITING: STRUCTURAL RELATIONSHIPS 96

Skill 6.1: Identify errors in the placement of phrases and clauses 96

Skill 6.2: Identify errors of misplaced and dangling modifiers 98

Skill 6.3: Identify errors in the use of coordinating and subordinating conjunctions 102

Skill 6.4: Recognize and correct sentence fragments and run-on sentences..107

Skill 6.5: Identify errors in the use of correlative conjunctions 114

Skill 6.6: Identify errors in parallel structure 114

COMPETENCY 7
LANGUAGE SKILLS FOR WRITING: WORD CHOICE.. 119

Skill 7.1: Identify errors in the use of idiomatic expressions 119

Skill 7.2: Identify errors in the use of frequently confused words..122

Skill 7.3: Identify wrong word use 129

Skill 7.4: Recognize and correct errors in redundancy 137

COMPETENCY 8
LANGUAGE SKILLS FOR WRITING: CAPITALIZATION AND PUNCTUATION 138

Skill 8.1: Identify errors in capitalization 138

Skill 8.2: Identify errors in punctuation 139

COMPETENCY 9
RESEARCH SKILLS 147

Skill 9.1: Assess the credibility and relevance of sources 147

Skill 9.2: Recognize the different elements of a citation 149

Skill 9.3: Recognize effective research strategies 149

Skill 9.4: Recognize information relevant to a particular research task 150

SAMPLE TEST
WRITING 151

Answer Key 171

DOMAIN III
MATHEMATICS 175

COMPETENCY 10
NUMBER AND QUANTITY 179

Skill 10.1: Understand ratio concepts and use ratio reasoning to solve problems................................179

Skill 10.2: Analyze proportional relationships and use them to solve real-world and mathematical problems 180

Skill 10.3: Apply understanding of multiplication and division to divide fractions by fractions..................183

Skill 10.4: Compute fluently with multi-digit numbers and find common factors and multiples 184

Skill 10.5: Apply understanding of operations with fractions to add, subtract, multiply, and divide rational number 191

Skill 10.6: Know that there are numbers that are not rational, and approximate them by rational numbers 196

Skill 10.7: Work with radicals and integer exponents 197

Skill 10.8: Reason quantitatively and use units to solve problem 198

COMPETENCY 11
ALGEBRA AND FUNCTIONS 201

Skill 11.1: Apply understanding of arithmetic to algebraic expressions 201

Skill 11.2: Solve real-life and mathematical problems using numerical and algebraic expressions 201

Skill 11.3: Use properties of operations to generate equivalent expressions..202

Skill 11.4: Understand the connections between proportional relationships, lines, and linear equations....................................205

Skill 11.5: Understand solving equations as a process of reasoning and explain the reasoning 207

Skill 11.6: Reason about and solve one-variable equations and inequalities 207

Skill 11.7: Solve equations and inequalities in one variable 208

Skill 11.8: Analyze and solve linear equations and pairs of simultaneous linear equations 210

Skill 11.9: Represent and solve equations and inequalities graphically 212

Skill 11.10: Interpreting functions 215

Skill 11.11: Building functions...216

COMPETENCY 12
GEOMETRY.. 219

Skill 12.1: Draw, construct, and describe geometrical figures and describe the relationships between them 219

Skill 12.2: Experiment with transformations in the plane 234

Skill 12.3: Understand and apply the Pythagorean theorem 236

Skill 12.4: Understand and apply theorems about circles..237

Skill 12.5: Solve real-life and mathematical problems involving angle measure, area, surface area, and volume 237

Skill 12.6: Explain volume formulas and use them to solve problems 238

Skill 12.7: Apply geometric concepts in modeling situations..239

COMPETENCY 13
STATISTICS AND PROBABILITY 240

Skill 13.1: Develop understanding of statistical variability 240

Skill 13.2: Summarize and describe distributions..240

Skill 13.3: Use random sampling to draw inferences about a population 245

Skill 13.4: Investigate chance processes and develop, use, and evaluate probability models 246

Skill 13.5: Investigate patterns of association in bivariate data 250

Skill 13.6: Summarize, represent, and interpret data on a single count or measurement variable 254

Skill 13.7: Interpret linear models 258

Skill 13.8: Understand and evaluate random processes underlying statistical experiments 258

Skill 13.9: Use probability to evaluate outcomes of decisions 259

SAMPLE TEST

MATHEMATICS 260

Answer Key 269

PRAXIS

CORE ACADEMIC SKILLS FOR EDUCATORS
5712, 5722, 5732

X

SECTION 1

ABOUT XAMONLINE

XAMonline—A Specialty Teacher Certification Company

Created in 1996, XAMonline was the first company to publish study guides for state-specific teacher certification examinations. Founder Sharon Wynne found it frustrating that materials were not available for teacher certification preparation and decided to create the first single, state-specific guide. XAMonline has grown into a company of over 1,800 contributors and writers and offers over 300 titles for the entire PRAXIS series and every state examination. No matter what state you plan on teaching in, XAMonline has a unique teacher certification study guide just for you.

XAMonline—Value and Innovation

We are committed to providing value and innovation. Our print-on-demand technology allows us to be the first in the market to reflect changes in test standards and user feedback as they occur. Our guides are written by experienced teachers who are experts in their fields. And our content reflects the highest standards of quality. Comprehensive practice tests with varied levels of rigor means that your study experience will closely match the actual in-test experience.

To date, XAMonline has helped nearly 600,000 teachers pass their certification or licensing exams. Our commitment to preparation exceeds simply providing the proper material for study—it extends to helping teachers **gain mastery** of the subject matter, giving them the **tools** to become the most effective classroom leaders possible, and ushering today's students toward a **successful future**.

SECTION 2

ABOUT THIS STUDY GUIDE

Purpose of This Guide

Is there a little voice inside of you saying, "Am I ready?" Our goal is to replace that little voice and remove all doubt with a new voice that says, "I AM READY. **Bring it on!**" by offering the highest quality of teacher certification study guides.

Organization of Content

You will see that while every test may start with overlapping general topics, each is very unique in the skills they wish to test. Only XAMonline presents custom content that analyzes deeper than a title, a subarea, or an objective. Only XAMonline presents content and sample test assessments along with **focus statements**, the deepest-level rationale and interpretation of the skills that are unique to the exam.

Title and field number of test

→Each exam has its own name and number. XAMonline's guides are written to give you the content you need to know for the specific exam you are taking. You can be confident when you buy our guide that it contains the information you need to study for the specific test you are taking.

Subareas

→These are the major content categories found on the exam. XAMonline's guides are written to cover all of the subareas found in the test frameworks developed for the exam.

Objectives

→These are standards that are unique to the exam and represent the main subcategories of the subareas/content categories. XAMonline's guides are written to address every specific objective required to pass the exam.

Focus statements

→These are examples and interpretations of the objectives. You find them in parenthesis directly following the objective. They provide detailed examples of the range, type, and level of content that appear on the test questions. **Only XAMonline's guides drill down to this level.**

How Do We Compare with Our Competitors?

XAMonline—drills down to the focus statement level.
CliffsNotes and REA—organized at the objective level
Kaplan—provides only links to content
MoMedia—content not specific to the state test

Each subarea is divided into manageable sections that cover the specific skill areas. Explanations are easy to understand and thorough. You'll find that every test answer contains a rejoinder so if you need a refresher or further review after taking the test, you'll know exactly to which section you must return.

How to Use This Book

Our informal polls show that most people begin studying up to eight weeks prior to the test date, so start early. Then ask yourself some questions: How much do you really know? Are you coming to the test straight from your teacher-education program or are you having to review subjects you haven't considered in ten years? Either way, take a **diagnostic or assessment test** first. Also, spend time on sample tests so that you become accustomed to the way the actual test will appear.

This guide comes with an online diagnostic test of 30 questions found online at *www.XAMonline.com*. It is a little boot camp to get you up for the task and reveal things about your compendium of knowledge in general. Although this guide is structured to follow the order of the test, you are not required to study in that order. By finding a time-management and study plan that fits your life you will be more effective. The results of your diagnostic or self-assessment test can be a guide for how to manage your time and point you toward an area that needs more attention.

After taking the diagnostic exam, fill out the **Personalized Study Plan** page at the beginning of each chapter. Review the competencies and skills covered in that chapter and check the boxes that apply to your study needs. If there are sections you already know you can skip, check the "skip it" box. Taking this step will give you a study plan for each chapter.

Week	Activity
8 weeks prior to test	Take a diagnostic test found at www.XAMonline.com
7 weeks prior to test	Build your Personalized Study Plan for each chapter. Check the "skip it" box for sections you feel you are already strong in. ✗ SKIP IT ☐
6-3 weeks prior to test	For each of these four weeks, choose a content area to study. You don't have to go in the order of the book. It may be that you start with the content that needs the most review. Alternately, you may want to ease yourself into plan by starting with the most familiar material.
2 weeks prior to test	Take the sample test, score it, and create a review plan for the final week before the test.
1 week prior to test	Following your plan (which will likely be aligned with the areas that need the most review) go back and study the sections that align with the questions you may have gotten wrong. Then go back and study the sections related to the questions you answered correctly. If need be, create flashcards and drill yourself on any area that makes you anxious.

SECTION 3
ABOUT THE PRAXIS EXAMS

What Is PRAXIS?

PRAXIS II tests measure the knowledge of specific content areas in K-12 education. The test is a way of insuring that educators are prepared to not only teach in a particular subject area, but also have the necessary teaching skills to be effective. The Educational Testing Service administers the test in most states and has worked with the states to develop the material so that it is appropriate for state standards.

PRAXIS Points

1. The PRAXIS Series comprises more than 140 different tests in over seventy different subject areas.

2. Over 90% of the PRAXIS tests measure subject area knowledge.

3. The purpose of the test is to measure whether the teacher candidate possesses a sufficient level of knowledge and skills to perform job duties effectively and responsibly.

4. Your state sets the acceptable passing score.

5. Any candidate, whether from a traditional teaching-preparation path or an alternative route, can seek to enter the teaching profession by taking a PRAXIS test.

6. PRAXIS tests are updated regularly to ensure current content.

Often **your own state's requirements** determine whether or not you should take any particular test. The most reliable source of information regarding this is either your state's Department of Education or the Educational Testing Service. Either resource should also have a complete list of testing centers and dates. Test dates vary by subject area and not all test dates necessarily include your particular test, so be sure to check carefully.

If you are in a teacher-education program, check with the Education Department or the Certification Officer for specific information for testing and testing timelines. The Certification Office should have most of the information you need.

If you choose an alternative route to certification you can either rely on our Web site at *www.XAMonline.com* or on the resources provided by an alternative certification program. Many states now have specific agencies devoted to alternative certification and there are some national organizations as well:

National Center for Education Information
http://www.ncei.com/Alt-Teacher-Cert.htm

National Associate for Alternative Certification
http://www.alt-teachercert.org/index.asp

Interpreting Test Results

Contrary to what you may have heard, the results of a PRAXIS test are not based on time. More accurately, you will be scored on the raw number of points you earn in relation to the raw number of points available. Each question is worth one raw point. It is likely to your benefit to complete as many questions in the time allotted, but it will not necessarily work to your advantage if you hurry through the test.

Follow the guidelines provided by ETS for interpreting your score. The web site offers a sample test score sheet and clearly explains how the scores are scaled and what to expect if you have an essay portion on your test.

Scores are usually available by phone within a month of the test date and scores will be sent to your chosen institution(s) within six weeks. Additionally, ETS now makes online, downloadable reports available for 45 days from the reporting date.

It is **critical** that you be aware of your own state's passing score. Your raw score may qualify you to teach in some states, but not all. ETS administers the test and assigns a score, but the states make their own interpretations and, in some cases, consider combined scores if you are testing in more than one area.

What's on the Test?

PRAXIS tests vary from subject to subject and sometimes even within subject area. Subject areas are divided into smaller categories, and each given category includes a range of 5-15 skills. The weight of each category varies from test to test.

For PRAXIS Core Academic Skills for Educators, the breakdowns are as follows:

5712 - Reading lasts for 85 minutes and consists of approximately 56 multiple-choice questions based on reading passages and statements.

5712: READING		
% of test	Category	# of test questions
35%	Key Ideas and Details	17-22 Multiple-choice
30%	Craft, Structure, and Language Skills	14-19 Multiple-choice
35%	Integration of Knowledge and Ideas	17-22 Multiple-choice

5722 - Writing lasts for 100 minutes, consisting of 40 minutes for approximately 40 multiple-choice questions and one hour for 2 essay questions.

	5722: WRITING	
% of test	**Category**	**# of test questions**
60%	Text Types, Purposes, and Production	6-12 Multiple-choice; 2 Essay
40%	Language and Research Skills for Writing	28-34 Multiple-choice

5732 - Mathematics lasts for 85 minutes and consists of approximately 56 multiple-choice questions. An on-screen calculator is available for this test.

	5732: MATHEMATICS	
% of test	**Category**	**# of test questions**
30%	Number and Quantity	17 Multiple-choice
30%	Algebra and Functions	17 Multiple-choice
20%	Geometry	11 Multiple-choice
20%	Statistics and Probability	11 Multiple-choice

Question Types

You're probably thinking, enough already, I want to study! Indulge us a little longer while we explain that there is actually more than one type of multiple-choice question. You can thank us later after you realize how well prepared you are for your exam.

1. **Complete the Statement.** The name says it all. In this question type you'll be asked to choose the correct completion of a given statement. For example:

> The Dolch Basic Sight Words consist of a relatively short list of words that children should be able to:
>
> A. Sound out
>
> B. Know the meaning of
>
> C. Recognize on sight
>
> D. Use in a sentence

The correct answer is B. In order to check your answer, test out the statement by adding the choices to the end of it.

2. **Which of the Following.** One way to test your answer choice for this type of question is to replace the phrase "which of the following" with your selection. Use this example:

> **Which of the following words is one of the twelve most frequently used in children's reading texts:**
>
> A. There
>
> B. This
>
> C. The
>
> D. An

Don't look! Test your answer. _____ is one of the twelve most frequently used in children's reading texts. Did you guess C? Then you guessed correctly.

3. **Roman Numeral Choices.** This question type is used when there is more than one possible correct answer. For example:

> **Which of the following two arguments accurately supports the use of cooperative learning as an effective method of instruction?**
>
> I. Cooperative learning groups facilitate healthy competition between individuals in the group.
>
> II. Cooperative learning groups allow academic achievers to carry or cover for academic underachievers.
>
> III. Cooperative learning groups make each student in the group accountable for the success of the group.
>
> IV. Cooperative learning groups make it possible for students to reward other group members for achieving.
>
> A. I and II
>
> B. II and III
>
> C. I and III
>
> D. III and IV

Notice that the question states there are **two** possible answers. It's best to read all the possibilities first before looking at the answer choices. In this case, the correct answer is D.

4. **Negative Questions.** This type of question contains words such as "not," "least," and "except." Each correct answer will be the statement that does **not** fit the situation described in the question. Such as:

> **Multicultural education is not**
>
> A. An idea or concept
>
> B. A "tack-on" to the school curriculum
>
> C. An educational reform movement
>
> D. A process

Think to yourself that the statement could be anything but the correct answer. This question form is more open to interpretation than other types, so read carefully and don't forget that you're answering a negative statement.

5. **Questions that Include Graphs, Tables, or Reading Passages.** As always, read the question carefully. It likely asks for a very specific answer and not a broad interpretation of the visual. Here is a simple (though not statistically accurate) example of a graph question:

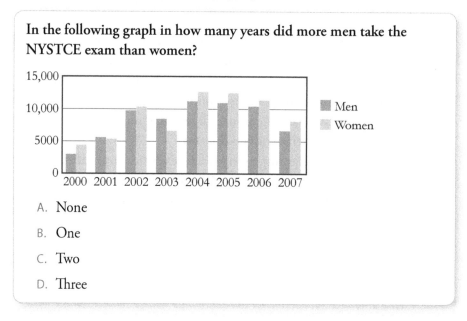

> **In the following graph in how many years did more men take the NYSTCE exam than women?**
>
> A. None
>
> B. One
>
> C. Two
>
> D. Three

It may help you to simply circle the two years that answer the question. Make sure you've read the question thoroughly and once you've made your determination, double check your work. The correct answer is C.

SECTION 4
HELPFUL HINTS

Study Tips

1. **You are what you eat.** Certain foods aid the learning process by releasing natural memory enhancers called CCKs (cholecystokinin) composed of tryptophan, choline, and phenylalanine. All of these chemicals enhance the neurotransmitters associated with memory and certain foods release memory enhancing chemicals. A light meal or snacks of one of the following foods fall into this category:

   - Milk
   - Rice
   - Eggs
   - Fish
   - Nuts and seeds
   - Oats
   - Turkey

   The better the connections, the more you comprehend!

2. **See the forest for the trees.** In other words, get the concept before you look at the details. One way to do this is to take notes as you read, paraphrasing or summarizing in your own words. Putting the concept in terms that are comfortable and familiar may increase retention.

3. **Question authority.** Ask why, why, why? Pull apart written material paragraph by paragraph and don't forget the captions under the illustrations. For example, if a heading reads *Stream Erosion* put it in the form of a question (Why do streams erode? What is stream erosion?) then find the answer within the material. If you train your mind to think in this manner you will learn more and prepare yourself for answering test questions.

4. **Play mind games.** Using your brain for reading or puzzles keeps it flexible. Even with a limited amount of time your brain can take in data (much like a computer) and store it for later use. In ten minutes you can: read two paragraphs (at least), quiz yourself with flash cards, or review notes. Even if you don't fully understand something on the first pass, your mind stores it for recall, which is why frequent reading or review increases chances of retention and comprehension.

5. **The pen is mightier than the sword.** Learn to take great notes. A by-product of our modern culture is that we have grown accustomed to getting our information in short doses. We've subconsciously trained ourselves to assimilate information into neat little packages. Messy notes fragment the flow of information. Your notes can be much clearer with proper formatting. *The Cornell Method* is one such format. This method was popularized in *How to Study in College*, Ninth Edition, by Walter Pauk. You can benefit from the method without purchasing an additional book by simply looking up the method online. Below is a sample of how *The Cornell Method* can be adapted for use with this guide.

← 2" → **Cue Column**	← 6" → **Note Taking Column**
	1. Record: During your reading, use the note-taking column to record important points.
	2. Questions: As soon as you finish a section, formulate questions based on the notes in the right-hand column. Writing questions helps to clarify meanings, reveal relationships, establish community, and strengthen memory. Also, the writing of questions sets the state for exam study later.
	3. Recite: Cover the note-taking column with a sheet of paper. Then, looking at the questions or cue-words in the question and cue column only, say aloud, in your own words, the answers to the questions, facts, or ideas indicated by the cue words.
	4. Reflect: Reflect on the material by asking yourself questions.
	5. Review: Spend at least ten minutes every week reviewing all your previous notes. Doing so helps you retain ideas and topics for the exam.
↕ 2"	**Summary** After reading, use this space to summarize the notes from each page.

*Adapted from How to Study in College, Ninth Edition, by Walter Pauk, ©2008 Wadsworth

6. **Place yourself in exile and set the mood.** Set aside a particular place and time to study that best suits your personal needs and biorhythms. If you're a night person, burn the midnight oil. If you're a morning person set yourself up with some coffee and get to it. Make your study time and place as free from distraction as possible and surround yourself with what you need, be it silence or music. Studies have shown that music can aid in concentration, absorption, and retrieval of information. Not all music, though. Classical music is said to work best

7. **Get pointed in the right direction.** Use arrows to point to important passages or pieces of information. It's easier to read than a page full of yellow highlights. Highlighting can be used sparingly, but add an arrow to the margin to call attention to it.

8. **Check your budget.** You should at least review all the content material before your test, but allocate the most amount of time to the areas that need the most refreshing. It sounds obvious, but it's easy to forget. You can use the study rubric above to balance your study budget.

The proctor will write the start time where it can be seen and then, later, provide the time remaining, typically fifteen minutes before the end of the test.

Testing Tips

1. **Get smart, play dumb.** Sometimes a question is just a question. No one is out to trick you, so don't assume that the test writer is looking for something other than what was asked. Stick to the question as written and don't overanalyze.

2. **Do a double take.** Read test questions and answer choices at least twice because it's easy to miss something, to transpose a word or some letters. If you have no idea what the correct answer is, skip it and come back later if there's time. If you're still clueless, it's okay to guess. Remember, you're scored on the number of questions you answer correctly and you're not penalized for wrong answers. The worst case scenario is that you miss a point from a good guess.

3. **Turn it on its ear.** The syntax of a question can often provide a clue, so make things interesting and turn the question into a statement to see if it changes the meaning or relates better (or worse) to the answer choices.

4. **Get out your magnifying glass.** Look for hidden clues in the questions because it's difficult to write a multiple-choice question without giving away part of the answer in the options presented. In most questions you can readily eliminate one or two potential answers, increasing your chances of answering correctly to 50/50, which will help out if you've skipped a question and gone back to it (see tip #2).

5. **Call it intuition.** Often your first instinct is correct. If you've been studying the content you've likely absorbed something and have subconsciously retained the knowledge. On questions you're not sure about trust your instincts because a first impression is usually correct.

6. **Graffiti.** Sometimes it's a good idea to mark your answers directly on the test booklet and go back to fill in the optical scan sheet later. You don't get extra points for perfectly blackened ovals. If you choose to manage your test this way, be sure not to mismark your answers when you transcribe to the scan sheet.

7. **Become a clock-watcher.** You have a set amount of time to answer the questions. Don't get bogged down laboring over a question you're not sure about when there are ten others you could answer more readily. If you choose to follow the advice of tip #6, be sure you leave time near the end to go back and fill in the scan sheet.

Do the Drill

No matter how prepared you feel it's sometimes a good idea to apply Murphy's Law. So the following tips might seem silly, mundane, or obvious, but we're including them anyway.

1. **Remember, you are what you eat, so bring a snack.** Choose from the list of energizing foods that appear earlier in the introduction.

2. **You're not too sexy for your test.** Wear comfortable clothes. You'll be distracted if your belt is too tight or if you're too cold or too hot.

3. **Lie to yourself.** Even if you think you're a prompt person, pretend you're not and leave plenty of time to get to the testing center. Map it out ahead of time and do a dry run if you have to. There's no need to add road rage to your list of anxieties.

4. **Bring sharp number 2 pencils.** It may seem impossible to forget this need from your school days, but you might. And make sure the erasers are intact, too.

5. **No ticket, no test.** Bring your admission ticket as well as **two** forms of identification, including one with a picture and signature. You will not be admitted to the test without these things.

6. **You can't take it with you.** Leave any study aids, dictionaries, notebooks, computers, and the like at home. Certain tests **do** allow a scientific or four-function calculator, so check ahead of time to see if your test does.

7. **Prepare for the desert.** Any time spent on a bathroom break **cannot** be made up later, so use your judgment on the amount you eat or drink.

8. **Quiet, Please!** Keeping your own time is a good idea, but not with a timepiece that has a loud ticker. If you use a watch, take it off and place it nearby but not so that it distracts you. And **silence your cell phone**.

To the best of our ability, we have compiled the content you need to know in this book and in the accompanying online resources. The rest is up to you. You can use the study and testing tips or you can follow your own methods. Either way, you can be confident that there aren't any missing pieces of information and there shouldn't be any surprises in the content on the test.

If you have questions about test fees, registration, electronic testing, or other content verification issues please visit *www.ets.org*.

Good luck!

Sharon Wynne
Founder, XAMonline

DOMAIN I
READING

PERSONALIZED STUDY PLAN

KNOWN MATERIAL/ SKIP IT

PAGE	COMPETENCY AND SKILL	
3	**1: Key Ideas and Details**	☑
	1.1: Draw inferences from and understand implications of the directly stated content of a reading selection	☑
	1.2: Identify summaries or paraphrases of the main idea or primary purpose of a reading selection	☑
	1.3: Identify summaries or paraphrases of supporting ideas	☑
	1.4: Identify how and why ideas, people, occurrences, and details interact within and inform a text	☑
10	**2: Craft, Structure, and Language Skills**	☑
	2.1: Determine the author's attitude toward material in a reading selection through word choices that reflect meaning and tone	☑
	2.2: Identify the key transition words and phrases and how they are used to denote meaning	☑
	2.3: Identify how a reading selection is organized in terms of cause/effect, compare/contrast, problem/solution, etc.	☑
	2.4: Assess how point of view or purpose shapes the content and style of a text	☑
	2.5: Determine the role than an idea, reference, or piece of information plays in an author's discussion or argument	☑
	2.6: Determine whether an idea reference, or piece of information in an author's discussion or argument is valid or relevant	☑
	2.7: Identify the meanings of words as they are used in the context of a reading selection	☑
	2.8: Determine the meaning of unknown and multiple-meaning words and phrases by using context clues	☑
	2.9: Understand figurative language and nuances in word meanings	☑
	2.10: Understand a range of words and phrases sufficient for reading at the college and career readiness level	☑
22	**3: Integration of Knowledge and Ideas**	☐
	3.1: Analyze content presented in diverse media and formats, including visually and quantitatively, as well as in words	☑
	3.2: Identify and evaluate the argument and specific claims in a text, including the validity of reasoning as well as the relevance and sufficiency of the evidence	☐
	3.3: Determine whether evidence strengthens, weakens, or is relevant to the arguments in a reading selection	☐
	3.4: Determine the logical assumptions upon which an argument or conclusion is based	☐
	3.5: Draw conclusions from material presented in a reading selection	☐
	3.6: Analyze how two or more texts address similar themes or topics in order to build knowledge and/or compare approaches the authors take	☐

COMPETENCY 1
KEY IDEAS AND DETAILS

SKILL 1.1 Draw inferences from and understand implications of the directly stated content of a reading selection

An **INFERENCE** is sometimes called an "educated guess" because it requires going beyond the strictly obvious to create additional meaning by taking the text one logical step further. Inferences and conclusions are based on the content of the passage—that is, on what the passage says or how the writer says it—and are derived by reasoning.

Inference is an essential and automatic component of most reading. Examples include making educated guesses about the meaning of unknown words, the author's main idea, or the existence of bias. Such is the essence of inference. You use your own ability to reason in order to figure out what the writer is implying.

Consider the following example. Assume you are an employer, and you are reading over the letters of reference submitted by a prospective employee for the position of clerk/typist in your real estate office. The position requires the applicant to be neat, careful, trustworthy, and punctual. You come across this letter of reference submitted by an applicant:

> To Whom It May Concern:
>
> Todd Finley has asked me to write a letter of reference for him. I am well qualified to do so because he worked for me for three months last year. His duties included answering the phone, greeting the public, and producing some simple memos and notices on the computer. Although Todd initially had few computer skills and little knowledge of telephone etiquette, he did acquire some during his stay with us. Todd's manner of speaking, both on the telephone and with the clients who came to my establishment, could be described as casual. He was particularly effective when communicating with peers. Please contact me by telephone if you wish to have further information about my experience with Todd.

Here the writer implies, rather than openly states, the main idea. This letter calls attention to itself because there is a problem with its tone. A truly positive letter would say something such as, "I have the distinct honor of recommending Todd Finley." Here, however, the letter simply verifies that Todd worked in the office. Second, the praise is obviously lukewarm. For example, the writer says that Todd

INFERENCE: an educated guess based on given facts and premises

"was particularly effective when communicating with peers." An educated guess translates that statement into a nice way of saying Todd was not serious about his communication with clients.

In order to draw inferences and make conclusions, a reader must use prior knowledge and apply it to the current situation. A conclusion or inference is never stated. The reader must rely on common sense.

Practice Questions

Read the following passages and select an answer.

1. Tim Sullivan had just turned fifteen. As a birthday present, his parents had given him a guitar and a certificate for ten guitar lessons. He had always shown a love of music and a desire to learn an instrument. Tim began his lessons, and before long, he was making up his own songs. At the music studio, Tim met Josh, who played the piano, and Roger, whose instrument was the saxophone. They all shared the same dream—to start a band—and each was praised by his teacher as having real talent. From this passage, one can infer that:

    A. Tim, Roger, and Josh are going to start their own band

    B. Tim is going to give up his guitar lessons

    C. Tim, Josh, and Roger will no longer be friends

    D. Josh and Roger are going to start their own band

2. The Smith family waited patiently around carousel number 7 for their luggage to arrive. They were exhausted after their five-hour trip and were anxious to get to their hotel. After about an hour, they realized that they no longer recognized any of the other passengers' faces. Mrs. Smith asked the person who appeared to be in charge if they were at the right carousel. The man replied, "Yes, this is it, but we finished unloading that baggage almost half an hour ago." From the man's response, we can infer that:

    A. The Smiths were ready to go to their hotel

    B. The Smiths' luggage was lost

    C. The man had the Smiths' luggage

    D. The Smiths were at the wrong carousel

Answer Key

1. **A**

Given the facts that Tim wanted to be a musician and start his own band, after he met others who shared the same dreams, we can infer that the friends joined in an attempt to make their dreams become a reality.

2. **B**

Because the Smiths were still waiting for their luggage, we know that they were not yet ready to go to their hotel. From the man's response, we know that they were not at the wrong carousel and that he did not have their luggage. Therefore, though not directly stated, it appears that their luggage was lost.

SKILL 1.2 Identify summaries or paraphrases of the main idea or primary purpose of a reading selection

The MAIN IDEA of a passage or paragraph is the basic message, idea, point, concept, or meaning that the author wants to convey to the reader. Understanding the main idea of a passage or paragraph is the key to understanding the more subtle components of the author's message. The main idea is what is being said about a topic or subject. Once you have identified the basic message, you will have an easier time answering other questions that test critical skills.

Main ideas are either stated or implied. A stated main idea is explicit: it is directly expressed in a sentence or two in the paragraph or passage. An implied main idea is suggested by the overall reading selection. In the first case, you need not pull information from various points in the paragraph or passage in order to form the main idea because the author already states it. If a main idea is implied, however, you must formulate—in your own words—a main idea statement by condensing the overall message contained in the material itself.

> **MAIN IDEA:** the basic message, idea, point, concept, or meaning that the author wants to convey to the reader

Sample Passage

Sometimes too much of a good thing can become a very bad thing indeed. In an earnest attempt to consume a healthy diet, dietary supplement enthusiasts have been known to overdose. Vitamin C, for example, long thought to help people ward off cold viruses, is currently being studied for its possible role in warding off cancer and other diseases that cause tissue degeneration. Unfortunately, an overdose of vitamin C—more than 10,000 mg—on a daily basis can cause nausea and diarrhea. Calcium supplements, commonly taken by women, are helpful in warding off osteoporosis. More than just a few grams a day, however, can lead to stomach upset and even kidney and bladder stones. Niacin, proven useful in reducing cholesterol levels, can be dangerous in large doses to those who suffer from heart problems, asthma, or ulcers.

The main idea expressed in this paragraph is:

   C. Supplements taken in excess can be a bad thing indeed.

   D. Dietary supplement enthusiasts have been known to overdose.

   E. Vitamins can cause nausea, diarrhea, and kidney or bladder stones.

   F. People who take supplements are preoccupied with their health.

Answer A is a paraphrase of the first sentence and provides a general framework for the rest of the paragraph: excess supplement intake is bad. The rest of the paragraph discusses the consequences of taking too many vitamins. Options B and C refer to major details, and Option D introduces the idea of preoccupation, which is not included in this paragraph.

Sample Test Questions and Rationale

For sample test questions and rationales requiring a reading passage, see page 31.

**SKILL Identify summaries or paraphrases of supporting ideas
1.3**

See Skill 6.4

SKILL 1.4 Identify how and why ideas, people, occurrences, and details interact within and inform a text

The **organization** of a written work includes two factors: the order in which the writer has chosen to present the different parts of the discussion or argument, and the relationships he or she constructs between these parts.

Written ideas need to be presented in a **logical order** so that a reader can follow the information easily and quickly. There are many different ways to order a series of ideas, but they all share one goal: to lead the reader along a desired path—while avoiding backtracking and skipping around—in order to give a clear, strong presentation of the writer's main idea. The following are some of the ways in which a paragraph may be organized:

WAYS TO ORGANIZE A WRITTEN WORK	
Organization	**Explanation**
Sequence of Events	In this type of organization, the details are presented in the order in which they have occurred. Paragraphs that describe a process or procedure, give directions, or outline a given time period (such as a day or a month) are often arranged chronologically.
Statement Support	In this type of organization, the main idea is stated and the rest of the paragraph explains or proves it. This type of organization is also referred to as *relative* or *order of importance*. This type of order is organized in four ways: most to least, least to most, most-least-most, and least-most-least.
Comparison-Contrast	The compare-contrast pattern is used when a paragraph describes the differences or similarities between two or more ideas, actions, events, or things. Usually, the topic sentence describes the basic relationship between the ideas or items, and the rest of the paragraph explains this relationship.
Classification	In this type of organization, the paragraph presents grouped information about a topic. The topic sentence usually states the general category, and the rest of the sentences show how various elements of the category have a common base and how they differ from the common base.
Cause and Effect	This pattern describes how two or more events are connected. The main sentence usually states the primary cause(s) and the primary effect(s) and how they are connected. The rest of the sentences explain the connection—how one event caused the next.
Spatial/Place	In this type of organization, certain descriptions are organized according to the location of items in relation to each other and to a larger context. The orderly arrangement guides the reader's eye as he or she mentally envisions the scene or place being described.
Example, Clarification, and Definition	These types of organization show, explain, or elaborate on the main idea. This can be done by showing specific cases, examining meaning multiple times, or describing one term extensively. Many times, all of these organizations follow the basic P.I.E. sequence: P—the point, or main idea, of the paragraph I—the information (data, details, facts) that supports the main idea E—the explanation or analysis of the information and how it proves, is related to, or connects to the main idea
Problem/Solution	In a problem-solution approach, information is organized into a description of the problem and a proposed solution. The problem will be shown to exist in one organized section; a proposed solution will be offered, discussed, and perhaps compared and contrasted to other potential solutions in order to prove that it is the most workable solution.

The relationship between sentences is the link that conceptually ties one sentence to another. The relationship may be explicit, in which case a transition or clue word helps identify the connection. The relation may be implicit, in which case you must closely examine the elements found in each sentence and often in the material between the sentences.

Most sentences cannot meaningfully stand alone. To read a passage without recognizing how each sentence is linked to those around it is to lose the passage's meaning.

Sentences can be connected to one another in many ways.

HOW SENTENCES ARE CONNECTED	
Addition	One sentence is "tacked on" to another without making one sentence depend upon the other. Both are equally important.
	*Joanna recently purchased a new stereo system, computer, and home alarm system. She **also** put a down payment on a new automobile.*
Clarification	One sentence restates the point of an earlier one but in different terms.
	*The national debt is growing continually. **In fact**, by next year it may be ten trillion dollars.*
Comparison/ Contrast	Connection is one of similarity or difference.
	*Shelley's strained relationship with his father led the poet to a life of rebellion. **Likewise**, Byron's Bohemian lifestyle may be traced to his ambivalence toward authority.*
Example	One sentence works to make another more concrete or specific.
	Sarah has always been an optimistic person. She believes that when she graduates from college, she will get the job of her choice. (implicit)
Location/Spatial Order	The relationship between sentences shows the placement of objects or items relative to each other in space.
	The park was darkened by the school building's shadow. However, the sun still splashed the front window with light. (implicit)
Cause/Effect	One event (cause) brings about the second event (effect).
	*General Hooker failed to anticipate General Lee's bold maneuver. **As a result**, Hooker's army was nearly routed by a smaller force.*
Summary	A summary sentence surveys and captures the most important points of the previous sentence(s).
	*Every Fourth of July, Ralph brings his whole family to the local parade; every Memorial Day, he displays the flag; and every November 4, he votes. **Overall**, he is a patriotic American.*
Time	The relationship describes the passage of time or various states of completion of events.
	*The car slid down the embankment. **Shortly thereafter**, curious onlookers had backed up traffic five miles.*

COMPETENCY 2
CRAFT, STRUCTURE, AND LANGUAGE SKILLS

> **SKILL** **Determine the author's attitude toward material in a reading**
> **2.1** **selection through word choices that reflect meaning and tone**

TONE: the author's attitude toward the subject matter

The **TONE** of a written passage is the author's attitude toward the subject matter. The tone (mood, feeling) is revealed through the qualities of the writing itself and is a direct product of such stylistic elements as language and sentence structure. The tone of the written passage is much like a speaker's voice; instead of being spoken, however, it is the product of words on a page.

Often, writers have an emotional stake in their subjects, and their purpose, either explicitly or implicitly, is to convey those feelings to the reader. In such cases, the writing is generally subjective; that is, it stems from opinions, judgments, values, ideas, and feelings. Both sentence structure (syntax) and word choice (diction) are instrumental tools in creating tone.

Tone may be thought of generally as positive, negative, or neutral. Below is a statement about snakes that demonstrates this.

> *Many species of snakes live here. Some of those species, both poisonous and non-poisonous, have habitats that coincide with those of human residents of the state.*

The voice of the writer in this statement is neutral. The sentences are declarative (not exclamations, fragments, or questions). The adjectives are few and nondescript—*many, some, poisonous* (balanced with *non-poisonous*). Nothing much in this brief paragraph would alert the reader to the feelings of the writer about snakes. The paragraph has a neutral, objective, detached, impartial tone.

If the writer's attitude toward snakes involved admiration, or even affection, the tone would generally be positive:

> *These snakes are a tenacious bunch. When they find their habitats invaded by humans, they cling to their home territories as long as they can, as if vainly attempting to fight off the onslaught of the human hordes.*

An additional message emerges in this paragraph—the writer quite clearly favors snakes over people. The writer uses adjectives such as tenacious to describe his or her feelings about snakes. The writer also humanizes the reptiles, making them brave, beleaguered creatures. Obviously, the writer is more sympathetic to snakes than to people in this paragraph.

If the writer's attitude toward snakes involved active dislike and fear, then the tone would also reflect that attitude by being negative:

> *Countless species of snakes, some more dangerous than others, still lurk on the urban fringes of towns and cities. They will often invade domestic spaces, terrorizing people and their pets.*

Here, obviously, the snakes are the villains. They *lurk*, they *invade*, and they *terrorize*. The tone of this paragraph might be defined as *distressed*.

In the same manner, a writer can use language to portray characters as good or bad. A writer uses positive and negative adjectives to convey the manner of a character.

SKILL 2.2 Identify the key transition words and phrases and how they are used to denote meaning

Even if the sentences that make up a given paragraph or passage are arranged in logical order, the document as a whole can still seem choppy, and the various ideas disconnected. TRANSITIONS—words that signal relationships between ideas—can help improve the flow of a document. Transitions can help achieve clear and effective presentation of information by establishing connections between sentences, paragraphs, and sections of a document. With transitions, each sentence builds on the ideas in the last, and each paragraph has clear links to the preceding one. As a result, the reader receives clear directions on how to piece together the writer's ideas in a logically coherent argument. By signaling how to organize, interpret, and react to information, transitions enable writers to explain their ideas effectively and elegantly. Below is a list of common transitional expressions.

TRANSITIONS: words that signal relationships between ideas

COMMON TRANSITIONS	
Logical Relationship	**Transitional Expression**
Similarity	also, in the same way, just as … so too, likewise, similarly
Exception/Contrast	but, however, in spite of, on the one hand … on the other hand, nevertheless, nonetheless, notwithstanding, in contrast, on the contrary, still, yet, although
Sequence/Order	first, second, third, … next, then, finally, until
Time	after, afterward, at last, before, currently, during, earlier, immediately, later, meanwhile, now, presently, recently, simultaneously, since, subsequently, then
Example	for example, for instance, namely, specifically, to illustrate
Emphasis	even, indeed, in fact, of course, truly
Place/Position	above, adjacent, below, beyond, here, in front, in back, nearby, there
Cause and Effect	accordingly, consequently, hence, so, therefore, thus, as a result, because, consequently, hence, if…then, in short
Additional Support or Evidence	additionally, again, also, and, as well, besides, equally important, further, furthermore, in addition, moreover, then
Conclusion/ Summary	finally, in a word, in brief, in conclusion, in the end, in the final analysis, on the whole, thus, to conclude, to summarize, in sum, in summary
Statement Support	most important, more significant, primarily, most essential
Addition	again, also, and, besides, equally important, finally, furthermore, in addition, last, likewise, moreover, too
Clarification	actually, clearly, evidently, in fact, in other words, obviously, of course, indeed

The following example shows good logical order and transitions. The transition words are highlighted in bold.

*No one really knows how Valentine's Day started. There are several legends, **however**, which are often told. The **first** attributes Valentine's Day to a Christian priest who lived in Rome during the third century under the rule of Emperor Claudius. Rome was at war and, **apparently,** Claudius felt that married men did not fight as well as bachelors. **Consequently**, Claudius banned marriage for the duration of the war. **But** Valentinus, the priest, risked his life to marry couples secretly in violation of Claudius' law. The **second** legend is **even more** romantic. In this story, Valentinus is a prisoner, having been condemned to death for refusing to worship pagan deities. **While** in jail, he fell in love with his jailer's daughter, who happened to be blind. Daily, he prayed for her sight to return and miraculously, it did. On February 14, the day that he was condemned to die, he was allowed to write the young woman a note. **In this farewell letter**, he promised eternal love and signed at the bottom of the page the now famous words, "Your Valentine."*

SKILL 2.3   **Identify how a reading selection is organized in terms of cause/ effect, compare/contrast, problem/solution, etc.**

See Skill 1.4

SKILL 2.4   **Assess how point of view or purpose shapes the content and style of a text**

See Skill 2.1

SKILL 2.5   **Determine the role than an idea, reference, or piece of information plays in an author's discussion or argument**

See Skill 3.2

SKILL 2.6   **Determine whether an idea reference, or piece of information in an author's discussion or argument is valid or relevant**

See Skill 3.2

SKILL 2.7 Identify the meanings of words as they are used in the context of a reading selection

FACTS: verifiable statements that report what has happened or what exists

OPINIONS: statements that must be supported in order to be accepted, such as beliefs, values, judgments, or feelings

JUDGMENTS: opinions, decisions, or declarations based on observation or reasoning that express approval or disapproval

FACTS are verifiable statements. **OPINIONS** are statements that must be supported in order to be accepted, such as beliefs, values, judgments, or feelings. Facts are objective statements used to support subjective opinions. For example, "Jane is a bad girl" is an opinion. However, "Jane hit her sister with a baseball bat" is a fact upon which the opinion is based. **JUDGMENTS** are opinions, decisions, or declarations based on observation or reasoning that express approval or disapproval. Facts report what has happened or what exists and come from observation, measurement, or calculation. Facts can be tested and verified, whereas opinions and judgments cannot. They can only be supported with facts.

Most statements cannot be so clearly distinguished. "I believe that Jane is a bad girl" is a fact. The speaker knows what he or she believes. However, it obviously includes a judgment that could be disputed by another person who might believe otherwise. Judgments are not usually so firm. They are, rather, plausible opinions that provoke thought or lead to factual development.

Mickey Mantle replaced Joe DiMaggio, a Yankees centerfielder, in 1952.

This is a fact. If necessary, evidence can be produced to support this statement.

First-year players are more ambitious than seasoned players are.

This is an opinion. There is no proof to support that everyone feels this way.

Practice Questions

1. The Inca were a group of Indians who ruled an empire in South America.

   A. fact

   B. opinion

2. The Inca were clever.

   A. fact

   B. opinion

3. The Inca built very complex systems of bridges.

   A. fact

   B. opinion

Answer Key

1. **A**

   Research can prove this statement true.

2. **B**

   It is doubtful that all people who have studied the Inca agree with this statement. Therefore, no proof is available.

3. **A**

   As with question number one, research can prove this statement true.

SKILL 2.8 Determine the meaning of unknown and multiple-meaning words and phrases by using context clues.

CONTEXT CLUES help readers determine the meanings of words with which they are not familiar. The CONTEXT of a word is the sentence or sentences that surround the word.

Read the following sentences and attempt to determine the meanings of the words in bold print.

> The **luminosity** of the room was so incredible that there was no need for lights.

If there was no need for lights, then one must assume that the word luminosity has something to do with giving off light. The definition of luminosity is "the emission of light."

> Jamie could not understand Joe's feelings. His mood swings made understanding him somewhat of an **enigma**.

The fact that he could not be understood made him somewhat of a puzzle. The definition of enigma is "a mystery or puzzle."

Familiarity with terms ROOTS (the basic elements of words) and prefixes (affixes that are added to the fronts of words to form derivative words) can help you determine the meanings of unknown words.

CONTEXT CLUES: help readers determine the meanings of words with which they are not familiar

CONTEXT: the sentence or sentences that surround a word

ROOTS: the basic elements of words

Following are some common roots and prefixes. It might be useful to review these.

SOME COMMON ROOTS AND THEIR MEANINGS		
Root	**Meaning**	**Example**
aqua	water	aqualung
astro	stars	astrology
bio	life	biology
carn	meat	carnivorous
circum	around	circumnavigate

Table continued on next page

Root	**Meaning**	**Example**
geo	earth	geology
herb	plant	herbivorous
mal	bad	malicious
neo	new	neonatal
tele	distant	telescope

SOME COMMON PREFIXES AND THEIR MEANINGS		
Prefix	**Meaning**	**Example**
un-	not	unnamed
re-	again	reenter
il-	not	illegible
pre-	before	preset
mis-	incorrectly	misstate
in-	not	informal
anti-	against	antiwar

SOME COMMON PREFIXES AND THEIR MEANINGS		
de-	opposite	derail
post-	after	postwar
ir-	not	irresponsible

Word Forms

Sometimes a very familiar word can appear as a different part of speech, as in the examples below.

You may have heard that fraud involves a criminal misrepresentation, so when this word appears in the adjective form fraudulent, you can make an educated guess as to its meaning. (Example: He was suspected of fraudulent activities.)

You probably know that something out-of-date is obsolete; therefore, when you read about "built-in obsolescence," you can detect the meaning of the unfamiliar word.

Recall that the context for a word is the written passage that surrounds it. Sometimes the writer offers synonyms—words that have nearly the same meaning. Context clues can appear within the sentence itself, within the preceding and/or following sentence(s), or in the passage as a whole.

Sentence Clues

Often, a writer will actually define a difficult or particularly important word for you the first time it appears in a passage. Phrases such as *that is, such as, which is*, or *is called* might announce the writer's intention to give just the definition you need. Occasionally, a writer will simply use a synonym (a word that means the same thing) or near-synonym joined by the word *or*. Look at the following examples:

The credibility, that is to say the believability, of the witness was called into question by evidence of previous perjury.

Nothing would assuage or lessen the child's grief.

Punctuation at the sentence level is often a clue to the meaning of a word. Commas, parentheses, quotation marks, and dashes tell the reader that the writer is offering a definition.

> *A tendency toward hyperbole, extravagant exaggeration, is a common flaw among persuasive writers.*

> *Political apathy—lack of interest—can lead to the death of the state.*

A writer might simply give an explanation in other words that you can understand in the same sentence:

> *The xenophobic townspeople were suspicious of every foreigner.*

Writers also explain a word in terms of its opposite at the sentence level:

> *His incarceration was ended, and he was elated to be out of jail.*

Adjacent Sentence Clues

The context for a word goes beyond the sentence in which it appears. At times, the writer uses adjacent (adjoining) sentences to present an explanation or definition:

> *The 200 dollars for the car repair would have to come out of the contingency fund. Fortunately, Angela's father had taught her to keep some money set aside for just such emergencies.*

Analysis: The second sentence offers a clue to the definition of contingency as used in this sentence: "emergencies." Therefore, a fund for contingencies would be money tucked away for unforeseen and/or urgent events.

Entire Passage Clues

On occasion, you must look at an entire paragraph or passage to figure out the definition of a word or term. In the following paragraph, notice how the word *nostalgia* undergoes a form of extended definition throughout the selection rather than in just one sentence.

The word nostalgia links the Greek words for "away from home" and "pain." If you are feeling nostalgic, then you are probably in some physical distress or discomfort, suffering from a feeling of alienation and separation from loved ones or loved places. Nostalgia is that awful feeling you remember from the first time you went away to camp or spent the weekend with a friend's family—homesickness, or some condition even more painful than that. However, in common use, nostalgia has come to have associations that are more sentimental. A few years back, for example, a nostalgic craze had to do with the 1950s. We resurrected poodle skirts and saddle shoes, built new restaurants to look like old ones, and tried to make chicken à la king just as Mother probably never made it. In TV situation comedies, we recreated a pleasant world that probably never existed and relished our nostalgia, longing for a homey, comfortable, lost time.

SKILL 2.9 Understand figurative language and nuances in word meanings

There are various forms of figurative language and nuances in word meanings. Some of the major forms of figurative language are:

- ⊠SIMILE: Direct comparison between two things. "My love is like a red-red rose." The words "like" or "as" denote a simile. "She's as pretty as a picture," is a simile, likening a woman to a painting, using the word "as."

- ⊠METAPHOR: Indirect comparison between two things; the use of a word or phrase denoting one kind of object or action in place of another to suggest a comparison between them. While poets use them extensively, they are also integral to everyday speech. For example, a person may be said to be "drowning in debt." Of course, he or she is not literally drowning, but figuratively he or she may feel overwhelmed and unable to get his or her head "above water" financially.

- ⊠PARALELLISM: The arrangement of ideas in phrases, sentences, and paragraphs that balance one element with another of equal importance and similar wording. An example from Francis Bacon's *Of Studies*: "Reading maketh a full man, conference a ready man, and writing an exact man."

- ⊠PERSONIFICATION: Attributing human characteristics to an inanimate object, an abstract quality, or animal. John Bunyan exemplified this by writing characters named Death, Knowledge, Giant Despair, Sloth, and Piety in his *Pilgrim's Progress*. The Cheshire Cat in *Alice in Wonderland* is another example of personification as the cat grins and talks.

- ⊠EUPHEMISM: The substitution of an agreeable or inoffensive term for one that might offend or suggest something unpleasant. Many euphemisms, such as "passed away" are used to refer to "died" to avoid using the real word. Calling a bathroom a "powder room" is another example of a euphemism.

- ⊠HYPERBOLE: Deliberate exaggeration for effect or comic effect. "I'm starving to death; let's eat" or "I am expiring from boredom" are hyperbole.

- ⊠CLIMAX: A number of phrases or sentences are arranged in ascending order of rhetorical forcefulness to build up to a powerful conclusion. Here is an example from Herman Melville's *Moby Dick*:

All that most maddens and torments; all that stirs up the lees of things; all truth with malice in it; all that cracks the sinews and cakes the brain; all the subtle demonisms of life and thought; all evil, to crazy Ahab, were visibly personified and made practically assailable in Moby Dick.

- ⊠BATHOS: A ludicrous attempt to portray pathos; that is, to evoke pity, sympathy, or sorrow. It may result from inappropriately dignifying the commonplace, elevating language to describe something trivial, or greatly exaggerating pathos.

- ⊠OXYMORON: A contradiction in terms deliberately employed for effect. It is usually seen in a qualifying adjective whose meaning is contrary to that of the noun it modifies, such as "wise folly."

- ⊠IRONY: Expressing something other than and particularly opposite to the literal meaning, such as words of praise when the author or speaker intends blame. In poetry, it is often used as a sophisticated or resigned awareness of contrast between what is and what ought to be and expresses a controlled pathos without sentimentality. This form of indirection avoids overt praise or censure. An early example: the Greek comic character Eiron, a clever underdog who by his wit repeatedly triumphs over the boastful character Alazon.

- ⊠ALLITERATION: The repetition of consonant sounds in two or more neighboring words or syllables. In its simplest form, it reinforces one or two consonant sounds. For example, Shakespeare's "Sonnet #12": "When I do count the clock that tells the time."

Some poets have used more complex patterns of alliteration by creating consonants both at the beginning of words and at the beginning of stressed syllables within words. For example, Shelley's "Stanza Written in Dejection Near Naples": "The City's voice itself is soft like Solitude's."

- ⊠ONOMATOPOEIA: The naming of a thing or action by a vocal imitation of the sound associated with it, such as buzz or hiss or the use of words whose sound suggests the sense. This is a good example from "The Brook" by Tennyson:

I chatter over stony ways;
In little sharps and trebles,
I bubble into eddying bays,
I babble on the pebbles.

SKILL **Understand a range of words and phrases sufficient for reading at**
2.10 **the college and career readiness level**

See Skill 2.8

COMPETENCY 3
INTEGRATION OF KNOWLEDGE AND IDEAS

SKILL 3.1 Analyze content presented in diverse media and formats, including visually and quantitatively, as well as in words

Technology allows for the presentation of information through diverse media. Audio and video stimuli may be used to present information. In addition to a reading passage, information may be delivered in visual formats such as graphs, tables, or maps.

The Practice Exercise below is an example of a quantitative visual format.

Practice Excercise: Visual Quantitative Format

Which conclusion about Blisstown is best supported by the data in the table below?

1. **Restaurant Visits in Blisstown 2001-2013**

Type of Restaurant	2011	2012	2013
Italian	10,000	12,000	15,000
Chinese	8,000	8,000	8,000
American	12,000	15,000	18,000

A. Most Chinese restaurants will go out of business in Blisstown by 2015

B. Blisstown has a sizable and growing Italian population

C. American is the most popular type of restaurant food in Blisstown

D. Italian restaurants will overtake American restaurants in Blisstown by 2015

E. Chinese restaurants have an unstable clientele

Answer Key

1. **C**

   Option A is not logical, for restaurant visits in Blisstown are steady. Option B appears logical, but in fact the table measures restaurant visits rather than demographic composition of restaurant visitors. Option C is supported by the data. Option D is not supported by the momentum of the data. The data supports the very opposite of the conclusion of Option E.

SKILL 3.2 Identify and evaluate the argument and specific claims in a text, including the validity of reasoning as well as the relevance and sufficiency of the evidence.

To evaluate an argument and specific claims in a text, one must have some knowledge of logic. Logic is valid reasoning. In addition to the relevance and sufficiency of evidence presented in an argument, arguments must follow logical courses and make claims based upon rationales.

Some of the statements made in support of an argument are simple statements. A simple statement represents a simple idea that can be described as either true or false, but not both.

If a simple statement is joined by a connective word to another statement, it becomes a compound statement. In logic, a hypothesis statement is often followed by a conclusion, making a compound statement. This kind of statement is usually written in "if-then" form. If the condition of the first part of the statement is true (the "if" clause), then the conclusion may be drawn from it (the conclusion is the "then" clause). The conclusion part of the compound statement is conditional upon the factuality of the hypothesis part of the compound statement. Therefore, these kinds of statements are sometimes called conditional statements.

This is an example of such a statement: "If all cats have an instinct to chase mice, then Laddie the cat must have an instinct to chase mice." The "if" part of the statement is the hypothesis of this compound statement. The "then" part of the statement is the conclusion of this compound statement. The "then" part of the statement is conditional upon the "if" part of the statement being true.

The logic of the statement may be restated as follows: Since Laddie is a cat and all cats have an instinct to chase mice, then it follows logically that Laddie the cat has an instinct to chase mice.

These kinds of statements are cues as to the argument and claims in a text. Their logic or lack of it show the validity of the reasoning in the argument.

SIMPLE STATEMENT: represents a simple idea that can be described as either true or false, but not both.

COMPOUND STATEMENTS: two simple statements joined by a connective (and, or, not, if…then, and if and only if, etc.).

HYPOTHESIS: the if clause of an if-then statement.

CONCLUSION: the then clause of an if-then statement.

DEDUCTIVE REASONING can help determine the validity of the reasoning behind an argument and the specific claims in a text.

Deductive reasoning is the process of arriving at a conclusion based on statements or premises. If the statements or premises are true, the conclusion will be reliably true.

An argument is **VALID** when the conclusion follows necessarily from the premises. An argument is **INVALID** or a fallacy when the conclusion does not follow from the premises.

Here are examples of four standard forms of valid arguments in deductive reasoning. They are Modus ponens, Modus tollens, Syllogisms, and the Distinctive Syllogisms.

Modus Ponens follows this form:
    Premise: If A, then B
    Premise: A.
    Conclusion: Therefore, B.

If Anna is a member of the Dining Club, she goes to restaurants. (Premise)

Anna is a member of the Dining Club. (Premise)

Therefore, Anna goes to restaurants. (Conclusion)

Modus tollens follows this form:
    Premise: If A, then B.
    Premise: Not B.
    Conclusion: Therefore, not A.

Where there's smoke, there's fire. (Premise)

There is no fire. (Premise)

Therefore, there is no smoke. (Conclusion)

Syllogisms follow this form:
Major Premise: If A, then B.
Minor Premise: If B, then C.
Conclusion: Therefore, if A, then C.

All human beings die. (Major premise)

Clarissa is a human being. (Minor premise)

Therefore, Clarissa will die. (Conclusion)

Disjunctive Syllogisms follow this form:
Premise: Either A or B.
Premise: Not A.
Conclusion: Therefore, B.

We must save the environment either through voluntary compliance or with legal penalties. (Premise)

Volunatry compliance has not produced results. (Premise)

Therefore, we must use legal penalties. (Conclusion)

Note that an argument can be valid when it comes to deductive reasoning without being sound. Its soundness depends upon the truth of its premises. Therefore, it is important to weigh the evidence as to its relevance and sufficiency.

The main idea of a passage may contain a wide variety of supporting information, but it is important that each sentence be related to the main idea. When a sentence contains information that bears little or no connection to the main idea, it is said to be IRRELEVANT. It is important to assess continually whether or not a sentence contributes to the overall task of supporting the main idea. When a sentence is deemed irrelevant, it is best either to omit it from the passage or to make it relevant by one of the following strategies:

> **IRRELEVANT:** bears little or no connection to the main idea

1. **Adding detail:** Sometimes a sentence can seem out of place if it does not contain enough information to link it to the topic. Adding specific information can show how the sentence relates to the main idea.

2. **Adding an example:** This is especially important in passages in which information is being argued or compared and contrasted. Examples can support the main idea and give the document credibility.

3. **Using diction effectively:** It is important to understand connotation, avoid ambiguity, and avoid too much repetition when selecting words.

4. **Adding transitions:** Transitions are extremely helpful for making sentences relevant because they are specifically designed to connect one idea to another. They can also reduce a paragraph's choppiness.

The following passage has several irrelevant sentences that are highlighted in **bold**:

> The New City Planning Committee is proposing a new capitol building to represent the multicultural face of New City. **The current mayor is a Democrat.** The new capitol building will be on 10th Street across from the grocery store and next to the recreational center. It will be within walking distance to the subway and bus depot, as the designers want to emphasize the importance of public transportation. Aesthetically, the building will have a contemporary design, featuring a brushed-steel exterior and large, floor-to-ceiling windows. **It is important for employees to have a connection with the outside world even when they are in their offices.** Inside the building, the walls will be moveable. This will not only facilitate a multitude of creative floor plans, but it will also create a focus on open communication and flow of information. **It sounds a bit gimmicky to me.** Finally, the capitol will feature a large outdoor courtyard full of lush greenery and serene fountains. **Work will now seem like Club Med to those who work at the New City capitol building!**

SKILL 3.3 Determine whether evidence strengthens, weakens, or is relevant to the arguments in a reading selection

See Skill 3.2

SKILL 3.4 Determine the logical assumptions upon which an argument or conclusion is based

See Skill 3.2

SKILL 3.5 Draw conclusions from material presented in a reading selection

See Skills 1.1, 3.2

SKILL **Analyze how two or more texts address similar themes or topics in order**
3.6 **to build knowledge and/or compare approaches the authors take**

Authors may use different approaches to the same or a similar topic. They may have differing points of view or present different interpretations of evidence or even different sets of evidence, including factors other authors have not considered or have dismissed as unimportant. Reading critically is an important skill when comparing and contrasting different viewpoints and ultimately drawing one's own conclusion. Critical reading and thinking are important too when applying the understanding gained in one reading selection to other reading selections or situations.

Practice Excercise: Comparing and Contrasting Two Passages

Passage 1

In Arthur Miller's famous play *The Crucible*, farmer John Proctor is accused of being involved in witchcraft. The reader gets the distinct impression that this accusation comes because of his refusal of the sexual advances of one of the foremost accusers. Wrong and unfair as the accusation is, John Proctor takes a strong moral stand.

Based upon real events and characters in Salem, Massachusetts during the famous Salem Witch Trials in 1693, the play raises the moral point of whether or not a person should confess to wrongdoing, even when innocent, to avoid punishment.

During the Salem Witch Trials, if a person accused of being a witch confessed to being so, he or she would be forgiven and released. He or she was also expected to "name names" of other people involved in witchcraft. Since the punishment for witchcraft was death, the temptation to confess to being a witch was strong, as was the temptation to solidify one's position with the judges by being willing to point out other "witches."

However, the false confessions of respectable people only added to the fear and paranoia in Salem Village. People felt they were indeed surrounded by evil powers if such pillars of the community were practicing witchcraft.

In *The Crucible*, John Proctor refuses to confess to being a witch. He stands strong and goes to his death. Historians note that the stances of respectable people who refused to confess to being witches helped to stop the madness as they showed that the accusations were false and unfair.

Practice Excercise: Comparing and Contrasting Two Passages (cont.)

Passage 2

John Proctor's stance in *The Crucible*, while admirable, did not take into account his full situation. His wife, who had also been accused of being a witch, was released from the death penalty because she was pregnant with his child. He was to be a father, yet he let himself be put to death, leaving his wife alone, tainted by accusation, and unable to support herself.

Is a white lie so terrible when one is facing a false and unfair accusation and going to be put to death for something one did not do? Could anyone blame John Proctor for not caring what the hysterical community thought? Surely some among them were bright enough to know that he was not a witch, nor was the respectable Rebecca Nurse, who also refused to confess to being a witch. People should have been reasonable enough and have thought things through enough themselves without anyone having to be a martyr to the insanity of the accusations of a bunch of hysterical teenage girls who, coincidentally, only seemed to name people they didn't like, as witches.

The injustice should have been obvious to everyone. John Proctor should not have had to bow to it by giving his life.

Proctor is inspired by the saintly Rebecca Nurse, but Rebecca Nurse is an elderly woman. She has had many children and grandchildren and has lived many years. She is known far and wide for her piety, assuring her a place in a benevolent afterlife. John Proctor's situation is totally different. He is a young man, has fathered his very first child, and also has some important years ahead of him as far as making up to his wife for the adultery he committed with Abigail, one of the chief accusers, several years before the story takes place. He should be given the years and experiences a Rebecca Nurse had to be a better man in the community and to redeem his life.

Practice Questions

1. The authors of the passage agree that

   A. John Proctor took an admirable stand in refusing to confess

   B. John Proctor was guilty of other things in his life

   C. John Proctor should have named names

   D. John Proctor is a non-fictional character

2. Unlike the author of Passage 1, the author of Passage 2 mentions

   A. John Proctor refused to confess to being a witch

   B. There was a sexualized relationship between John Proctor and one of the foremost accusers

   C. John Proctor's wife was pregnant

   D. The naming of names of others involved in witchcraft was an important aspect of being set free

3. Which of the following recommendations for John Proctor given by the author of Passage 2 might have been the result of him giving his life?

   A. John's admiration for Rebecca Nurse

   B. John Proctor's redemption of his life

   C. The exoneration of Rebecca Nurse

   D. The discrediting of Abigail and the other teenage accusers

4. The Crucible was written as a literary protest to Senator Joe McCarthy's strong-arm tactics in rooting out liberal people from the entertainment industry in the 1950s. Many were accused of being communists and were then "blackballed" in the industry and unable to find work. Because he has his hero Proctor give his life, what can we extrapolate was Miller's opinion on how people should deal with being accused of being communists and asked to name the names of other entertainers who had liberal tendencies?

   A. That they should go along, confess, name names, and save their own livelihoods

   B. That they should look to the example of John Proctor's wife, who was released out of mercy for her unborn child

   C. That they should change professions

   D. That they should not cooperate by confessing or by naming names

Question Unclear at First

Answer Key

1. **A**

   In Passage 1, the author uses the words "John Proctor takes a strong moral stand." In Passage 2, the author says that John Proctor's stance in The Crucible was "admirable."

2. **C**

   The author of Passage 1 does not mention this at all; the author of Passage 2 uses it as a justification for John Proctor to have saved his own life by confessing.

3. **B**

   The author of Passage 2 expresses that John proctor needs to "redeem his life." The author recommends he do that by living on, taking care of his family, and living to an old age, like Rebecca Nurse, as a respected and kindly person in the community. However, giving his life in order to save the community from the madness, as is spoken of in Passage 1, also is a redemptive act for John Proctor's.

4. **D**

   The wording of the question gives hints to the answer here. The play was a literary "protest," which would imply non-cooperation. John Proctor is called Miller's "hero" and therefore his actions of non-cooperation are meant to be models of how to behave in such challenging situations. That is, Miller seemed to imply that those accused of being communists should not confess to it falsely to save their own livelihoods or name names of others to get out of trouble themselves.

SAMPLE TEST
READING

DIRECTIONS: Read the following paragraph and answer the questions that follow.

This writer has often been asked to tutor hospitalized children with cystic fibrosis. While undergoing all the precautionary measures to see these children (i.e. scrubbing thoroughly and donning sterilized protective gear for the child's protection), she has often wondered why their parents subject these children to the pressures of schooling and trying to catch up on what they have missed because of hospitalization, which is a normal part of cystic fibrosis patients' lives. These children undergo so many tortuous treatments a day that it seems cruel to expect them to learn as normal children do, especially with their life expectancies being as short as they are.

1. **What is the main idea of this passage?**

   A. There is much preparation involved in visiting a patient with cystic fibrosis.

   B. Children with cystic fibrosis are incapable of living normal lives.

   C. Certain concessions should be made for children with cystic fibrosis.

   D. Children with cystic fibrosis die young.

2. **What is the author's purpose?**

   A. To inform

   B. To entertain

   C. To describe

   D. To narrate

3. **What type of organizational pattern is the author using?**

   A. Classification

   B. Explanation

   C. Comparison and contrast

   D. Cause and effect

4. **What kind of relationship is found within the last sentence, which starts with "These children undergo ..." and ends with "... as short as they are"?**

   A. Comparison and contrast

   B. Statement support

   C. Spatial/Place

   D. Classification

5. **What is meant by the word "precautionary" in the second sentence?**

   A. Careful

   B. Protective

   C. Medical

   D. Sterilizing

6. **How is the author so familiar with the procedures used when visiting a child with cystic fibrosis?**

   A. She has read about it

   B. She works in a hospital

   C. She is the parent of one

   D. She often tutors them

7. Does the author present an argument that is valid or invalid concerning the schooling of children with cystic fibrosis?

   A. Valid

   B. Invalid

8. The author states that it is "cruel" to expect children with cystic fibrosis to learn as "normal" children do. Is this a fact or an opinion?

   A. Fact

   B. Opinion

9. What is the author's tone?

   A. Sympathetic

   B. Cruel

   C. Disbelieving

   D. Cheerful

10. Is there evidence of bias in this paragraph?

    A. Yes

    B. No

DIRECTIONS: Read the following passage and answer the questions that follow.

Disciplinary practices have been found to affect diverse areas of child development, such as the acquisition of moral values, obedience to authority, and performance at school. Even though the dictionary has a specific definition of the word "discipline," it is still open to interpretation by people of different cultures.

There are four types of disciplinary styles: assertion of power, withdrawal of love, reasoning, and permissiveness. Assertion of power involves the use of force to discourage unwanted behavior. Withdrawal of love involves making the love of a parent conditional on a child's good behavior. Reasoning involves persuading the child to behave one way rather than another. Permissiveness involves allowing the child to do as he or she pleases and face the consequences of his/her actions.

11. What is the author's purpose in writing this?

    A. To describe

    B. To narrate

    C. To entertain

    D. To inform

12. What is the main idea of this passage?

    A. Different people have different ideas of what discipline is

    B. Permissiveness is the most widely-used disciplinary style

    C. Most people agree on their definition of. discipline

    D. There are four disciplinary styles

13. Name the four types of disciplinary styles.

    A. Reasoning, power assertion, morality, and permissiveness

    B. Morality, reasoning, permissiveness, and withdrawal of love

    C. Withdrawal of love, permissiveness, assertion of power, and reasoning

    D. Permissiveness, morality, reasoning, and power assertion

14. **What does the technique of reasoning involve?**

    A. Persuading the child to behave in a certain way

    B. Allowing the child to do as he/she pleases

    C. Using force to discourage unwanted behavior

    D. Making love conditional on good behavior

15. **What organizational structure is used in the first sentence of the second paragraph?**

    A. Addition

    B. Cause and effect

    C. Clarification

    D. Example

16. **What is the overall organizational pattern of this passage?**

    A. Statement support

    B. Cause and effect

    C. Classification

    D. Summary

17. **What is the meaning of the word "diverse" in the first sentence?**

    A. Many

    B. Related to children

    C. Disciplinary

    D. Moral

18. **The author states "assertion of power involves the use of force to discourage unwanted behavior." Is this a fact or an opinion?**

    A. Fact

    B. Opinion

19. **Is this passage biased?**

    A. Yes

    B. No

20. **What is the author's tone?**

    A. Disbelieving

    B. Angry

    C. Informative

    D. Optimistic

21. **From reading this passage, we can conclude that:**

    A. The author is a teacher

    B. The author has many children

    C. The author has written a book about discipline

    D. The author has done a lot of research on discipline

DIRECTIONS: Read the following passage and answer the questions that follow.

One of the most difficult problems plaguing American education is the assessment of teachers. No one denies that teachers should be answerable for what they do, but what exactly does that mean? The Oxford American Dictionary defines accountability as the obligation to give a reckoning or explanation for one's actions.

Does a student have to learn for teaching to have taken place? Historically, teaching has not been defined in this restrictive manner; the teacher was thought to be responsible for the quantity and quality of material covered and the way in which it was presented. However, some definitions of teaching now imply that students must learn in order for teaching to have taken place.

As a teacher who tries my best to keep current on all the latest teaching strategies, I believe that those teachers who do not bother even to pick up an educational journal every once in a while should be kept under close watch. There are many teachers out there who have been teaching for decades and who refuse to change their ways even if research has proven that their methods are outdated and ineffective. There is no place in the profession of teaching for these types of individuals. It is time that the American educational system clean house, for the sake of our children.

22. **What is the main idea of the passage?**

   A. Teachers should not be answerable for what they do

   B. Teachers who do not do their job should be fired

   C. The author is a good teacher

   D. Assessment of teachers is a serious problem in society today

23. **What is the author's purpose in writing this?**

   A. To entertain

   B. To narrate

   C. To describe

   D. To persuade

24. **Where does the author get her definition of "accountability"?**

   A. Webster's Dictionary

   B. Encyclopedia Britannica

   C. Oxford Dictionary

   D. World Book Encyclopedia

25. **The author states that teacher assessment is a problem for**

   A. Elementary schools

   B. Secondary schools

   C. American education

   D. Families

26. **What is the author's overall organizational pattern?**

   A. Classification

   B. Cause and effect

   C. Definition

   D. Comparison and contrast

27. **What is the organizational pattern of the second paragraph?**

   A. Cause and effect

   B. Classification

   C. Sequence of events

   D. Explanation

28. **What is meant by the word "plaguing" in the first sentence?**

   A. Causing problems

   B. Causing illness

   C. Causing anger

   D. Causing failure

29. What is the meaning of the word "reckoning" in the third sentence?

  A. Thought

  B. Answer

  C. Obligation

  D. Explanation

30. Is this a valid argument?

  A. Yes

  B. No

31. Teachers who do not keep current on educational trends should be fired. Is this a fact or an opinion?

  A. Fact

  B. Opinion

32. The author's tone is one of:

  A. Disbelief

  B. Excitement

  C. Support

  D. Concern

33. Is there evidence of bias in this passage?

  A. Yes

  B. No

34. From the passage, one can infer that:

  A. The author considers herself a good teacher

  B. Poor teachers will be fired

  C. Students have to learn for teaching to take place

  D. The author will be fired

DIRECTIONS: Read the following paragraph and answer the questions that follow.

Mr. Smith gave instructions for the painting to be hung on the wall. Then, it leaped forth before his eyes: the little cottages on the river, the white clouds floating over the valley, and the green of the towering mountain ranges that were seen in the distance. The painting was so vivid that it seemed almost real. Mr. Smith was now certain that the painting had been worth money.

35. What is the main idea of this passage?

  A. The painting that Mr. Smith purchased is expensive

  B. Mr. Smith purchased a painting

  C. Mr. Smith was pleased with the quality of the painting he had purchased

  D. The painting depicted cottages and valleys

36. The author's purpose is to:

  A. Inform

  B. Entertain

  C. Persuade

  D. Narrate

37. What does the author mean by the expression "it leaped forth before his eyes"?

  A. The painting fell off the wall

  B. The painting appeared so real it was almost three-dimensional

  C. The painting struck Mr. Smith in the face

  D. Mr. Smith was hallucinating

38. **What is the meaning of the word "vivid" in the third. sentence?**

   A. Lifelike
   B. Dark
   C. Expensive
   D. Big

39. **Is this passage biased?**

   A. Yes
   B. No

40. **From the last sentence, one can infer that:**

   A. The painting was expensive
   B. The painting was cheap
   C. Mr. Smith was considering purchasing the painting
   D. Mr. Smith thought the painting was too expensive and decided not to purchase it

DIRECTIONS: Read the following selection and answer the questions below, selecting the best choice of the options presented.

Mornings, he likes to sit in his new leather chair by his new living room window, looking out across the rooftops and chimney pots, the clotheslines and telegraph lines and office towers. It's the first time Manhattan, from high above, hasn't crushed him with desire. On the contrary the view makes him feel smug. All those people down there, striving, hustling, pushing, shoving, busting to get what Willie's already got. In spades. He lights a cigarette, blows a jet of smoke against the window. Suckers.

41. **The subject in this passage is:**

   A. a character, and seems to be the lead of the story.
   B. a supporting character.
   C. has an attitude of a criminal.
   D. is female.

42. **What kind of description is the author providing of this scene?**

   A. Backstory of the character.
   B. A characterization of what the character is like.
   C. A narrative in the first person.
   D. The unreliable narrative about a character.

43. **What types of words are "striving, hustling, pushing, shoving, bustling"?**

   A. Adjectives
   B. Adverbs
   C. Nouns
   D. Gerunds

44. **If you had to explain the phrase "crushed him" in the paragraph above and context of the paragraph, what would be the best appropriate explanation?**

   A. The city sustained him with all the opportunity available.
   B. The city called to him to be part of its life.
   C. The city complimented him for everything he has achieved.
   D. The city had energized him to get what he felt he deserved.

45. **Replacing the word "smug" with an antonym in context would have which of the following used?**

   A. Sleepy

   B. Prideful

   C. Humble

   D. Self-satisfied

46. **When the author uses the phrase, "In spades," which of the following is best representing what he is referencing?**

   A. The apartment where Willie is living.

   B. The personal satisfaction of accumulated wealth.

   C. Modern comforts in his home.

   D. The loved ones surrounding him.

47. **By using the introductory word "Mornings," the author achieves what?**

   A. An optimistic tone for the passage.

   B. A simple description of time of day, or chronology for the passage.

   C. It's the start of the book, so he sets the passage at "day one."

   D. A and C.

DIRECTIONS: Read the passage and answer the following questions carefully.

The history of all hitherto existing society is the history of class struggles. Freeman and slave, patrician and plebeian, lord and serf, guildmaster and journeyman, in a word, oppressor and oppressed, stood in constant opposition to one another, carried on an uninterrupted, now hidden, now open fight, a fight that each time ended, either in a revolutionary reconstitution of society at large, or in the common ruin of the contending classes.

In the earlier epochs of history, we find almost everywhere a complicated arrangement of society into various orders, a manifold gradation of social rank. In ancient Rome we have patricians, knights, plebeians, slaves; in the Middle Ages, feudal lords, vassals, guildmasters, journeymen, apprentices, serfs; in almost all of these classes, again, subordinate gradations.

The modern bourgeois society that has sprouted from the ruins of feudal society, has not done away with class antagonisms. It has but established new classes, new conditions of oppression, new forms of struggle in place of the old ones.

Our epoch, the epoch of the bourgeoisie, possesses, however, this distinctive feature: It has simplified the class antagonisms. Society as a whole is more and more splitting up into two great hostile camps, into two great classes directly facing each other - bourgeoisie and proletariat...

48. **The first sentence can best be paraphrased as...**

   A. Every future societal shall deal with issues of class

   B. Education of history is essential for a society to develop

   C. Struggle between classes is the most important aspect of history

   D. In the past, class struggles were very common

   Answer C. Struggle between classes is the most important aspect of history

   With the opening line, the author is explaining that class struggles have defined history. C is the best answer.

49. This piece could best be described as a...

    A. Didactic
    B. Allegory
    C. Extended metaphor
    D. Warning

    Answer A. Didactic.

    The piece's main goal is to educate. It does not warn or entreat, and it does not deal with its subjects allegorically or in an extended metaphor.

50. In context, "manifold" can be assumed to mean...

    A. Assertive
    B. Oppressive
    C. Ludicrous
    D. Numerous

51. Through repetition, this piece, particularly the second paragraph ("Freeman and slaves," etc.) makes effective use of...

    A. Juxtaposition
    B. Pathos
    C. Appeal to authority
    D. Logic

52. What is the author's attitude towards class as a concept?

    A. It is a necessary evil
    B. It is an inevitability
    C. It is a tool of oppression
    D. It is useful, but often misused

53. The author's prose in this piece appeals to the reader through its...

    A. Factual accuracy
    B. Simplicity
    C. Superior tone
    D. Vernacular

54. What can we assume will be the subject of this longer piece?

    A. The volatile history of class struggle
    B. The need to improve conditions for the lower class
    C. The contemporary struggle of the upper and lower classes
    D. The methods by which the upper class created such a dualistic society

55. What best describes the tone of this piece?

    A. Emphatic
    B. Dithering
    C. Scholarly
    D. Fearful

ANSWER KEY			
1. C	15. D ✗	29. D	43. C ✗
2. C ✗	16. C	30. B ✗	44. D
3. B ✗	17. A	31. B	45. C ✗
4. B ✗	18. A	32. D	46. B ✗
5. B	19. B	33. A	47. A ✗
6. D	20. C	34. A	48. C ✗
7. B ✗	21. D	35. C	49. A ✗
8. B	22. D	36. D	50. D
9. A	23. D	37. B	51. A
10. A	24. C	38. A	52. C ✗
11. D	25. C	39. B ✗	53. B ✗
12. A	26. C	40. A	54. C ✗
13. C	27. D ✗	41. A	55. A ✗
14. A	28. A	42. C ✗	56.

36/55 = 65.45%

18 minutes
6/14

Sample Test Questions and Rationale

DIRECTIONS: Read the following paragraph, and answer the questions that follow.

This writer has often been asked to tutor hospitalized children with cystic fibrosis. While undergoing all the precautionary measures to see these children (i.e. scrubbing thoroughly and donning sterilized protective gear for the child's protection), she has often wondered why their parents subject these children to the pressures of schooling and trying to catch up on what they have missed because of hospitalization, which is a normal part of cystic fibrosis patients' lives. These children undergo so many tortuous treatments a day that it seems cruel to expect them to learn as normal children do, especially with their life expectancies being as short as they are.

1. **What is the main idea of this passage?**

   A. There is much preparation involved in visiting a patient with cystic fibrosis.

   B. Children with cystic. fibrosis are incapable of living normal lives.

   C. Certain concessions should be made for children with cystic fibrosis.

   D. Children with cystic fibrosis die young.

   Answer: C. Certain concessions should be made for children with cystic fibrosis.

   The correct answer is C. The author states that she wonders, "why parents subject these children to the pressures of schooling" and that "it seems cruel to expect them to learn as normal children do." In making these statements, she appears to be expressing the belief that these children should not have to do what "normal" children do. They have enough to deal with—their illness itself.

2. **What is the author's purpose?**

   A. To inform

   B. To entertain

   C. To describe

   D. To narrate

   Answer: C. To describe

   The correct answer is C. The author is simply describing her experience in working with children with cystic fibrosis.

3. **What type of organizational pattern is the author using?**

   A. Classification

   B. Explanation

   C. Comparison and contrast

   D. Cause and effect

   Answer: B. Explanation

   The correct answer is B. The author mentions tutoring children with cystic fibrosis in her opening sentence and goes on to "explain" some of the issues that are involved with her job.

Sample Test Questions and Rationale (cont.)

4. What kind of relationship is found within the last sentence, which starts with "These children undergo..." and ends with "...as short as they are"?

   A. Comparison and contrast

   B. Statement support

   C. Spatial/Place

   D. Classification

   but why is it not a comparison?

Answer: B. Statement Support

The correct answer is B. In mentioning that their life expectancies are short, she supports her belief that it is cruel to expect them to learn as normal children do.

5. What is meant by the word "precautionary" in the second sentence?

   A. Careful

   B. Protective

   C. Medical

   D. Sterilizing

Answer: B. Protective

The correct answer is B. The writer uses expressions such as "protective gear" and "child's protection" to emphasize this.

6. How is the author so familiar with the procedures used when visiting a child with cystic fibrosis?

   A. She has read about it

   B. She works in a hospital

   C. She is the parent of one

   D. She often tutors them

Answer: D. She often tutors them.

The correct answer is D. The writer states this fact in the opening sentence.

7. Does the author present an argument that is valid or invalid concerning the schooling of children with cystic fibrosis?

   A. Valid

   B. Invalid

Answer: B. Invalid

The correct answer is B. Even though the writer's argument makes good sense to most readers, it is biased and it lacks real evidence.

Sample Test Questions and Rationale (cont.)

8. The author states that it is "cruel" to expect children with cystic fibrosis to learn as "normal" children do. Is this a fact or an opinion?

A. Fact

B. Opinion

Answer: B. Opinion

The correct answer is B. The fact that she states that it "seems" cruel indicates there is no evidence to support this belief.

9. What is the author's tone?

A. Sympathetic

B. Cruel

C. Disbelieving

D. Cheerful

Answer: A. Sympathetic

The correct answer is A. The author states that "it seems cruel to expect them to learn as normal children do," thereby indicating that she feels sorry for them.

10. Is there evidence of bias in this paragraph?

A. Yes

B. No

Answer: A. Yes

The correct answer is A. The writer clearly feels sorry for these children and gears her writing in that direction.

Sample Test Questions and Rationale (cont.)

DIRECTIONS: Read the following passage, and answer the questions that follow.

Disciplinary practices have been found to affect diverse areas of child development, such as the acquisition of moral values, obedience to authority, and performance at school. Even though the dictionary has a specific definition of the word "discipline," it is still open to interpretation by people of different cultures.

There are four types of disciplinary styles: assertion of power, withdrawal of love, reasoning, and permissiveness. Assertion of power involves the use of force to discourage unwanted behavior. Withdrawal of love involves making the love of a parent conditional on a child's good behavior. Reasoning involves persuading the child to behave one way rather than another. Permissiveness involves allowing the child to do as he or she pleases and face the consequences of his or her actions.

11. **What is the author's purpose in writing this?**

    A. To describe

    B. To narrate

    C. To entertain

    D. To inform

    Answer: D. To inform

    The correct answer is D. The author is providing the reader with information about disciplinary practices.

12. **What is the main idea of this passage?**

    A. Different people have different ideas of what discipline is

    B. Permissiveness is the most widely used disciplinary style

    C. Most people agree on their definition of discipline

    D. There are four disciplinary styles

Answer: A. Different people have different ideas of what discipline is.

The correct answer is A. Choice C is not true; the opposite is stated in the passage. Choice B could be true, but we have no evidence of this. Choice D is just one of the many facts listed in the passage.

13. **Name the four types of disciplinary styles.**

    A. Reasoning, power assertion, morality, and permissiveness

    B. Morality, reasoning, permissiveness, and withdrawal of love

    C. Withdrawal of love, permissiveness, assertion of power, and reasoning

    D. Permissiveness, morality, reasoning, and power assertion

Answer: C. Withdrawal of love, permissiveness, assertion of power, and reasoning.

The correct answer is C. This is directly stated in the second paragraph.

Sample Test Questions and Rationale (cont.)

14. **What does the technique of reasoning involve?**

    A. Persuading the child to behave in a certain way

    B. Allowing the child to do as he/she pleases

    C. Using force to discourage unwanted behavior

    D. Making love conditional on good behavior

    Answer: A. Persuading the child to behave in a certain way.

    The correct answer is A. This fact is directly stated in the second paragraph.

15. **What organizational structure is used in the first sentence of the second paragraph?**

    A. Addition

    B. Cause and effect

    C. Clarification

    D. Example

    Answer: D. Example

    The correct answer is D. The author simply states and gives examples of the types of disciplinary styles.

16. **What is the overall organizational pattern of this passage?**

    A. Statement support

    B. Cause and effect

    C. Classificatio.

    D. Summary

Answer: C. Classification

The correct answer is C. The author has taken a subject, in this case discipline, and developed it point by point.

17. **What is the meaning of the word "diverse" in the first sentence?**

    A. Many

    B. Related to children

    C. Disciplinary

    D. Moral

    Answer: A. Many

    The correct answer is A. Any of the other choices would be redundant in this sentence.

18. **The author states "assertion of power involves the use of force to discourage unwanted behavior." Is this a fact or an opinion?**

    A. Fact

    B. Opinion

    Answer: A. Fact

    The correct answer is A. The author appears to have done extensive research on this subject.

Sample Test Questions and Rationale (cont.)

19. **Is this passage biased?**

    A. Yes

    B. No

    Answer: B. No

    The correct answer is B. If the reader were so inclined, he could research discipline and find this information.

20. **What is the author's tone?**

    A. Disbelieving

    B. Angry

    C. Informative

    D. Optimistic

    Answer: C. Informative

    The correct answer is C. The author appears to be simply stating the facts.

21. **From reading this passage, we can conclude that:**

    A. The author is a teacher

    B. The author has many children

    C. The author has written a book about discipline

    D. The author has done a lot of research on discipline

    Answer: D. The author has done a lot of research on discipline.

    The correct answer is D. Given all the facts mentioned in the passage, this is the only inference one can make.

Sample Test Questions and Rationale (cont.)

DIRECTIONS: Read the following passage, and answer the questions that follow.

One of the most difficult problems plaguing American education is the assessment of teachers. No one denies that teachers should be answerable for what they do, but what exactly does that mean? The Oxford American Dictionary defines accountability as the obligation to give a reckoning or explanation for one's actions.

Does a student have to learn for teaching to have taken place? Historically, teaching has not been defined in this restrictive manner; the teacher was thought to be responsible for the quantity and quality of material covered and the way in which it was presented. However, some definitions of teaching now imply that students must learn in order for teaching to have taken place.

As a teacher who tries my best to keep current on all the latest teaching strategies, I believe that those teachers who do not bother even to pick up an educational journal every once in a while should be kept under close watch. There are many teachers out there who have been teaching for decades and who refuse to change their ways even if research has proven that their methods are outdated and ineffective. There is no place in the profession of teaching for these types of individuals. It is time that the American educational system clean house, for the sake of our children.

22. **What is the main idea of the passage?**

   A. Teachers should not be answerable for what they do

   B. Teachers who do not do their job should be fired

   C. The author is a good teacher

   D. Assessment of teachers is a serious problem in society today

Answer: D. Assessment of teachers is a serious problem in society today.

The correct answer is D. Most of the passage is dedicated to elaborating on why teacher assessment is such a problem.

23. **What is the author's purpose in writing this?**

   A. To entertain

   B. To narrate

   C. To describe

   D. To persuade

Answer: D. To persuade

The correct answer is D. The author does some describing, but the majority of her statements seem to be geared towards convincing the reader that teachers who are lazy or who do not keep current should be fired.

Sample Test Questions and Rationale (cont.)

24. Where does the author get her definition of "accountability"?

    A. Webster's Dictionary

    B. Encyclopedia Britannica

    C. Oxford Dictionary

    D. World Book Encyclopedia

    Answer: C. Oxford Dictionary

    The correct answer is C. This is directly stated in the third sentence of the first paragraph.

25. The author states that teacher assessment is a problem for

    A. Elementary schools

    B. Secondary schools

    C. American education

    D. Families

    Answer: C. American Education

    The correct answer is C. This is directly stated in the first sentence of the first paragraph.

26. What is the author's overall organizational pattern?

    A. Classification

    B. Cause and effect

    C. Definition

    D. Comparison and contrast

Answer: C. Definition

The correct answer is C. The author identifies teacher assessment as a problem and spends the rest of the passage defining why it is considered a problem.

27. What is the organizational pattern of the second paragraph?

    A. Cause and effect

    B. Classification

    C. Sequence of events

    D. Explanation

Answer: D. Explanation

The correct answer is D. The author goes on to explain further what she meant by "...what exactly does that mean?" in the first paragraph.

28. What is meant by the word "plaguing" in the first sentence?

    A. Causing problems

    B. Causing illness

    C. Causing anger

    D. Causing failure

Answer: A. Causing problems

The correct answer is A. The first paragraph makes this definition clear.

Sample Test Questions and Rationale (cont.)

29. What is the meaning of the word "reckoning" in the third sentence?

    A. Thought

    B. Answer

    C. Obligation

    D. Explanation

    Answer: D. Explanation

    The correct answer is D. The meaning of this word is directly stated in the same sentence.

30. Is this a valid argument?

    A. Yes

    B. No

    Answer: B. No

    The correct answer is B. In the third paragraph, the author appears to be resentful of lazy teachers.

31. Teachers who do not keep current on educational trends should be fired. Is this a fact or an opinion?

    A. Fact

    B. Opinion

    Answer: B. Opinion

    The correct answer is B. There may be those who feel they can be good teachers by using old methods.

32. The author's tone is one of:

    A. Disbelief

    B. Excitement

    C. Support

    D. Concern

    Answer: D. Concern

    The correct answer is D. The author appears concerned with the future of education.

33. Is there evidence of bias in this passage?

    A. Yes

    B. No

    Answer: A. Yes

    The correct answer is A. The entire third paragraph is the author's opinion on the matter.

34. From the passage, one can infer that:

    A. The author considers herself a good teacher

    B. Poor teachers will be fired

    C. Students have to learn for teaching to take place

    D. The author will be fired

    Answer: A. The author considers herself a good teacher.

    The correct answer is A. The first sentence of the third paragraph alludes to this.

Sample Test Questions and Rationale (cont.)

DIRECTIONS: Read the following paragraph, and answer the questions that follow.

Mr. Smith gave instructions for the painting to be hung on the wall. Then, it leaped forth before his eyes: the little cottages on the river, the white clouds floating over the valley, and the green of the towering mountain ranges that were seen in the distance. The painting was so vivid that it seemed almost real. Mr. Smith was now certain that the painting had been worth money.

35. **What is the main idea of this passage?**

    A. The painting that Mr. Smith purchased is expensive.

    B. Mr. Smith purchased a painting.

    C. Mr. Smith was pleased with the quality of the painting he had purchased.

    D. The painting depicted cottages and valleys.

    Answer: C. Mr. Smith was pleased with the quality of the painting he had purchased.

    The correct answer is C. Every sentence in the paragraph alludes to this fact

36. **The author's purpose is to:**

    A. Inform

    B. Entertain

    C. Persuade

    D. Narrate

    Answer: D. Narrate

    The correct answer is D. The author is simply narrating or telling the story of Mr. Smith and his painting.

37. **What does the author mean by the expression "it leaped forth before his eyes"?**

    A. The painting fell off the wall.

    B. The painting appeared so real it was almost three-dimensional.

    C. The painting struck Mr. Smith in the face.

    D. Mr. Smith was hallucinating.

    Answer: B. The painting appeared so real it was almost three-dimensional.

    The correct answer is B. This is almost directly stated in the third sentence.

38. **What is the meaning of the word "vivid" in the third sentence?**

    A. Lifelike

    B. Dark

    C. Expensive

    D. Big

    Answer: A. Lifelike

    The correct answer is A. The second half of the same sentence reinforces this.

Sample Test Questions and Rationale (cont.)

39. Is this passage biased?

A. Yes

B. No

Answer: B. No

The correct answer is B. The author appears to be just telling what happened when Mr. Smith had his new painting hung on the wall.

40. From the last sentence, one can infer that:

A. The painting was expensive

B. The painting was cheap

C. Mr. Smith was considering purchasing the painting

D. Mr. Smith thought the painting was too expensive and decided not to purchase it

Answer: A. The painting was expensive.

The correct answer is A. Choice B is incorrect because, had the painting been cheap, chances are that Mr. Smith would not have considered his purchase. Choices C and D are ruled out by the fact that the painting had already been purchased. The author makes this clear when she says, "...the painting had been worth the money."

Sample Test Questions and Rationale (cont.)

DIRECTIONS: Read the following selection and answer the questions below, selecting the best choice of the options presented.

Mornings, he likes to sit in his new leather chair by his new living room window, looking out across the rooftops and chimney pots, the clotheslines and telegraph lines and office towers. It's the first time Manhattan, from high above, hasn't crushed him with desire. On the contrary the view makes him feel smug. All those people down there, striving, hustling, pushing, shoving, busting to get what Willie's already got. In spades. He lights a cigarette, blows a jet of smoke against the window. Suckers.

41. **The subject in this passage is:**

    A. a character, and seems to be the lead of the story.

    B. a supporting character.

    C. has an attitude of a criminal.

    D. is female.

    Answer A. A character, and seems to be the lead of the story.

    The female pronoun is used, so D is inaccurate. B is not accurate as he is the focus of the passage. Of A and C, there is no support for this character being a criminal. Remember not to make assumptions when you answer questions.

42. **What kind of description is the author providing of this scene?**

    A. Backstory of the character.

    B. A characterization of what the character is like.

    C. A narrative in the first person.

    D. The unreliable narrative about a character.

    Answer C. A narrative in the first person.

Backstory isn't accurate because a current scene is described. B uses the same root-word twice, which is usually an indication that it is not a correct guess. There is nothing to suggest the character is unreliable. This leaves options C and E and neither the author nor character are persuading the reader toward a conclusion.

43. **What types of words are "striving, hustling, pushing, shoving, bustling"?**

    A. Adjectives

    B. Adverbs

    C. Nouns

    D. Gerunds

    Answer C. Nouns   6

Backstory isn't accurate because a current scene is described. B uses the same root-word twice, which is usually an indication that it is not a correct guess. There is nothing to suggest the character is unreliable. This leaves option C in which neither the author nor character are persuading the reader toward a conclusion.

Sample Test Questions and Rationale (cont.)

44. If you had to explain the phrase "crushed him" in the paragraph above and context of the paragraph, what would be the best appropriate explanation?

    A. The city sustained him with all the opportunity available.

    B. The city called to him to be part of its life.

    C. The city complimented him for everything he has achieved.

    D. The city had energized him to get what he felt he deserved.

Answer D. The city had energized him to get what he felt he deserved.

This tests your reading comprehension.

45. Replacing the word "smug" with an antonym in context would have which of the following used?

    A. Sleepy

    B. Prideful

    C. Humble

    D. Self-satisfied

Answer C. Humble

This involves knowing the words meanings as well as reading carefully as the question asked for antonym.

46. When the author uses the phrase, "In spades," which of the following is best representing what he is referencing?

    A. The apartment where Willie is living.

    B. The personal satisfaction of accumulated wealth.

    C. Modern comforts in his home.

    D. The loved ones surrounding him.

Answer B. The personal satisfaction of accumulated wealth.

The context and reading comprehension bring you to the correct answer. Nothing implying loved ones, modern comforts or the mere large apartment relate to the question.

47. By using the introductory word "Mornings," the author achieves what?

    A. An optimistic tone for the passage.

    B. A simple description of time of day, or chronology for the passage.

    C. It's the start of the book, so he sets the passage at "day one."

    D. A and C.

Answer A. An optimistic tone for the passage.

Context of the tone of the passage shows the character speaking is in a good mood, but it does not mean that it actually is morning and there is no indication that it is the start of the book.

Sample Test Questions and Rationale (cont.)

DIRECTIONS: Read the passage and answer the following questions carefully.

The history of all hitherto existing society is the history of class struggles. Freeman and slave, patrician and plebeian, lord and serf, guildmaster and journeyman, in a word, oppressor and oppressed, stood in constant opposition to one another, carried on an uninterrupted, now hidden, now open fight, a fight that each time ended, either in a revolutionary reconstitution of society at large, or in the common ruin of the contending classes.

In the earlier epochs of history, we find almost everywhere a complicated arrangement of society into various orders, a manifold gradation of social rank. In ancient Rome we have patricians, knights, plebeians, slaves; in the Middle Ages, feudal lords, vassals, guild- masters, journeymen, apprentices, serfs; in almost all of these classes, again, subordinate gradations.

The modern bourgeois society that has sprouted from the ruins of feudal society, has not done away with class antagonisms. It has but established new classes, new conditions of oppression, new forms of struggle in place of the old ones.

Our epoch, the epoch of the bourgeoisie, possesses, however, this distinctive feature: It has simplified the class antagonisms. Society as a whole is more and more splitting up into two great hostile camps, into two great classes directly facing each other - bourgeoisie and proletariat…

48. The first sentence can best be paraphrased as…

A. Every future societal shall deal with issues of class

B. Education of history is essential for a society to develop

C. Struggle between classes is the most important aspect of history

D. In the past, class struggles were very common

Answer C. Struggle between classes is the most important aspect of history

With the opening line, the author is explaining that class struggles have defined history. C is the best answer.

49. This piece could best be described as a…

A. Didactic

B. Allegory

C. Extended metaphor

D. Warning

Answer A. Didactic.

The piece's main goal is to educate. It does not warn or entreat, and it does not deal with its subjects allegorically or in an extended metaphor.

Sample Test Questions and Rationale (cont.)

50. In context, "manifold" can be assumed to mean...

A. Assertive

B. Oppressive

C. Ludicrous

D. Numerous

Answer D. Numerous

"Manifold" is a synonym for "various", "diverse" or "many".

51. Through repetition, this piece, particularly the second paragraph ("Freeman and slaves," etc.) makes effective use of...

A. Juxtaposition

B. Pathos

C. Appeal to authority

D. Logic

Answer A. Juxtaposition

The repetitions, such as "freedman and slave" or "guildmaster and journeyman", create juxtapositions the author uses for rhetorical effect.

52. What is the author's attitude towards class as a concept?

A. It is a necessary evil

B. It is an inevitability

C. It is a tool of oppression

D. It is useful, but often misused

Answer C. It is a tool of oppression

The author is primarily concerned with class hierarchies as a tool of oppression, stating how the modern era of bourgeoisie vs. proletariat struggle is simplified in its antagonism. He feels class struggle is oppressive.

53. The author's prose in this piece appeals to the reader through its...

A. Factual accuracy

B. Simplicity

C. Superior tone

D. Vernacular

Answer B. Simplicity

The author uses primarily simple language in this treatise. It makes opinion-based assertions and relies less on factual accuracy, so A is inappropriate. Likewise, the piece does not strive to superior or overly familiar, so C and D do not apply.

Sample Test Questions and Rationale (cont.)

54. **What can we assume will be the subject of this longer piece?**

    A. The volatile history of class struggle

    B. The need to improve conditions for the lower class

    C. The contemporary struggle of the upper and lower classes

    D. The methods by which the upper class created such a dualistic society

    Answer C. The contemporary struggle of the upper and lower classes

    The author ends on his point about bourgeoisie vs. proletariat, suggesting that this is the topic he will pursuing for the longer essay.

55. **What best describes the tone of this piece?**

    A. Emphatic

    B. Dithering

    C. Scholarly

    D. Fearful

    Answer A. Emphatic

    The author makes many emphatic points throughout the piece, even in points that could best be characterized as opinion. He is stating things strongly, with no room for argument.

DOMAIN II
WRITING

PERSONALIZED STUDY PLAN

KNOWN MATERIAL/ SKIP IT

PAGE	COMPETENCY AND SKILL	
59	**4: Text Types, Purposes and Production**	☐
	4.1: Producing an Argumentative Essay	☐
	4.2: Producing Informative or Explanatory Texts	☐
	4.3: The Revision and Editing Process in Text Production	☐
	4.4: Apply Knowledge of Language and its Functions to EnhanceMeaning and Style when Revising	☐
	4.5: Revising to Maintain Consistency in Style and Tone	☐
75	**5: Language Skills for Writing Grammatical Relationships**	☐
	5.1: Identify errors in the use of adjectives and adverbs	☐
	5.2: Identify errors in noun noun agreement	☐
	5.3: Identify errors in pronoun-antecedent agreement	☐
	5.4: Identify errors in pronoun case	☐
	5.5: Identify errors in the use of intensive pronouns	☐
	5.6: Identify errors in pronoun number and person	☐
	5.7: Identify errors in the use of vague pronouns	☐
	5.8: Recognize and correct errors in subject-verb agreement	☐
	5.9: Recognize and correct inappropriate shifts in verb tense	☐
96	**6: Language and Research Skills for Writing: Structural Relationships**	☐
	6.1: Identify errors in the placement of phrases and clauses	☐
	6.2: Identify errors of misplaced and dangling modifiers	☐
	6.3: Identify errors in the use of coordinating and subordinating conjunctions	☐
	6.4: Recognize and correct sentence fragments and run-on sentences	☐
	6.5: Identify errors in the use of correlative conjunctions	☐
	6.6: Identify errors in parallel structure	☐
116	**7: Language Skills for Writing: Word Choice**	☐
	7.1: Identify errors in the use of idiomatic expressions	☐
	7.2: Identify errors in the use of frequently confused words	☐
	7.3: Identify wrong word use	☐
	7.4: Recognize and correct errors in redundancy	☐
138	**8: Language Skills for Writing: Capitalization and Punctuation**	☐
	8.1: Identify errors in capitalization	☐
	8.2: Identify errors in punctuation	☐
147	**9: Research Skills**	☐
	9.1: Assess the credibility and relevance of sources	☐
	9.2: Recognize the different elements of a citation	☐
	9.3: Recognize effective research strategies	☐
	9.4: Recognize information relevant to a particular research task	☐

COMPETENCY 4
TEXT TYPES, PURPOSES AND PRODUCTION

SKILL Producing an Argumentative Essay
4.1

An excellent argumentative essay presents its argument with clarity and coherence, using relevant, valid, and sufficient evidence. Such an essay also:

- Is written on the level of educated adults and adheres to the assignment given

- Presents and develops ideas in a logical organizational pattern while explaining them clearly and pointing out connections between the ideas while providing original thinking and creative insights

- States outright or else clearly implies the author's stance or thesis and stays consistent with this throughout

- Provides supporting ideas, reasons, details and examples that are logically connected and on point.

- Shows the author's ability and facility in the use of the English language and uses a variety of sentence structures

- Is mostly free of errors in regard to sentence structure, syntax, grammar, punctuation, spelling, et cetera and adheres to the standards of written English

To develop a complete essay, spend a few minutes planning. Jot down your ideas and quickly sketch an outline. Although you may feel under pressure to begin writing, you will write more effectively if you plan your major points.

Prewriting

Before actually writing, you will need to generate content and develop a writing plan. The following are three prewriting techniques that can be helpful:

Brainstorming

When brainstorming, quickly create a list of words and ideas that are connected to the topic. Let your mind roam free to generate as many relevant ideas as possible in a few minutes. For example, on the topic of computers you may write:

> computer—modern invention
>
> types—personal computers, microchips in calculators and watches
>
> wonder—acts like an electronic brain
>
> uses—science, medicine, offices, homes, schools
>
> problems—too much reliance; the machines are not perfect

This list could help you focus on the topic, and it states the points you could develop in the body paragraphs. The brainstorming list keeps you on track and is well worth the few minutes it takes to jot down the ideas. While you have not yet ordered the ideas, seeing them on paper is an important step.

Questioning

Questioning helps you focus as you mentally ask a series of exploratory questions about the topic. You may use the most basic questions: who, what, where, when, why, and how.

> **"What** is my subject?"
>
> [computers]
>
> **"What** types of computers are there?"
>
> [personal computers, microchip computers]
>
> **"Why** have computers been a positive invention?"
>
> [act as an electronic brain in machinery and equipment; help solve complex scientific problems]
>
> **"How** have computers been a positive invention?"
>
> [used to make improvements in:
> * science (space exploration, moon landings)
> * medicine (MRIs, CT scans, surgical tools, research models)
> * business (PCs, FAX, telephone equipment)
> * education (computer programs for math, languages, science, social studies)
> * personal tasks (family budgets, tax programs, healthy diet plans)]

> **"How** can I show that computers are good?"
>
> [cite numerous examples]
>
> **"What** problems do I see with computers?"
>
> [too much reliance; not yet perfect]
>
> **"What** personal experiences would help me develop examples to respond to this topic?
>
> [my own experiences using computers]

Of course, you may not have time to write out the questions completely. You might just write the words who, what, where, why, and how and the major points next to each. An abbreviated list might look as follows:

What: *computers/modern wonder/making life better*

How: *through technological improvements: lasers, calculators, CT scans, MRIs*

Where: *in science and space exploration, medicine, schools, offices*

In a few moments, your questions should help you focus on the topic and generate interesting ideas and points to make in the essay. Later in the writing process, you can look back at the list to be sure you have made the key points you intended.

Clustering

Some visual thinkers find clustering an effective prewriting method. When clustering, you draw a box in the center of your paper and write your topic within that box. Then, you draw lines from the center box connecting it to small satellite boxes that contain related ideas. Note the cluster below on computers:

SAMPLE CLUSTER

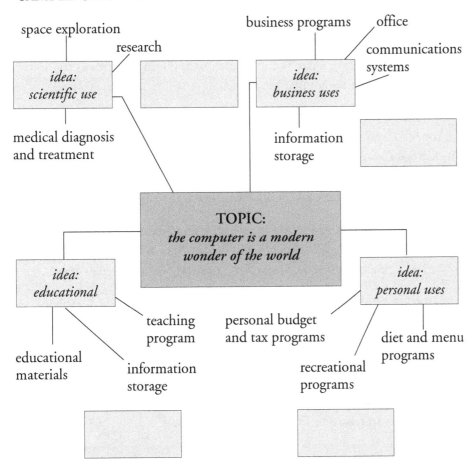

Sample Question Prompt for a
PPST Argumentative Essaay

Directions: Read the opinion stated below and discuss ways in which you disagree or agree with it. Support your views with reasons and examples from your own reading, knowledge, experience, or observations on the topic at hand.

Prompt:

Several highly intelligent thinkers wanted a great deal of freedom for the individual, including the freedom from strict obedience of the law. In the Declaration of Independence, Thomas Jefferson asserted the human "right to revolution" if a government becomes too tyrannical. Henry David Thoreau said that the best government is that which governs the least. Dr. Martin Luther King said people had an obligation to break unjust laws. These great thinkers were right because it is the rule-breakers who make society better.

Sample Response:

While I agree that it is often the rule-breakers who advance society, I disagree that the great thinkers mentioned thought anyone should enjoy freedom from strict obedience of the law. All three were deeply moral men concerned with justice. Law attempts to achieve justice. Doing away with law, government, and rules would result in anarchy and chaos. However, in these men's thinking, justice should be the foundation of law.

I am reminded of Sir Thomas More's statement in Robert Bolton's play "A Man for All Seasons." When More's passionate son-in-law said he would do away with all law to protect morality, More replied that if all laws were struck down, no one could stand in the winds that would be unleashed. Certainly all of us depend upon laws to protect ourselves, our rights, and our property.

The Declaration of Independence was in itself an attempt to codify into law the colonies' freedom from the injustices of Great Britain. Thomas Jefferson was himself a lawyer and a government representative. He clearly believed in the rule of law.

Thoreau was a great free thinker and the author of "On Civil Disobedience," an essay that urged non-cooperation with the government when it is unjust. This essay was written in reaction to the injustice of slavery. Thoreau believed that a person's conscience was higher than the law and that when it came to an issue like slavery, which was legal in some states at the time, the good citizen had a duty to listen to conscience rather than an unjust law. His position was clearly only in regard to flagrantly immoral laws.

Sample Question Prompt for a
PPST Argumentative Essaay (cont.)

Almost as a continuation of the argument, and nearly one hundred years later, Dr. Martin Luther King reflected on the nature of law and a just society. In general, he came down on the side of the law. He believed that while morality could not be legislated by making laws, a society could regulate behavior by enforcing laws that called for decent behavior toward others. As Dr. Martin Luther King put it, "Law cannot change the heart but it can restrain the heartless." At the same time, in his letter from Birmingham Jail, Dr. King talked about how it is obligatory for a moral person to break unjust laws. He did, however, insist that a person who is breaking an unjust law must meekly and bravely accept the consequences of breaking that law. In jail at the time for leading a marching demonstration without a parade permit, Dr. King asserted rightly that justice was a higher law than the parade ordinance.

Analysis

This argumentative essay is clearly written and is written to an audience of educated adults who would be familiar with several of the famous persons named: Thomas Jefferson, Henry David Thoreau, Dr. Martin Luther King, and Sir Thomas More. Three out of four of those famous persons were mentioned in the prompt, so the argumentative essay sample responds directly to the prompt.

After the insertion of the insightful note about Sir Thomas More and the importance of the rule of law, the writer systematically talks about each of the famous persons and their ideas about obedience to law and the requirements of justice. Each paragraph supports the thesis stated clearly in the first paragraph: that anarchy and chaos would be the results of widespread disobedience to the law and that the famous men mentioned did not advocate lawlessness but the higher law of justice.

The supporting details and examples elaborate on the complex thinking of the figures who were noted in the essay prompt, explaining why their rebellion against certain laws still fit into a larger mental framework in each man that believed in the rule of law.

The vocabulary and varied sentence structures show ability and facility in the English language, and the essay in mostly free of grammatical and other errors according to standards of written English.

The essay writer displays competence in writing this essay.

SKILL 4.2 Producing Informative or Explanatory Texts

An excellent informative/explanatory essay examines, analyzes, and selects as significant complex ideas and information from sources. Such an essay also:

- Is written with clarity and coherence

- Is written on the level of educated adults; adheres to the assignment given

- Effectively draws out supportive evidence and insights from informational sources

- Presents ideas in a logical organizational pattern while explaining them clearly and pointing out relationships between the ideas

- Synthesizes and integrates the information from more than one source without lapsing into plagiarism; properly attributes sources

- States outright or else clearly implies a stance or thesis and stays consistent with this throughout

- Shows the author's ability and facility with a variety of sentence structures and language usage

- Is mostly free of errors in regard to sentence structure, syntax, grammar, punctuation, spelling, et cetera and adheres to the standards of written English

Sample Question Prompt for a
PPST Informative/Explanatory Essay

Directions: Carefully read the two selections and write an essay about the major points of issue discussed in the two sources and the significance of these major points. You must use both sources for information in addition to your own reading, knowledge, experience, or observations on the topic at hand. Remember to cite the source when you are quoting directly, paraphrasing, or summing up the source's information.

Source 1: McGinty, Terry. "Legislating Green." *University of Telmont Law Review*, 37:1 (2009): 272. Web. 12 Dec. 2014.

Laws should restrain those who are careless toward the environment so that they behave respectfully toward it. This is for the common good, not only in our country, but all over the world. Planet Earth is shared; it is not ours to destroy because the money-minded find landfills cheaper than recycling. It is not ours to destroy because industry says water and air pollution are collateral damage to be expected in the name of profits.

Right now recycling is voluntary in many communities. It should be federally mandated everywhere. For many communities, a mandatory recycling program has had an immediate effect. By just recycling glass, aluminum cans, and plastic bottles, we have reduced the volume of disposable trash by one-third, thus extending the useful life of local landfills by over a decade. Imagine the difference if those dramatic results were achieved nationwide.

The amount of reusable items we thoughtlessly dispose of is staggering. For example, Americans dispose of enough steel every day to supply Detroit car manufacturers for three months. Additionally, we dispose of enough aluminum annually to rebuild the nation's air fleet. These statistics, available from the Environmental Protection Agency (EPA), should encourage us to watch what we throw away.

Clearly, recycling in our homes and communities directly improves the environment. Therefore, it should be mandated by law in every state and every community.

Sample Question Prompt for a
PPST Informative/Explanatory Essay (cont.)

Source 2: Luften, Samuel T., *The Power of Education*, New York. Post Publishing, 2010. 79-80. Web. 14 Dec. 2013.

Another way in which the power of education may be demonstrated is when it comes to recycling. Recycling should be a way of life, not something we do once a week because we will be fined if we do not. It is the decisions of each individual that impact the environment most dramatically. The environmentally conscious person who decides to "Use it up, wear it out, make it do, and do without" so as not to consume, consume, consume natural resources in the production of ever more and ever newer goods is a far more efficient environmentalist than the person who (begrudgingly) separates his plastic from his aluminum cans and thinks he's done enough.

There are so many ideological and political issues involved in environmental protection through law, we may be sure that many laws are passed for reasons other than pure concern for the environment. Unfortunately, the environmental crisis continues despite policies and laws on the books.

An example is the federal Clean Water Act. Enacted in the 1970s, the Clean Water Act was intended to clean up polluted waters throughout the nation and to provide safe drinking water for everyone. However, even with the Clean Water Act in place, dangerous medical waste has washed onto public beaches in Florida and, recently, several people died from the polluted drinking water in Madison, Wisconsin.

Additionally, contradictory government policies often work against resource protection. For example, some state welfare agencies give new mothers money only for disposable, not cloth, diapers. In fact, consumer groups found that cloth diapers are cheaper initially and save money over time as we struggle with the crisis of bulging landfills.

If they are to work at all, government policies and laws should at least be consistent with research as to what really aids the environment rather than being affected by funding and special interest groups. (Believe it or not, the disposable diaper industry is a huge industry, and state contracts are extremely lucrative.)

Rather than trusting politicians and government to do our environmental protection for us, we should put our faith in nonprofit organizations that lobby for meaningful, enforceable legal changes. Most of us do not have time to write letters, send telegrams, or study every issue concerning the environment. We can join several organizations that act as watchdogs for us all. For example, organizations such as Greenpeace, the Cousteau Society, and the Sierra Club all offer memberships for low fees. By supporting these organizations, we ensure that they have the necessary resources to keep working for all of us and do not have to alter their standards because they must accept funding from special interest groups.

Sample Question Prompt for a
PPST Informative/Explanatory Essay (cont.)

Sample Response:

The two authors share a major area of concern with regard to the environment, namely that people should recycle. They differ in their interpretation of the most efficient way to ensure that people recycle: through federal mandate or through raised consciousness. In his piece, Terry McGinty believes that "recycing should be mandated by law in every state and every community ("Legislating Green"). In his book *The Power of Education*, Samuel T. Luften asserts that recycling is an individual lifestyle choice and depends more upon education than ordinances.

McGinty asserts that "laws should restrain those who are careless toward the environment so that they behave respectfully toward it" (McGinty). Because recycling is currently voluntary in some municipalities, McGinty believes it should be federally mandated. McGinty cites local figures of 33% reduction of the volume of disposable trash in a community, and asks the reader to extrapolate those results nationwide (McGinty). McGinty also notes that the EPA has found that Americans throw away enough steel and aluminum each year to save billions on the production of automobiles and airplanes. (McGinty) His essay frequently appeals to the macro level, speaking of Planet Earth as shared by the world's inhabitants and relating local statistics to national visions.

Luften, on the other hand, believes that environmental legislation is so fraught with politics and money interests that it sometimes works against itself. In spite of the Clean Water Act, he says, water has been dangerously polluted in examples like Florida and Wisconsin (Luften). What is more, government policies are often affected by monetary interests, such as the disposable diaper industry, which convinced some state welfare agencies to "give new mothers money only for disposable, not cloth, diapers" in spite of cloth diapers' proven lesser environmental impact (Luften). To combat monetary and political interests affecting legislation, Luften recommends that citizens support non-profit groups dedicated to the environment.

Both authors support and see the need for environmental protection. McGinty believes in the power of government to help; Luften prefers the power of educated individual choices and monetarily and politically disinterested non-profits to bring about environmental improvement. Yet in fact, the ultimate answer is probably not "either/or" but "both/and." Surely some governmental regulation of environmental standards has worked well to improve the environment, even as it is up to the individual to make the buying, re-using, and recycling choices that, multiplied many times over, determine the size of humanity's carbon footprint on our earth.

Sample Question Prompt for a
PPST Informative/Explanatory Essay (cont.)

Analysis:

This response clearly depicts the main concern of the essay writers of sources 1 and 2 and their different approaches to addressing this shared concern. This is stated succinctly and clearly in the first paragraph, and it sets up the organization of the essay.

The sample essay is organized well. The first paragraph presents the area of mutual concern and summarizes each Source author's position. The following paragraphs treat each author's point of view and supporting details and ideas separately and then analyzes them together, synthesizing their points of view into a concluding original insight.

The Sources are properly attributed, and all direct language from the sources is put in quotation marks. The vocabulary and sentence structure are sophisticated, and the essay is generally free of errors and lives up to the standards of written English.

Through its vocabulary, references, and insights, the essay is written to an audience of educated adults and addresses the assignment given. The writer of the essay draws out evidence and insights from both sources and makes significant connections between the two sources and their areas of main concerns as well as their differing solutions to a shared area of significance. The essay writer draws his or her own conclusion based upon the evidence from each Source. The essay upholds standards of written English and shows a facility and ability with a variety of sentence structures.

SKILL 4.3 The Revision and Editing Process in Text Production

Good writers are good readers. Competencies 1, 2, and 3 of Reading, Domain 1, give excellent background in how to write and revise well.

It is important to know that revising and editing are more than just looking for typographical errors or tweaking word use. Revising and editing both develop and strengthen a piece of writing. As they revise and edit, students need to ask themselves the following questions:

- Is the reasoning coherent?

- Is the point established?

- Does the introduction make the reader want to read the discourse?

- What is the thesis? Is it proven?

- What is the purpose? Is it clear? Is it useful, valuable, and interesting?

- Is the style of writing so wordy that it exhausts the reader and interferes with engagement?

- Is the writing so spare that it is boring?

- Are the sentences too uniform in structure?

- Are there too many simple sentences?

- Are too many of the complex sentences of the same structure?

- Are the compounds truly compounds or are they unbalanced?

- Are parallel structures truly parallel?

- Is the title appropriate?

- Does the writing show creativity or does it seem boring?

- Is the language appropriate? Is it too formal? Too informal? If jargon is used, is it appropriate?

An important part of revisions to stay on topic. Every paragraph of the essay and every sentence within each paragraph should support the thesis. A good thesis gives structure to your essay and helps focus your thoughts.

Writing the Thesis

THESIS: the controlling idea of an essay

After focusing on the topic and generating your ideas, you will form your THESIS, the controlling idea of your essay. The thesis is your general statement to the reader that expresses your point of view and guides your essay's purpose and scope. A strong thesis will enable you either to explain your subject or to take an arguable position about it. A good thesis statement is neither too narrow nor too broad.

Subject and Assertion of the Thesis

From the statement of the general topic, you analyzed the topic in terms of its two parts: subject and assertion. On the teacher certification exam, your thesis or viewpoint on a particular topic is stated in two important points:

> The **subject** of the paper and the **assertion** about the subject

SUBJECT OF THE THESIS: relates directly to the topic prompt but expresses the specific area you have chosen to discuss

The SUBJECT OF THE THESIS relates directly to the topic prompt but expresses the specific area you have chosen to discuss. (Remember, the exam topic will be general and will allow you to choose a particular subject related to the topic.) For example, the computer is one of many modern inventions you might choose to write about.

The ASSERTION OF THE THESIS is your viewpoint, or opinion, about the subject. The assertion provides the motive or purpose for your essay, and it may be an arguable point or one that explains or illustrates a point of view.

ASSERTION OF THE THESIS: your viewpoint, or opinion, about the subject

For example, you may present an argument for or against a particular issue. You may contrast two people, objects, or methods to show that one is better than the other. You may analyze a situation in all aspects and make recommendations for improvement. You may assert that a law or policy should be adopted, changed, or abandoned. You may also explain to your reader, as in the computer example, that a situation or condition exists; rather than argue a viewpoint, you would use examples to illustrate your assertion about the essay's subject.

Guidelines for Writing Thesis Statements

The following guidelines are not a formula for writing thesis statements, but rather are general strategies for making your thesis statement clear and effective.

1. State a particular point of view about the topic with both a subject and an assertion. The thesis should give the essay purpose and scope and thus provide the reader a guide. If the thesis is vague, your essay may be undeveloped because you do not have an idea to assert or a point to explain. Weak thesis statements are often framed as facts, questions, or announcements:

A. Avoid a fact statement as a thesis. While a fact statement may provide a subject, it generally does not include a point of view about the subject that provides the basis for an extended discussion. Example: *Recycling saved our community over $10,000 last year.* This fact statement provides a detail, not a point of view. Such a detail might be found within an essay, but it does not state a point of view.

B. Avoid framing the thesis as a vague question. In many cases, rhetorical questions do not provide a clear point of view for an extended essay. Example: *How do people recycle?* This question neither asserts a point of view nor helpfully guides the reader to understand the essay's purpose and scope.

C. Avoid the "announcer" topic sentence that merely states the topic you will discuss. Example: *I will discuss ways to recycle.* This sentence states the subject, but the scope of the essay is only suggested. Again, this statement does not assert a viewpoint that guides the essay's purpose. It merely "announces" that the writer will write about the topic.

2. Start with a workable thesis. You might revise your thesis as you begin writing and discover your own point of view.

3. If feasible and appropriate, perhaps state the thesis in multi-point form, expressing the scope of the essay. By stating the points in parallel form, you clearly lay out the essay's plan for the reader. Example: *To improve the environment, we can recycle our trash, elect politicians who see the environment as a priority, and support lobbying groups that work for environmental protection.*

4. Because of the exam time limit, place your thesis in the first paragraph to key the reader to the essay's main idea.

When forming or revising your thesis, look at your prewriting strategy--clustering, questioning, or brainstorming. Then, decide which two or three major areas you will discuss. Remember, you must limit the scope of the essay because of the time factor.

From these major areas, you will have formed an outline. An outline lists the main points as topics for each paragraph.

Check that each paragraph in the essay focuses on the main point of the essay as a whole. The point should be clear to readers, and all parts of an essay should support it.

The topic sentence of each paragraph should be a one-sentence, general summary of the paragraph's main point, relating both back toward the thesis and toward the content of the paragraph. A good topic sentence also provides transition from the previous paragraph. Eliminate sentences that do not support the topic sentence. (A topic sentence is sometimes unnecessary if the paragraph continues a developing idea clearly introduced in a preceding paragraph or if the paragraph appears in a narrative of events, where generalizations might interrupt the flow of the story.)

If there is not enough evidence to support the claim a topic sentence is making, do not fall into the trap of wandering or introducing new ideas within the paragraph. Either find more evidence, or adjust the topic sentence to corroborate with the available evidence.

Make sure your essay has an introduction, body paragraphs full of concrete, interesting information and supporting details developed from the topic sentence, and a conclusion to tie the essay together.

Introduction: Put your thesis statement into a clear, coherent opening paragraph. One effective device is to use a funnel approach, in which you begin with a brief description of the broader issue and then move on to a clearly focused, specific thesis statement.

Body paragraphs: Your paragraphs should contain concrete, interesting information and supporting details to support your point of view. As often as possible, create images in your readers' minds. Fact statements add weight to your opinions, especially when you are trying to convince the reader of your viewpoint. Because every good thesis has an assertion, you should offer specifics, anecdotes, facts, data, expert opinions, and other details to show or prove that assertion.

While you know what you mean, your reader does not. On the exam, you must explain and develop ideas as fully as possible in the time allowed. Revising can help bring more clarity to the expression of your ideas.

Conclusion: End your essay with a straightforward concluding paragraph that ties together the essay's content and leaves the reader with a sense of its completion. The conclusion should reinforce the main points and offer some insight into the topic, provide a sense of unity by relating the essay to the thesis, and signal clear closure of the essay.

See Skill 4.5

SKILL 4.4 Apply Knowledge of Language and its Functions to Enhance Meaning and Style when Revising

To ensure understanding and interest, it is important to use language in a captivating style and to explain things clearly so that meaning comes through.

Enhancing Interest through Style

- Start out with an attention-grabbing introduction. This sets an engaging tone for an entire piece and it will be more likely to pull in the reader.

- Use dynamic vocabulary and varied sentence beginnings. Keep readers on their toes. If they can predict what you are going to say next, switch it up.

- Avoid using clichés (cold as ice, the best thing since sliced bread, nip it in the bud, etc.). These are easy shortcuts, but they are not memorable, interesting, or convincing.

Ensuring Understanding through Clarity of Meaning

- Avoid using the words "clearly," "obviously," and "undoubtedly." Often, things that are clear or obvious to the author are not as apparent to the reader. Instead of using these words, make your point so strongly that it is clear on its own.

- Use the word that best fits the meaning you intend even if it is longer or a little less common. Try to find a balance and go with a familiar yet precise word.

- When in doubt, explain further.

See Competencies 5-8

SKILL 4.5 **Revising to Maintain Consistency in Style and Tone**

One way to remain on point in a piece of writing is to maintain a consistent point of view throughout. Maintaining a consistent point of view will suggest revisions to do with style and tone as well as what to edit out and what to leave in. Point of view defines the focus a writer assumes in relation to a given topic. Point of view relates to matters of person, tense, tone, and number.

Another way to maintain consistency is to stay in the same person mode. We recommend writing in the third person, as it is considered the most formal. If you do decide to use a less formal person mode (I, you, or we) in an essay, be careful not to shift between first, second, and third person from sentence to sentence or paragraph to paragraph. Be consistent.

It is also important to stick to one tense, for the most part. However, in an essay about the history of environmental protection, for example, it might be necessary to include a paragraph about the future benefits or consequences of protecting the earth.

The tone of an essay varies greatly with the purpose, subject, and audience. It is best to assume a formal tone for an essay. (*See Domain I, Skill 2.1*)

Words change when their meanings are singular or plural. Make sure that you do not shift number needlessly; if a meaning is singular in one sentence, do not make it plural in a subsequent sentence.

COMPETENCY 5
LANGUAGE SKILLS FOR WRITING GRAMMATICAL RELATIONSHIPS

SKILL Identify errors in the use of adjectives and adverbs
5.1

An excellent**ADJECTIVES** are words that modify or describe nouns or pronouns. Adjectives usually precede the words they modify but not always; for example, an adjective may occur after a linking verb.

ADVERBS are words that modify verbs, adjectives, or other adverbs. They cannot modify nouns. Adverbs answer such questions as how, why, when, where, how much, or how often. Many adverbs are formed by adding *-ly*.

> **ADJECTIVES:** words that modify or describe nouns or pronouns

> **ADVERBS:** words that modify verbs, adjectives, or other adverbs

Error: *The birthday cake tasted sweetly.*

Problem: *Tasted* is a linking verb; the modifier that follows should be an adjective, not an adverb.

Correction: *The birthday cake tasted sweet.*

Error: *You have done good with this project.*

Problem: *Good* is an adjective and cannot be used to modify a verb phrase such as *have done.*

Correction: *You have done well with this project.*

Error: *The coach was positive happy about the team's chance of winning.*

Problem: The adjective *positive* cannot be used to modify another adjective, *happy*. An adverb is needed instead.

Correction: *The coach was positively happy about the team's chance of winning.*

Error: *The fireman acted quick and brave to save the child from the burning building.*

Problem: *Quick* and *brave* are adjectives and cannot be used to describe a verb. Adverbs are needed instead.

Correction: *The fireman acted quickly and bravely to save the child from the burning building.*

Practice Exercise: Adjectives and Adverbs

Choose the option that corrects an error in the underlined portion(s). If no error exists, choose "No change is necessary."

5. Moving <u>quick</u> throughout the house, the burglar <u>removed</u> several priceless antiques before <u>carelessly</u> dropping his wallet.

   A. quickly

   B. remove

   C. careless

   D. No change is necessary

6. The car <u>crashed</u> <u>loudly</u> into the retaining wall before spinning <u>wildly</u> on the sidewalk.

   A. crashes

   B. loudly

   C. wild

   D. No change is necessary

7. The airplane <u>landed</u> <u>safe</u> on the runway after <u>nearly</u> colliding with a helicopter.

   A. land

   B. safely

   C. near

   D. No change is necessary

8. The <u>horribly</u> <u>bad</u> special effects in the movie disappointed us <u>great</u>.

   A. horrible

   B. badly

   C. greatly

   D. No change is necessary

9. The man promised to obey <u>faithfully</u> the rules of the social club.

   A. faithful

   B. faithfulness

   C. faith

   D. No change is necessary

Answer Key

1. **A.**

   The adverb *quickly* is needed to modify *moving*. Option B is incorrect because it uses the wrong form of the verb. Option C is incorrect because the adverb *carelessly*, not the adjective *careless*, is needed before the verb *dropping*.

2. **D.**

   The sentence is correct as it is written. The adverbs *loudly* and *wildly* are needed to modify *crashed* and *spinning*. Option A incorrectly uses the verb *crashes* instead of the participle *crashing*, which acts as an adjective.

3. **B.**

   The adverb *safely* is needed to modify the verb *landed*. Option

   A is incorrect because *land* is a noun. Option C is incorrect because *near* is an adjective, not an adverb.

4. **C.**

   The adverb *greatly* is needed to modify the verb *disappointed*. Option A is incorrect because *horrible* is an adjective, not an adverb. Option B is incorrect because the adverb *horribly* needs to modify the adjective *bad*.

5. **D.**

   The adverb *faithfully* is the correct modifier of the verb *promised*. Option A is an adjective used to modify nouns. Neither Option B nor Option C, both of which are nouns, is a modifier.

Sample Test Questions and Rationale

For sample test questions and rationales requiring a reading passage, see page 151.

When comparisons are made, the correct form of the adjective or adverb must be used. The **COMPARATIVE FORM** is used for two items. The **SUPERLATIVE FORM** is used for more than two items.

COMPARATIVE FORM:
used to compare two items

SUPERLATIVE FORM:
used to compare more than two items

	Comparative	Superlative
slow	slower	slowest
young	younger	youngest
tall	taller	tallest

With some words, *more* and *most* are used to make comparisons instead of *-er* and *-est*.

	Comparative	Superlative
energetic	more energetic	most energetic
quick	more quickly	most quickly

Comparisons must be made between similar structures or items. In the sentence "My house is similar in color to Steve's," one house is being compared to another house, as understood by the use of the possessive *Steve's*.

On the other hand, if the sentence reads "My house is similar in color to Steve," the comparison would be faulty because it would be comparing the house to Steve, not to Steve's house.

Error: *Last year's rides at the carnival were bigger than this year.*

Problem: In the sentence as it is worded, the rides at the carnival are being compared to this year, not to this year's rides.

Correction: *Last year's rides at the carnival were bigger than this year's.*

Practice Exercise: Logical Comparisons

Choose the sentence that logically and correctly expresses the comparison.

1. A. This year's standards are higher than last year.

   B. This year's standards are more high than last year.

   C. This year's standards are higher than last year's.

2. A. Tom's attitudes are very different from his father's.

   B. Toms attitudes are very different from his father.

   C. Tom's attitudes are very different from his father.

3. A. John is the stronger member of the gymnastics team.

   B. John is the strongest member of the gymnastics team.

   C. John is the most strong member of the gymnastics team.

4. A. Tracy's book report was longer than Tony's.

   B. Tracy's book report was more long than Tony's.

   C. Tracy's book report was longer than Tony.

5. A. Becoming a lawyer is as difficult as, if not more difficult than, becoming a doctor.

   B. Becoming a lawyer is as difficult, if not more difficult, than becoming a doctor.

   B. Becoming a lawyer is difficult, if not more difficult, than becoming a doctor.

6. A. Better than any movie of the modern era, *Schindler's List* portrays the destructiveness of hate.

   B. More better than any movie of the modern era, *Schindler's List* portrays the destructiveness of hate.

   C. Better than any other movie of the modern era, *Schindler's List* portrays the destructiveness of hate.

Answer Key

1. **C**

   Option C is correct because the comparison is between this year's standards and last year's (*standards* is understood). Option A compares the standards to last year. In Option B, the faulty comparative *more high* should be *higher*.

2. **A**

   Option A is correct because Tom's attitudes are compared to his father's (*attitudes* is understood). Option B deletes the apostrophe that is necessary to show possession (*Tom's*), and the comparison is faulty because *attitudes* is compared to *father*. While Option C uses the correct possessive, it retains the faulty comparison shown in Option B.

3. **B**

   In Option B, John is correctly the strongest member of a team that consists of more than two people. Option A uses the comparative *stronger* (comparison of two items) rather than the superlative *strongest* (comparison of more than two items). Option C uses a faulty superlative, *most strong*.

4. **A**

   Option A is correct because the comparison is between Tracy's book report and Tony's (book report). Option B uses the faulty comparative *more long* instead of *longer*. Option C wrongly compares Tracy's book report to Tony.

5. **A**

   In Option A, the dual comparison is correctly stated: *as difficult as, if not more difficult than*. Remember to test the dual comparison by taking out the intervening comparison. Option B deletes the necessary *as* after the first *difficult*. Option C deletes the *as* before and after the first *difficult*.

6. **C**

   Option C includes the necessary word *other* in the comparison *better than any other movie*. The comparison in Option A is not complete, and Option B uses the faulty comparative *more better*.

Sample Test Question and Rationale

DIRECTIONS: Choose the sentence that logically and correctly expresses the comparison.

(Easy)

1. A. The Empire State Building in New York is taller than buildings in the city.

   B. The Empire State Building in New York is taller than any other building in the city.

   C. The Empire State Building in New York is tallest than other buildings in the city.

Answer: B. The Empire State Building in New York is taller than any other building in the city.

Because the Empire State Building is a building in New York City, the phrase *any other* must be included. Option A is incorrect because the Empire State Building is implicitly compared to itself since it is one of the buildings. Option C is incorrect because *tallest* is the incorrect form of the adjective.

SKILL 5.2 Identify errors in noun noun agreement

In a sentence the initial noun should be in agreement with any following nouns related to the same issue.

For example, in the sentence: "The Bounty mutineers, unlike those who remained with the captain of the ship, forever changed their relationship with Great Britain" there is noun noun disagreement. "Mutineers" is a plural noun, and "their" is a plural pronoun, therefore the word "relationship" should also be plural. Corrected, the sentence would read "The Bounty mutineers, unlike those who remained with the captain of the ship, forever changed their relationships with Great Britain."

Here is another example: "Two of Barbara Bush's sons became a governor."

Because the sentence refers to "two . . . sons" the word "governor" should also be plural. The sentence should read "Two of Barbara Bush's sons became governors."

General information on nouns includes:

Plural Nouns

A good dictionary is an invaluable resource that can replace the need to learn complex spelling rules based on phonics or letter doubling, especially when the exceptions to these rules have not been mastered by adulthood. Learning to use a dictionary and thesaurus will be a rewarding use of time.

Most plurals of nouns that end in hard consonants or in hard consonant sounds followed by a silent *e* are made by adding -*s*. Plurals of some words ending in vowels are formed by adding only -*s*.

> fingers, numerals, banks, bugs, riots, homes, gates, radios, bananas

For nouns that end in soft consonant sounds—*s, j, x, z, ch,* and *sh*—the plurals are formed by adding -*es*. Plurals of some nouns ending in *o* are formed by adding -*es*.

> dresses, waxes, churches, brushes, tomatoes

For nouns ending in *y* preceded by a vowel, just add -*s*.

> boys, alleys

For nouns ending in *y* preceded by a consonant, change the *y* to *i* and add -*es*.

> babies, corollaries, frugalities, poppies

Some nouns' plurals are formed irregularly or remain the same.

> sheep, deer, children, leaves, oxen

Some nouns derived from foreign words, especially Latin words, are made plural in two different ways. Sometimes the meanings are the same; other times the two plural forms are used in slightly different contexts. It is always wise to consult the dictionary.

> appendices, appendixes   criterion, criteria
> indexes, indices   crisis, crises

Make the plurals of closed (solid) compound words in the usual way.

> timelines, hairpins
> cupfuls, handfuls

Make the plurals of open or hyphenated compounds by adding the change in inflection to the word that changes in number.

> *fathers-in-law, courts-martial, masters of art, doctors of medicine*

Make the plurals of letters, numbers, and abbreviations by adding *-s*.

> *fives and tens, IBMs, 1990s,* **ps** *and* **qs** *(Note that letters are italicized.)*

Possessive Nouns

Make the possessives of singular nouns by adding an apostrophe followed by the letter *s* (*'s*).

> *baby's bottle, mother's job, elephant's eye, teacher's desk,*
> *sympathizer's protests, week's postponement*

Make the possessives of singular nouns ending in *s* by adding either an apostrophe or an apostrophe followed by the letter *s*, depending upon common usage or sound. When the possessive sounds awkward, use a prepositional phrase instead. Even with the sibilant ending, with a few exceptions, it is advisable to use the *'s* construction.

> *dress's color, species' characteristics (or characteristics of the species),*
> *James' hat (or James's hat), Dolores's shirt*

Make the possessives of plural nouns ending in *s* by adding an apostrophe after the *s*.

> *horses' coats, jockeys' times, four days' time*

Make the possessives of plural nouns that do not end in *s* by adding *'s*, just as with singular nouns.

> *children's shoes, deer's antlers, cattle's horns*

Make the possessives of compound nouns by adding the inflection at the end of the word or phrase.

> *the mayor of Los Angeles' campaign, the mailman's new truck, the mailmen's new trucks, my father-in-law's first wife, the keepsakes' values, several daughters-in-law's husbands*

SKILL 5.3	**Identify errors in pronoun-antecedent agreement**

Rules for Clearly Identifying Pronoun Reference

Make sure that the antecedent reference is clear and cannot refer to something else.

A "distant relative" is a relative pronoun or a relative clause that has been placed too far away from the antecedent to which it refers. It is a common error to place a verb between the relative pronoun and its antecedent.

Note: *Because a gerund functions as a noun, any noun preceding it and operating as a possessive adjective must reflect the necessary inflection. However, if the gerundive following the noun is a participle, no inflection is added.*

The general was perturbed by the private's sleeping on duty. (The word sleeping is a gerund, the object of the preposition by.)
—but—
The general was perturbed to see the private sleeping on duty. (The word sleeping is a participle modifying private.)

Error: *Return the books to the library that are overdue.*

Problem: The relative clause *that are overdue* refers to the books and should be placed immediately after the antecedent.

Correction: *Return the books that are overdue to the library.*
—OR—
Return the overdue books to the library.

A pronoun should not refer to adjectives or possessive nouns

Adjectives, nouns, or possessive pronouns should not be used as antecedents. This will create ambiguity in sentences.

Error: *In Todd's letter, he told his mom he'd broken the priceless vase.*

Problem: In this sentence, the pronoun *he* seems to refer to the noun phrase *Todd's letter*, though it is probably meant to refer to the possessive noun *Todd's*.

Correction: *In his letter, Todd told his mom that he had broken the priceless vase.*

A pronoun should not refer to an implied idea

A pronoun must refer to a specific antecedent rather than an implied antecedent. When an antecedent is not stated specifically, the reader has to guess or assume the meaning of a sentence. Pronouns that do not have antecedents are called EXPLETIVES. "It" and "there" are the most common expletives, though other pronouns can become expletives as well. In informal conversation, expletives allow for casual presentation of ideas without supporting evidence. However, in more formal writing, it is best to be more precise.

EXPLETIVE: a pronoun that does not have an antecedent

Error: *She said that it is important to floss every day.*

Problem: The pronoun *it* refers to an implied idea.

Correction: *She said that flossing every day is important.*

Error: *Milt and Bette returned the books because they had missing pages.*

Problem: The pronoun *they* does not refer to the antecedent.

Correction: *The customers returned the books with missing pages.*

Using Who, That, and Which

Who, whom, and *whose* refer to human beings and can introduce either essential or nonessential clauses. *That* refers to things other than humans and is used to introduce essential clauses. *Which* refers to things other than humans and is used to introduce nonessential clauses.

Error: *The doctor that performed the surgery said the patient would recover fully.*

Problem: Since the relative pronoun is referring to a human, *who* should be used.

Correction: *The doctor who performed the surgery said the patient would recover fully.*

Error: *That ice cream cone that you just ate looked delicious.*

Problem: *That* has already been used, so you must use *which* to introduce the next clause, whether it is essential or nonessential.

Correction: *That ice cream cone, which you just ate, looked delicious.*

Identify Proper Case Forms

Pronouns, unlike nouns, change case forms. Pronouns must be in the subjective, objective, or possessive form, according to their function in the sentence.

PERSONAL PRONOUNS						
SUBJECTIVE (NOMINATIVE)			**POSSESSIVE**		**OBJECTIVE**	
	Singular	Plural	Singular	Plural	Singular	Plural
1st person	I	We	My	Our Ours	Me	Us
2nd person	You	You	Your Yours	Your Yours	You	You
3rd person	He She It	They	His Her/ Hers Its	Their Theirs	Him Her It	Them

RELATIVE PRONOUNS	
Who	Subjective/Nominative
Whom	Objective
Whose	Possessive

Error: *Tom and me have reserved seats for next week's baseball game.*

Problem: The pronoun *me* is the subject of the verb *have reserved* and should be in the subjective form.

Correction: *Tom and I have reserved seats for next week's baseball game.*

Error: *Mr. Green showed all of we students how to make paper hats.*

Problem: The pronoun *we* is the object of the preposition *of*. It should be in the objective form, us.

Correction: *Mr. Green showed all of us students how to make paper hats.*

Error: *Who's coat is this?*

Problem: The interrogative possessive pronoun is *whose*; *who's* is the contraction for *who is*.

Correction: *Whose coat is this?*

Practice Exercise: Pronoun Case

Choose the option that corrects an error in the underlined portion(s). If no error exists, choose "No change is necessary."

1. Even though Sheila and <u>he</u> had planned to be alone at the diner, <u>they</u> were joined by three friends of <u>their's</u> instead.

    A. him

    B. him and her

    C. theirs

    D. No change is necessary

2. Uncle Walter promised to give his car to <u>whomever</u> would guarantee to drive it safely.

    A. whom

    B. whoever

    C. them

    D. No change is necessary

3. Eddie and <u>him</u> gently laid <u>the body</u> on the ground next to <u>the sign</u>.

    A. he

    B. them

    C. it

    D. No change is necessary

4. Mary, <u>who</u> is competing in the chess tournament, is a better player than <u>me</u>.

    A. whose

    B. whom

    C. I

    D. No change is necessary

5. <u>We ourselves</u> have decided not to buy property in that development; however, our friends have already bought <u>themselves</u> some land.

    A. We, ourself,

    B. their selves

    C. their self

    D. No change is necessary

Answer Key

1. **C**

   The possessive pronoun *theirs* does not need an apostrophe. Option A is incorrect because the subjective pronoun *he* is needed in this sentence. Option B is incorrect because the subjective pronoun *they*, not the objective pronouns *him* and *her*, is needed.

2. **B**

   The subjective case *whoever*—not the objective case *whomever*—is the subject of the relative clause *whoever would guarantee to drive it safely*. Option A is incorrect because *whom* is an objective pronoun. Option C is incorrect because *car* is singular and takes the pronoun *it*.

3. **A**

   The subjective pronoun *he* is needed as the subject of the verb *laid*. Option B is incorrect because *them* is vague; the noun *body* is needed to clarify *it*. Option C is incorrect because *it* is vague, and the noun *sign* is necessary for clarification.

4. **C**

   The subjective pronoun *I* is needed because the comparison is understood. Option A incorrectly uses the possessive *whose*. Option B is incorrect because the subjective pronoun *who*, and not the objective *whom*, is needed.

5. **D**

   The reflexive pronoun *themselves* refers to the plural *friends*. Option A is incorrect because the plural we requires the reflexive *ourselves*. Option C is incorrect because the possessive pronoun *their* is never joined with either *self* or *selves*.

SKILL 5.4 Identify errors in pronoun case

See Skill 5.3

SKILL 5.5 Identify errors in the use of intensive pronouns

The intensive pronoun is the form that uses "self" or "selves" and is used for emphasis and/or clarification regarding its antecedent.

For example:

The Queen herself appeared at the charity ball to show royal support for it.

"Herself" is an intensive pronoun emphasizing its antecedent "The Queen."

I have often wondered whether I was in the wrong during the argument myself, even though I was not the first one to start shouting.

"Myself" is an intensive pronoun emphasizing its antecedent "I."

The supervisor told me that the children themselves had named their daycare center "Lollipop Daycare."

"Themselves" is an intensive pronoun clarifying its antecedent "the children".

We were frantic and when Lola was two hours late and were beginning to think of calling the police when Lola herself walked in the door and said, "I just stopped by a friend's! Why, were you worried?"

"Herself" is an intensive pronoun emphasizing and clarifying its antecedent "Lola".

Reflexive pronouns are similar to intensive pronouns in form: herself, himself, myself, yourself, itself, themselves, ourselves, yourselves. They are used when they are not only the subject of the sentence, but are also acted upon by the subject of a sentence, as in "He can only blame himself" or "I had to defend myself."

SKILL 5.6 Identify errors in pronoun number and person

See Skill 5.3

SKILL 5.7 Identify errors in the use of vague pronouns

See Skill 5.3

SKILL 5.8 **Recognize and correct errors in subject-verb agreement**

Past Tense and Past Participles

Both regular and irregular verbs must appear in their standard forms for each tense. Note: The *-ed* or *-d* ending is added to regular verbs in the past tense and to past participles.

REGULAR VERB FORMS		
Infinitive	Past Tense	Past Participle
Bake	Baked	Baked

IRREGULAR VERB FORMS		
Infinitive	Past Tense	Past Participle
Be	Was/Were	Been
Become	Became	Become
Break	Broke	Broken
Bring	Brought	Brought
Choose	Chose	Chosen
Come	Came	Come
Do	Did	Done
Draw	Drew	Drawn
Eat	Ate	Eaten
Fall	Fell	Fallen
Forget	Forgot	Forgotten
Freeze	Froze	Frozen
Give	Gave	Given
Go	Went	Gone

IRREGULAR VERB FORMS		
Infinitive	**Past Tense**	**Past Participle**
Grow	Grew	Grown
Have/Has	Had	Had
Hide	Hid	Hidden
Know	Knew	Known

Table continued on next page

Infinitive	**Past Tense**	**Past Participle**
Lay	Laid	Laid
Lie	Lay	Lain
Ride	Rode	Ridden
Rise	Rose	Risen
Run	Ran	Run
See	Saw	Seen
Steal	Stole	Stolen
Take	Took	Taken
Tell	Told	Told
Throw	Threw	Thrown
Wear	Wore	Worn
Write	Wrote	Written

Error: *She should have went to her doctor's appointment at the scheduled time.*

Problem: The past participle of the verb *to go* is *gone*. *Went* expresses the simple past tense.

Correction: *She should have gone to her doctor's appointment at the scheduled time.*

Error: *My train is suppose to arrive before two o'clock.*

Problem: The verb following *train* is a present tense passive construction, which requires the present tense verb *to be* and the past participle.

Correction: *My train is supposed to arrive before two o'clock.*

Error: *Linda should of known that the car wouldn't start after leaving it out in the cold all night.*

Problem: *Should of* is a nonstandard expression. *Of* is not a verb.

Correction: *Linda should have known that the car wouldn't start after leaving it out in the cold all night.*

Practice Exercise: Standard Verb Forms

Choose the option that corrects an error in the underlined portion(s). If no error exists, choose "No change is necessary."

1. My professor <u>had knew</u> all along that we would pass his course.

   A. know

   B. had known

   C. knowing

   D. No change is necessary

2. Kevin was asked to erase the vulgar words he <u>had wrote</u>.

   A. writes

   B. has write

   C. had written

   D. No change is necessary

3. Melanie <u>had forget</u> to tell her parents that she left the cat in the closet.

   A. had forgotten

   B. forgot

   C. forget

   D. No change is necessary

4. Craig always <u>leave</u> the house a mess when his parents aren't there.

   A. left

   B. leaves

   C. leaving

   D. No change is necessary

5. The store manager accused Kathy of <u>having stole</u> more than five hundred dollars from the safe.

   A. has stolen

   B. having stolen

   C. stole

   D. No change is necessary

Answer Key

1. **B**

   Option B is correct because the past participle needs the helping verb *had*. Option A is incorrect because *it* is in the infinitive tense. Option C incorrectly uses the present participle.

2. **C**

   Option C is correct because the past participle follows the helping verb *had*. Option A uses the verb in the present tense. Option B is an incorrect use of the verb.

3. **A**

   Option A is correct because the past participle uses the helping verb *had*. Option B uses the wrong form of the verb. Option C uses the wrong form of the verb.

4. **B**

   Option B correctly uses the present tense of the verb. Option A uses the verb in an incorrect way. Option C uses the verb without a helping verb such as *is*.

5. **B**

   Option B is correct because it is the past participle. Options A and C use the verb incorrectly.

Verb Tenses

Verb tenses must refer to the same time consistently, unless a change in time is required.

Error: *Despite the increased number of students attending school this year, overall attendance is higher last year at the sporting events.*

Problem: The verb *is* represents an inconsistent shift to the present tense when the action refers to a past occurrence.

Correction: *Despite the increased number of students attending school this year, overall attendance was higher last year at sporting events.*

Error: *My friend Lou, who just competed in the marathon, ran since he was twelve years old.*

Problem: Because Lou continues to run, the present perfect tense is needed.

Correction: *My friend Lou, who just competed in the marathon, has run since he was twelve years old.*

Error: *The mayor congratulated Wallace Mangham, who renovates the city hall last year.*

Problem: Although the speaker is talking in the present, the action of renovating the city hall was in the past.

Correction: *The mayor congratulated Wallace Mangham, who renovated the city hall last year.*

Practice Exercise: Shifts in Tense

Choose the option that corrects an error in the underlined portion(s). If no error exists, choose "No change is necessary."

1. After we <u>washed</u> the fruit that had <u>growing</u> in the garden, we knew there <u>was</u> a store that would buy the fruit.

   A. washing
   B. grown
   C. is
   D. No change is necessary

2. The tourists <u>used</u> to visit the Atlantic City boardwalk whenever they <u>vacationed</u> during the summer. Unfortunately, their numbers have <u>diminished</u> every year.

   A. use
   B. vacation
   C. diminish
   D. No change is necessary

3. When the temperature <u>drops</u> to below thirty-two degrees Fahrenheit, the water on the lake <u>freezes</u>, which <u>allowed</u> children to skate across it.

   A. dropped
   B. froze
   C. allows
   D. No change is necessary

4. The artists were <u>hired</u> to <u>create</u> a monument that would pay tribute to the men who were <u>killed</u> in World War II.

   A. hiring
   B. created
   C. killing
   D. No change is necessary

5. Emergency medical personnel rushed to the scene of the shooting, where many injured people <u>waiting</u> for treatment.

   A. wait
   B. waited
   C. waits
   D. No change is necessary

Answer Key

1. **B**

   The past participle *grown* is needed instead of *growing*, which is the progressive tense. Option A is incorrect because the past participle *washed* takes the *-ed*. Option C incorrectly replaces the past participle was with the present tense *is*.

2. **D**

   Option A is incorrect because *use* is the present tense. Option B incorrectly uses the present tense of the verb *vacation*. Option C incorrectly uses the present tense *diminish* instead of the past tense *diminished*.

3. **C**

   The present tense *allows* is necessary in the context of the sentence. Option A is incorrect because *dropped* is a past participle. Option B is incorrect because *froze* is also a past participle.

4. **D**

   Option A is incorrect because *hiring* is the present tense. Option B is incorrect because *created* is a past participle. In Option C, *killing* does not fit into the context of the sentence.

5. **B**

   In Option B, *waited* corresponds with the past tense *rushed*. In Option A, *wait* is incorrect because it is present tense. In Option C, *waits* is incorrect because the noun *people* is plural and requires the singular form of the verb.

SKILL 5.9 Recognize and correct inappropriate shifts in verb tense

See Skill 5.8

COMPETENCY 6
LANGUAGE AND RESEARCH SKILLS FOR WRITING: STRUCTURAL RELATIONSHIPS

SKILL Identify errors in the placement of phrases and clauses
6.1

Types of Clauses

CLAUSES are connected word groups that are composed of at least one subject and one verb. (A **SUBJECT** is the doer of an action or the element that is being joined. A **VERB** conveys either the action or the link.)

> *Students are waiting for the start of the assembly.*
>
> *(subject)   (verb)*
>
> *At the end of the play, students wait for the curtain to come down.*
>
> *(subject) (verb)*

CLAUSES: connected word groups that are composed of at least one subject and one verb

SUBJECT: the doer of an action or the element that is being joined

VERB: conveys either the action or the link

INDEPENDENT CLAUSES: can stand alone or they can be joined to other clauses

Clauses can be independent or dependent.

INDEPENDENT CLAUSES can stand alone or they can be joined to other clauses.

LINKING CLAUSES		
Independent clause	for and nor	Independent clause
Independent clause,	but or yet so	Independent clause
Independent clause	;	Independent clause
Dependent clause	,	Independent clause
Independent clause	,	Dependent clause

DEPENDENT CLAUSES, by definition, contain at least one subject and one verb. However, they cannot stand alone as a complete sentence. They are structurally dependent on the main clause.

> **DEPENDENT CLAUSES:** have a subject and a verb but cannot stand alone as a complete sentence

There are two types of dependent clauses:

1. Those with a subordinating conjunction

2. Those with a relative pronoun

> *Unless a cure is discovered, many more people will die of the disease.*
>
> *Dependent clause + Independent clause*
>
> *The White House has an official website, which contains press releases, news updates, and biographies of the president and vice president.*
>
> *(independent clause + relative pronoun + relative dependent clause)*

Fundamentals of Sentence Structure

TYPES OF SENTENCES	
Simple	Consists of one independent clause. *Joyce wrote a letter.*
Compound	Consists of two or more independent clauses. The two clauses are usually connected by a coordinating conjunction (and, but, or, nor, for, so, yet). Semicolons sometimes connect compound sentences. *Joyce wrote a letter, and Dot drew a picture.*
Complex	Consists of an independent clause plus one or more dependent clauses. The dependent clause may precede the independent clause or follow it. *While Joyce wrote a letter, Dot drew a picture.*
Compound-Complex	Consists of one or more dependent clauses plus two or more independent clauses. *When Mother asked the girls to demonstrate their newfound skills, Joyce wrote a letter, and Dot drew a picture.*

Note: Do not confuse compound sentence elements with compound sentences.

Simple sentence with compound subject:

> *Joyce and Dot wrote letters.*
>
> *The girl in row three and the boy next to her were passing notes across the aisle.*

Simple sentence with compound predicate:

> Joyce _wrote letters_ and _drew pictures_.
>
> The captain of the high school debate team _graduated with honors_ and _studied broadcast journalism in college_.

Simple sentence with compound object of preposition:

> Coleen graded the students' essays for _style_ and _mechanical accuracy_.

SKILL 6.2 Identify errors of misplaced and dangling modifiers

Particular phrases that are not placed near the one word they modify often result in misplaced modifiers. Particular phrases that do not relate to the subject being modified result in dangling modifiers.

Error: Weighing the options carefully, a decision was made regarding the punishment of the convicted murderer.

Problem: Who is weighing the options? No one capable of weighing is named in the sentence; thus, the participle phrase "weighing the options carefully" dangles. This problem can be corrected. By adding a subject of the sentence capable of doing the action.

Correction: Weighing the options carefully, the judge made a decision regarding the punishment for the convicted murderer.

Error: Returning to my favorite watering hole brought back many fond memories.

Problem: The person who returned is never indicated, and the participle phrase dangles. This problem can be corrected by creating a dependent clause from the modifying phrase.

Correction: When I returned from my favorite watering hole, many fond memories came back to me.

Error: One damaged house stood only to remind townspeople of the hurricane.

Problem: The placement of the misplaced modifier "only" suggests that the sole reason the house remained was to serve as a reminder. The faulty modifier creates ambiguity.

Correction: Only one damaged house stood, reminding townspeople of the hurricane.

Error: Recovered from the five-mile hike, the obstacle course was a piece of cake for the Boy Scout troop.

Problem: The obstacle course was not recovered from the five-mile hike, so the modifying phrase must be placed closer to the word "troop" that it modifies.

Correction: The obstacle course was a piece of cake for the Boy Scout Troop, which had just recovered from a five-mile hike.

Practice Exercise: Misplaced and Dangling Modifiers

Choose the sentence that expresses the thought most clearly and effectively and that has no error in structure.

1.
   A. Attempting to remove the dog from the well, the paramedic tripped and fell in also.

   B. As the paramedic attempted to remove the dog from the well, he tripped and fell in also.

   C. The paramedic tripped and fell in also attempting to remove the dog from the well.

2.
   A. To save the wounded child, a powerful explosion ripped through the operating room as the doctors worked.

   B. In the operating room, as the wounded child was being saved, a powerful explosion ripped through.

   C. To save the wounded child, the doctors worked as an explosion ripped through the operating room.

3.
   A. One hot July morning, a herd of giraffes screamed wildly in the jungle next to the wildlife habitat.

   B. One hot July morning, a herd of giraffes screamed in the jungle wildly next to the wildlife habitat.

   C. One hot July morning, a herd of giraffes screamed in the jungle next to the wildfife habitat, wildly.

4.
   A. Looking through the file cabinets in the office, the photographs of the crime scene revealed a new suspect in the investigation.

   B. Looking through the file cabinets in the office, the detective discovered photographs of the crime scene which revealed a new suspect in the investigation.

   C. A new suspect in the investigation was revealed in photographs of the crime scene that were discovered while looking through the file cabinets in the office.

Answer Key: Misplaced and Dangling Modifiers

1. **B**

   Option B corrects the dangling participle *attempting to remove the dog from the well* by creating a dependent clause introducing the main clause. In Option A, the introductory participle phrase *Attempting...well* does not refer to a paramedic, the subject of the main clause. The word *also* in Option C incorrectly implies that the paramedic was doing something besides trying to remove the dog.

2. **C**

   Option C corrects the dangling modifier *to save the wounded child* by adding the concrete subject *doctors worked*. Option A infers that an explosion was working to save the wounded child. Option B never tells who was trying to save the wounded child.

3. **A**

   Option A places the adverb *wildly* closest to the verb *screamed*, which it modifies. Both Options B and C incorrectly place the modifier away from the verb.

4. **B**

   Option B corrects the modifier *looking through the file cabinets in the office* by placing it next to the detective who is doing the looking. Option A sounds as though the photographs were looking; Option C has no one doing the looking.

SKILL 6.3 Identify errors in the use of coordinating and subordinating conjunctions

COORDINATION: means that ideas of equal importance are joined

SUBORDINATION: means that an idea of lesser importance is joined to one of greater importance

COORDINATION means that ideas of equal importance are joined. Coordinating conjunctions include the **FANBOYS—For, And, Nor, But, Or, Yet, So**. A comma precedes a coordinating conjunction that joins two independent clauses.

SUBORDINATION means that an idea of lesser importance is joined to one of greater importance. Dependent clauses are created in one of two ways—with subordinating conjunctions (although, when, until, since, because, if) or with relative pronouns (who, whom, which, that).

Error: *Because college students need to be diligent in their job search, the market is tight.*

Problem: The problem here is one of inappropriate or illogical subordination. The tight job market is not caused by the need for diligence among college students. Rather, the tight job market is a reason college students need to be diligent.

Correction: *Because the job market is tight, college students need to be diligent in their job search.*

Error: *The college newspaper is published every weekday, yet it is a useful source of information to students.*

Problem: These two independent clauses are equally important, but the wrong coordinating conjunction is used. The word *yet* implies a contradictory piece of information.

Correction: *The college newspaper is published every weekday, and it is a useful source of information to students.*

Error: *The college newspaper is run entirely and completely by students, and they are often journalism majors.*

Problem: This sentence is wordy and needs to subordinate the less important idea.

Correction: *The college newspaper is run entirely by students, who are often journalism majors.*

Practice Exercise: Coordination and Subordination

For the underlined sentences below, choose the option that expresses the meaning with the most fluency and the clearest logic. If the underlined sentence should not be changed, choose Option A.

1. **Charity fundraisers have had to be creative in their efforts to support their organizations. <u>At the arts fair each spring, some groups sell popcorn and drinks due to the fact that they need to raise money, and other groups sell homemade goods at the craft fairs held each fall.</u>**

   A. At the arts fair each spring, some groups sell popcorn and drinks due to the fact that they need to raise money, and other groups sell homemade goods at the craft fairs held each fall.

   B. To raise money, some groups sell popcorn and drinks at the spring arts fair while other groups sell homemade goods at the fall crafts fair.

   C. Because charities want to raise money at the arts fair held each spring, some groups sell popcorn and drinks, and in the fall other groups sell homemade goods at the craft fair.

   D. Due to the fact that charities want to raise money, at the spring arts fair, some groups sell popcorn and drinks, but other groups sell homemade goods at the crafts fair in the fall.

2. **The winter dragged on with recurrent cold fronts dashing our hopes of warm weather. <u>Then one morning we awoke, and we saw the deep purple of the redbud blooms, and there were the pink, white, and lilac-colored azaleas, and also the snow-white dogwoods.</u>**

   A. Then one morning we awoke, and we saw the deep purple of the redbud blooms, and there were the pink, white, and lilac-colored azaleas, and also the snow-white dogwoods.

   B. Then one morning we awoke seeing the deep purple of the redbud blooms, and then there were the pink, white, and lilac-colored azaleas and also the snow-white dogwoods.

   C. Then one morning we awoke to see the deep purple of the redbud blooms, the pink, white, and lilac-colored azaleas, and the snow-white dogwoods.

   D. The one morning we awoke to see the deep purple of the redbud blooms as well as the pink, white, and the lilac-colored azaleas. We also saw the snow-white dogwoods.

Practice Exercise: Coordination and Subordination (cont.)

3. In the last twenty years, laser technology has facilitated delicate heart operations. <u>Although once unimaginable, a laser beam that has given new life to many gravely-ill heart patients is a surgical technique that enables drilling tiny holes in the heart wall.</u>

   A. Although once unimaginable, a laser beam that has given new life to many gravely ill heart patients is a surgical technique that enables drilling tiny holes in the heart wall.

   B. It once seemed unimaginable, but laser beam surgery, in which holes are drilled in the heart wall, is a new surgical technique, although it has given hope to gravely ill heart patients.

   C. Bringing new hope to gravely ill heart patients, a once unimaginable surgical technique enables doctors to drill holes in the heart wall with a laser beam.

   D. Although once unimaginable and now a new hope to gravely ill heart patients, a new surgical technique uses a laser beam to drill holes in the heart wall.

4. To the dismay of NASA scientists, the Hubble telescope at first sent back out-of-focus pictures. <u>However, an extraordinary mission in December 1993 was when a space shuttle team accomplished restoring Hubble's "eye," and now the Hubble can send back pictures that are sharp and clear.</u>

   A. However, an extraordinary mission in December 1993 was when a space shuttle team accomplished restoring Hubble's "eye," and now the Hubble can send back pictures that are sharp and clear.

   B. However, now sending back sharp, clear pictures, the Hubble "eye" was restored in December 1993 by the extraordinary mission of a space shuttle team.

   C. However, the Hubble "eye" was restored in December 1993 in an extraordinary mission accomplished by a space shuttle team sending back sharp and clear images.

   D. However, in an extraordinary mission in December 1993, a space shuttle team restored Hubble's "eye," so it now sends back sharp, clear images.

Answer Key

1. **B**

   By using the infinitive phrase at the beginning of the dependent clause at the end, Option B most concisely and clearly expresses the idea of groups raising money for charities by selling food and homemade goods. Option A adds the wordy phrase "due to the fact that" and introduces the two sentences with a long prepositional phrase that only relates to the first independent clause. Option C creates a wordy dependent clause and coordinates the two sentences with a "but," indicating an inappropriate contrast.

2. **C**

   Option C most concisely coordinates the series of ideas expressed in the sentence. Option A coordinates three independent clauses that can be condensed. Option B overuses the words "and then" and includes the illogical idea "we awoke seeing." Option D creates two sentences that can be condensed to save words.

3. **C**

   Option C places the modifying words and phrases near the words they modify, and the main clause is concisely and clearly phrased. In Option A, the long relative clause after the subject *laser beam* is confusing. Option B creates a main clause out of an idea that should be subordinated for concise phrasing, and it adds a wordy modifying phrase after the subject *laser beam surgery*. Option D creates an awkward introductory modifying phrase.

4. **D**

   Option D places the prepositional phrase "in an extraordinary mission in December 1993" at the beginning of the sentence to avoid confusion, and the coordinating conjunction *so* emphasizes the cause-and-effect relationship of the team's repair of the "eye" and the improved pictures. Option A uses an awkward construction with "was when." Option B offers an illogical sequence with the result first and then the action of repair following. Option C misplaces the modifying phrase so that the team is "sending back sharp and clear images."

Sample Test Questions and Rationale

DIRECTIONS: For the underlined sentence(s), choose the option that expresses the meaning with the most fluency and the clearest logic within the context. If the underlined sentence should not be changed, choose Option A, which shows no change.

(Rigorous)

1. John wanted to join his friends on the mountain-climbing trip. <u>Seeing that the weather had become dark and stormy, John knew he would stay safe indoors.</u>

   A. Seeing that the weather had become dark and stormy, John knew he would stay safe indoors.

   B. The weather had become dark and stormy, and John knew he would stay indoors, and he would be safe.

   C. Because the weather had become dark and stormy, John knew he would stay indoors, where he would be safe.

   D. Because the weather had become dark, as well as stormy, John knew he would stay safe indoors.

   Answer: D. Because the weather had become dark, as well as stormy, John knew he would stay safe indoors.

   This sentence best subordinates the idea of dark and stormy weather to John's knowledge. Option A is incorrect because *seeing that* is an awkward construction. Option B does not subordinate any idea to any other. Option C is incorrect because the idea that John would be safe should not be subordinate to staying indoors.

(Average)

2. A few hours later, the storm subsided, so John left the cabin to join his friends. <u>Even though he was tired from the four-mile hike the day before, he climbed the mountain in a few hours.</u>

   A. Even though he was tired from the four-mile hike the day before, he climbed the mountain in a few hours.

   B. He was tired from the four-mile the day before; he climbed the mountain in a few hours.

   C. He climbed the mountain in a few hours, John was tired from the four-mile hike the day before.

   D. Seeing as he was tired from the day before, when he went on a four-mile hike, John climbed the mountain in a few hours.

   Answer: A. Even though he was tired from the four-mile hike the day before, he climbed the mountain in a few hours.

   The idea that John was tired from the four-mile hike the day before is subordinate to the idea of John climbing the mountain. Options B and C do not subordinate the idea of John being tired from the four-mile hike to John climbing the mountain. In Option D, the modifying phrase *Seeing as...* before makes no logical sense in the context of the sentence.

Recognize and correct sentence fragments and run-on sentences

Fragments

Fragments occur when word groups standing alone are missing either a subject or a verb, or when word groups containing a subject and verb and standing alone are made dependent through the use of subordinating conjunctions or relative pronouns.

Error: *The teacher waiting for the class to complete the assignment.*

Problem: This sentence is not complete because an *-ing* word alone does not function as a verb. When a helping verb is added (for example, *was waiting*), the fragment becomes a sentence.

Correction: *The teacher was waiting for the class to complete the assignment.*

Error: *Until the last toy was removed from the floor.*

Problem: Words such as *until, because, although, when,* and *if* make a clause dependent and thus incapable of standing alone. An independent clause must be added to make the sentence complete.

Correction: *Until the last toy was removed from the floor, the kids could not go outside to play.*

Error: *The city will close the public library. Because of a shortage of funds.*

Problem: The problem is the same as above. The dependent clause must be joined to the independent clause.

Correction: *The city will close the public library because of a shortage of funds.*

Error: *Anyone planning to go on the trip should bring the necessary items. Such as a backpack, boots, a canteen, and bug spray.*

Problem: The second word group is a phrase and cannot stand alone because there is neither a subject nor a verb. The fragment can be corrected by adding the phrase to the sentence.

Correction: *Anyone planning to go on the trip should bring the necessary items, such as a backpack, boots, a canteen, and bug spray.*

Practice Exercise: Fragments

Choose the option that corrects an error in the underlined portion(s). If no error exists, choose "No change is necessary."

1. Despite the lack of funds in the <u>budget it</u> was necessary to rebuild the roads that were damaged from the recent floods.

   A. budget: it

   B. budget, it

   C. budget; it

   D. No change is necessary

2. After determining that the fire was caused by faulty <u>wiring, the</u> building inspector said the construction company should be fined.

   A. wiring. The

   B. wiring the

   C. wiring; the

   D. No change is necessary

3. Many years after buying a grand <u>piano Henry</u> decided he'd rather play the violin instead.

   A. piano: Henry

   B. piano, Henry

   C. piano; Henry

   D. No change is necessary

4. Computers are being used more and more <u>frequently. because</u> of their capacity to store information.

   A. frequently because

   B. frequently, because

   C. frequently; because

   D. No change is necessary

5. Doug washed the floors <u>every day. to</u> keep them clean for the guests.

   A. every day to

   B. every day, to

   C. every day; to

   D. No change is necessary

Answer Key

1. **B**

    The clause that begins with *despite* is introductory and must be separated from the clause that follows by a comma. Option A is incorrect because a colon is used to set off a list or to emphasize what follows. In Option B, a comma incorrectly suggests that the two clauses are dependent.

2. **D**

    A comma correctly separates the dependent clause *After...wiring* at the beginning of the sentence from the independent clause that follows. Option A incorrectly breaks the two clauses into separate sentences, Option B omits the comma, and Option C incorrectly suggests that the phrase is an independent clause.

3. **B**

    The phrase *Henry decided... instead* must be joined to the independent clause. Option A incorrectly puts a colon before *Henry decided*, and Option C incorrectly separates the phrase as if it were an independent clause.

4. **A**

    The second clause *because... information* is dependent and must be joined to the first independent clause. Option B is incorrect because, as the dependent clause comes at the end of the sentence rather than at the beginning, a comma is not necessary. In Option C, a semicolon incorrectly suggests that the two clauses are independent.

5. **A**

    The second clause to *keep... guests* is dependent and must be joined to the first independent clause. Option B is incorrect because, as the dependent clause comes at the end of the sentence rather than at the beginning, a comma is not necessary. In Option C, a semicolon incorrectly suggests that the two clauses are independent.

Run-on Sentences and Comma Splices

Comma splices appear when a comma joins two sentences. Fused sentences appear when two sentences are run together with no punctuation at all.

Error:	*Dr. Sanders is a brilliant scientist, his research on genetic disorders won him a Nobel Prize.*
Problem:	A comma alone cannot join two independent clauses (complete sentences). The two clauses can be joined by a semicolon, joined by a conjunction and a comma, or separated into two sentences by a period.
Correction:	*Dr. Sanders is a brilliant scientist; his research on genetic disorders won him a Nobel Prize.* *-OR-* *Dr. Sanders is a brilliant scientist. His research on genetic disorders won him a Nobel Prize.* *-OR-* *Dr. Sanders is a brilliant scientist, and his research on genetic disorders won him a Nobel Prize.*
Error:	*Paradise Island is noted for its beaches they are long, sandy, and beautiful.*
Problem:	The first independent clause ends with the word *beaches*, and the second independent clause is fused to the first. The fused sentence error can be corrected in several ways: (1) One clause may be made dependent on another by inserting a subordinating conjunction or a relative pronoun (2) A semicolon may be used to combine two equally important ideas (3) The two independent clauses may be separated by a period (4) The independent clauses may be joined by a conjunction and a comma
Correction:	*Paradise Island is noted for its beaches, which are long, sandy, and beautiful.* *-OR-* *Paradise Island is noted for its beaches; they are long, sandy, and beautiful.* *-OR -* *Paradise Island is noted for its beaches. They are long, sandy, and beautiful.* *-OR-* *Paradise Island is noted for its beaches, for they are long, sandy, and beautiful.*

Error: *The number of hotels has increased, however, the number of visitors has grown also.*

Problem: The first sentence ends with the word increased, and a comma is not strong enough to connect it to the second sentence. The adverbial transition however does not function in the same way as a coordinating conjunction and cannot be used with commas to link two sentences. Several different corrections are available.

Correction: *The number of hotels has increased; however, the number of visitors has grown also.*

[Two separate but closely related sentences are created with the use of the semicolon.]
-OR-
The number of hotels has increased. However, the number of visitors has grown also.
[Two separate sentences are created.]
-OR-
Although the number of hotels has increased, the number of visitors has grown also.

[One idea is made subordinate to the other and separated with a comma.]
-OR-
The number of hotels has increased, but the number of visitors has grown also.
[The comma before the coordinating conjunction but is appropriate. The adverbial transition *however* does not function in the same way as the coordinating conjunction *but.*]

Practice Exercise: Fused Sentences and Comma Splices

Choose the option that corrects an error in the underlined portion(s). If no error exists, choose "No change is necessary."

1. Scientists are excited at the ability to clone a <u>sheep: however,</u> it is not yet known if the same can be done to humans.

   A. sheep, however,

   B. sheep. However,

   C. sheep, however;

   D. No change is necessary

2. Because of the rising cost of college <u>tuition the</u> federal government now offers special financial assistance, <u>such as loans,</u> to students.

   A. tuition, the

   B. tuition; the

   C. such as loans

   D. No change is necessary

3. As the number of homeless people continues to <u>rise, the major cities</u> such as <u>New York and Chicago,</u> are now investing millions of dollars in low-income housing.

   A. rise. The major cities

   B. rise; the major cities

   C. New York and Chicago

   D. No change is necessary

4. Unlike in <u>the 1950s, in most</u> households the husband and wife work full-time to make <u>ends meet in many</u> different career fields.

   A. the 1950s; in most

   B. the 1950s in most

   C. ends meet, in many

   D. No change is necessary

Answer Key

1. **B**

   Option B correctly separates two independent clauses. The comma in Option A after the word *sheep* creates a run-on sentence. The semicolon in Option C does not separate the two clauses because it occurs at an inappropriate point.

2. **A**

   The comma in Option A correctly separates the independent clause and the dependent clause. The semicolon in Option B is incorrect because one of the clauses is independent. Option C requires a comma to prevent a run-on sentence.

3. **C**

   Option C is correct because a comma creates a run-on sentence. Option A is incorrect because the first clause is dependent. The semicolon in Option B incorrectly separates the dependent clause from the independent clause.

4. **D**

   Option D correctly separates the two clauses with a comma. Option A incorrectly uses a semicolon to separate the clauses. The lack of a comma in Option B creates a run-on sentence. Option C puts a comma in an inappropriate place.

Identify errors in the use of correlative conjunctions

Correlative conjunctions are conjunctions which appear in tandem in a sentence, although separated by other words. Some examples are: either, or; neither, nor; both, and; whether, or; not only, but also; so that; between, and; as, as.

Correlative expressions need to be constructed grammatically in the same way. In other words, the grammatical structure surrounding one should be parallel with the other.

Using the correlative conjunctions as and as, we can see a faulty parallel construction in the following sentence:

Tim's biceps are not as developed as Brad.

Since Tim's biceps are being discussed, Brad's biceps should also be discussed, not Brad himself as a general topic. The correct construction would be:

Tim's biceps are not as developed as Brad's.

See Skill 6.6

Identify errors in parallel structure

Faulty Parallelism

Two or more elements stated in a single clause should be expressed with the same (or parallel) structure (e.g., all adjectives, all verb forms, or all nouns).

Error:	*She needed to be beautiful, successful, and have fame.*
Problem:	The phrase *to be* is followed by two different structures: beautiful and successful are adjectives, and have fame is a verb phrase.
Correction:	*She needed to be <u>beautiful</u>, <u>successful</u>, and <u>famous</u>.*
	(adjective) (adjective) (adjective)

-OR-)
She needed <u>beauty</u>, <u>success,</u> and <u>fame</u>.
    (noun) (noun)   (noun)

Error: *I plan either to sell my car during the spring or during the summer.*

Problem: Paired conjunctions (also called *correlative conjunctions,* such as *either-or, both-and, neither-nor,* and *not only-but also*) need to be followed with similar structures. In the sentence above, *either* is followed by *to sell my car during the spring,* while *or* is followed only by the phrase *during the summe*r.

Correction: *I plan to sell my car during either the spring or the summer.*

Error: *The President pledged to lower taxes and that he would cut spending to lower the national debt.*

Problem: Since the phrase *to lower taxes* follows the verb *pledged,* a similar structure of *to* is needed with the phrase *cut spending.*

Correction: *The President pledged to lower taxes and to cut spending to lower the national debt.*
-OR-
The President pledged that he would lower taxes and cut spending to lower the national debt.

Practice Exercise: Parallelism

Choose the sentence that expresses the thought most clearly and effectively and that has no error in structure.

1. A. Andy found the family tree, researches the Irish descendents, and he was compiling a book for everyone to read.

    B. Andy found the family tree, researched the Irish descendents, and compiled a book for everyone to read.

    C. Andy finds the family tree, researched the Irish descendents, and compiled a book for everyone to read.

2. A. In the last ten years, computer technology has advanced so quickly that workers have had difficulty keeping up with the new equipment and the increased number of functions.

    B. Computer technology has advanced so quickly in the last ten years that workers have had difficulty to keep up with the new equipment and by increasing number of functions.

    C. In the last ten years, computer technology has advanced so quickly that workers have had difficulty keeping up with the new equipment, and the number of functions are increasing.

3. A. The History Museum contains exhibits honoring famous residents, a video presentation about the state's history, an art gallery featuring paintings and sculptures, and they even display a replica of the State House.

    B. The State History Museum contains exhibits honoring famous residents, a video presentation about the state's history, an art gallery featuring paintings and sculptures, and even a replica of the State House.

    C. The State History Museum contains exhibits honoring famous residents, a video presentation about the state's history, an art gallery featuring paintings and sculptures, and there is even a replica of the State House.

Practice Exercise: Parallelism (cont.)

4. A. Either the criminal justice students had too much practical experience and limited academic preparation or too much academic preparation and little practical experience.

    B. The criminal justice students either had too much practical experience and limited academic preparation or too much academic preparation and little practical experience.

    C. The criminal justice students either had too much practical experience and limited academic preparation or had too much academic preparation and limited practical experience.

5. A. Filmmaking is an arduous process in which the producer hires the cast and crew, chooses locations for filming, supervises the actual production, and guides the editing.

    B. Because it is an arduous process, filmmaking requires the producer to hire a cast and crew and choose locations, supervise the actual production, and guides the editing.

    C. Filmmaking is an arduous process in which the producer hires the cast and crew, chooses locations for filming, supervises the actual production, and guided the editing.

Answer Key

1. **B**

   Option B uses parallelism by presenting a series of past tense Verbs: *found, researched, and compiled.* Option A interrupts the parallel structure of past tense verbs: found, researches, and *he was compiling.* Option C uses present tense verbs and then shifts to past tense: *finds, researched, and compiled.*

2. **A**

   Option A uses parallel structure at the end of the sentence: *the new equipment and the increased number of functions.* Option B creates a faulty structure with *to keep up with the new equipment and by increasing number of functions.* Option C creates faulty parallelism with *the number of functions are increasing* (and uses a plural verb for a singular noun).

3. **B**

   Option B uses parallelism by presenting a series of noun phrases acting as objects of the verb *contains.* Option A interrupts that parallelism by inserting *they even display,* and Option C interrupts the parallelism with the addition of *there is.*

4. **C**

   In the either-or parallel construction, look for a balance on both sides. Option C creates that balanced parallel structure: *either had ... or had.* Options A and B do not create the balance. In Option A, the structure is *Either the criminal justice students ... or too much.* In Option B, the structure is *either had ... or too much.*

5. **A**

   Option A uses parallelism by presenting a series of verbs with objects: *hires the cast and crew, chooses locations for filming, supervises the actual production, and guides the editing.* The structure of Option B incorrectly suggests that filmmaking chooses locations, supervises the actual production, and guides the editing. Option C interrupts the series of present tense verbs by inserting the participle *guided* instead of the present tense *guides.*

COMPETENCY 7
LANGUAGE SKILLS FOR WRITING: WORD CHOICE

SKILL **Identify errors in the use of idiomatic expressions**
7.1

An **IDIOMATIC EXPRESSION** is a group of words whose meaning, when considered as a whole, is something entirely different from the meaning of each individual word. This feature of idioms is called noncompositionality. For example, the expression "hit the hay" has nothing to do with literally hitting hay; it means to go to bed. In addition, idioms display nonsubstitutability, which means that one cannot replace a word in an idiom and maintain the idiom's meaning. For example, one cannot say "hit the straw" instead of "hit the hay," even though straw and hay could be considered synonyms. Lastly, idioms are nonmodifiable; if an idiom is modified with syntactic transformations, it loses its idiomatic meaning. "Katie hit the bale of hay with her car" changes the meaning.

Idioms are not hard and fast grammatical rules; rather, idioms are verbal habits that have become ingrained in standard English language usage. Learning correct usage of idiomatic expressions is about learning to trust your ear. Idioms come in the form of expressions such as "rain check" or "a penny for your thoughts" as well as phrases such as "in contrast to" and "not only … but."

> **IDIOMATIC EXPRESSION:** a group of words whose meaning, when considered as a whole, is something entirely different from the meaning of each individual word

SOME IDIOMS	
abide by	discriminate against
agreed to	in charge of
as…as	in contrast to
among	insist upon
between	neither… nor
concerned with	not only…. but also
different from	rely upon

Error: *I am having trouble deciding between the chocolate, vanilla, and* *strawberry milkshakes.*

Problem: Here, more than two items are being distinguished. In this case, you must use *among*, as *between* should only be used when comparing two items.

Correction: *I am having trouble deciding among the chocolate, vanilla, and strawberry milkshakes.*

Error: *Eugena has less game tokens than Charlie.*

Problem: *Less* is used to answer the question *"How much?"*, whereas *fewer* is used to answer the question *"How many?"*

Correction: *Eugena has fewer game tokens than Charlie.*

Error: *Sheryl is considered as the top executive in her field.*

Problem: This sentence sounds awkward. The proper expression would be *considered the* instead of *considered as the*.

Correction: *Sheryl is considered the top executive in her field.*

Error: *The geography final exam featured such topics like state capitals, the seven seas, and world climate.*

Problem: The correct expression should be *such…as* instead of *such… like*. *Like* should be used only with a direct comparison: Cara looks a lot like her sister.

Correction: *The geography final exam featured such topics as state capitals, the seven seas, and world climate.*
—OR—
The geography final exam featured topics such as state capitals, the seven seas, and world climate.

Practice Exercise: Identify Meanings of Idiomatic Expressions

Choose the option that explains the meaning of the underlined portion.

1. My parents took everyone out for my birthday and agreed to <u>foot the bill</u>.

   A. Kick the receipt

   B. Leave without paying

   C. Pay

2. On the first day of school, the teacher had planned several "getting-to-know-you" activities to help break the ice.

   A. Break up a block of ice

   B. Put everyone at ease

   C. Learn names

3. My boss gave me <u>the green light</u> to begin the project I'd proposed last week.

   A. Permission to start

   B. A large sum of money

   C. A hug

Answer Key

1. **C**
2. **B**

3. **A**

SKILL 7.2 **Identify errors in the use of frequently confused words**

HOMONYM: a word that is spelled and pronounced just like another word but that has a different meaning

HOMOGRAPHS: words that share the same spelling, regardless of how they are pronounced, and have different meanings

HOMOPHONES: words that are pronounced the same but may or may not have different spellings

HETERONYMS: (sometimes called heterophones) share the same spelling but have different pronunciations and meanings

CAPITONYMS: words that are spelled the same but have different meanings when capitalized

Recognize Commonly Confused or Misused Words or Phrases

Students frequently encounter problems with homonyms. Strictly speaking, a HOMONYM is a word that is spelled and pronounced just like another word but that has a different meaning. An example is the word *mean*, which can be a verb—"to intend"; an adjective—"unkind"; or a noun or adjective—"average."

HOMOGRAPHS are words that share the same spelling, regardless of how they are pronounced, and have different meanings. Words that are pronounced the same but may or may not have different spellings are called HOMOPHONES. HETERONYMS (sometimes called heterophones) share the same spelling but have different pronunciations and meanings. For example, the homographs *desert* (abandon) and *desert* (arid region) are heteronyms (pronounced differently), but the homographs *mean* (intend) and *mean* (average) are homophones because they are pronounced the same (they are also homonyms).

CAPITONYMS are words that are spelled the same but have different meanings when capitalized. A capitonym may or may not have different pronunciations; for example, *polish* (to make shiny) and *Polish* (from Poland).

Some of the most troubling homophones are those that are spelled differently but that sound the same. Some examples include its (third person singular neuter pronoun) and *it's* ("it is"); *there* (a location), *their* (third person plural pronoun), and *they're* ("they are"). Another common example is to, *too*, and *two*.

Some homonyms/homographs are particularly intriguing. *Fluke*, for instance, refers to a fish, a flatworm, the end parts of an anchor, the fins on a whale's tail, and a stroke of luck.

COMMONLY MISUSED WORDS		
Accept is a verb meaning "to receive or to tolerate."	**Except** is usually a preposition meaning "excluding."	**Except** is also a verb meaning "to exclude."
Advice is a noun meaning "recommendation."	**Advise** is a verb meaning "to recommend."	
Affect is usually a verb meaning "to influence."	**Effect** is usually a noun meaning "result." Effect can also be a verb meaning "to bring about."	
An **allusion** is "an indirect reference."	An **illusion** is "a misconception or false impression."	
Add is a verb meaning "to put together."	**Ad** is a noun that is the abbreviation for the word "advertisement."	
Ain't is a common, nonstandard contraction for the contraction "aren't."		
Allot is a verb meaning "to distribute."	**A lot** can act as an adverb that means "often," "to a great degree," or "a large quantity." (Example: She shops a lot.)	
Allowed is used as an adjective that means "permitted."	**Aloud** is an adverb that means "audible."	
Bare is an adjective that means "naked" or "exposed." It can also indicate a minimum.	As a noun, **bear** is a large mammal.	As a verb, **bear** means "to carry a heavy burden."
Capital refers to a city; capitol to "a building where lawmakers meet."	**Capital** also refers to "wealth" or "resources."	
A **chord** is a noun that refers to "a group of musical notes."	**Cord** is a noun meaning "rope" or "a long electrical line."	
Compliment is a noun meaning "a praising or flattering remark."	**Complement** is a noun that means "something that completes or makes perfect."	
Climactic is derived from climax, "the point of greatest intensity in a series or progression of events."	**Climatic** is derived from climate; it refers to meteorological conditions.	

Table continued on next page

Discreet is an adjective that means "tactful" or "diplomatic".	**Discrete** is an adjective that means "separate" or "distinct."	
Dye is a noun or verb used to indicate artificial coloring.	**Die** is a verb that means "to pass away."	**Die** is also a noun that means "a cube-shaped game piece."
Effect is a noun that means "outcome."	**Affect** is a verb that means "to influence."	
Elicit is a verb meaning "to bring out" or "to evoke."	**Illicit** is an adjective meaning "unlawful."	
Emigrate means "to leave one country or region to settle in another."	**Immigrate** means "to enter another country and reside there."	
Gorilla is a noun meaning "a large great ape."	**Guerrilla** is "a member of a band of irregular soldiers."	
Hoard is a verb that means "to accumulate" or "store up."	A **horde** is "a large group."	
Lead is a verb that means "to guide" or "to serve as the head of." It is also a noun that is a type of metal.		
Medal is a noun that means "an award that is strung round the neck."	**Meddle** is a verb that means "to involve oneself in a matter without right or invitation."	**Metal** is "an element such as silver or gold." **Mettle** is a noun meaning "toughness" or "courage."
Morning is a noun indicating "the time between midnight and midday."	**Mourning** is a verb or noun pertaining to "the period of grieving after a death."	
Past is a noun meaning "a time before now" (past, present, and future).	**Passed** is the past tense of the verb "to pass."	
Piece is a noun meaning "portion."	**Peace** is a noun meaning "the opposite of war or serenity."	
Peak is a noun meaning "the tip" or "height to reach the highest point."	**Peek** is a verb that means "to take a brief look."	**Pique** is a verb meaning "to incite or raise interest."

Table continued on next page

Principal is a noun most commonly meaning "the chief or head," and it also means "a capital sum of money."	**Principle** is a noun meaning "a basic truth or law."	
Rite is a noun meaning "a special ceremony."	**Right** is an adjective meaning "correct" or "the opposite direction of left."	**Write** is a verb meaning "to compose in writing."
Than is a conjunction used in comparisons; **then** is an adverb denoting time. Examples: That pizza is more <u>than</u> I can eat. Tom laughed, and <u>then</u> we recognized him.	To remember the correct use of these words, you can use the following: **Than** is used to *compare*; both words have the letter a in them. **Then** tells *when*; both words are spelled the same, except for the first letter.	
There is an adverb specifying place; it is also an expletive. Adverb: Sylvia is lying there unconscious. Expletive: <u>There</u> are two plums left.	**Their** is a possessive pronoun.	**They're** is a contraction of "they are." Fred and Jane finally washed <u>their</u> car. <u>They're</u> later than usual today.
To is a preposition.	**Too** is an adverb.	**Two** is a number.
Your is a possessive pronoun;	**You're** is a contraction of "you are."	

PROBLEM PHRASES	
CORRECT	**INCORRECT**
Supposed to	Suppose to
Used to	Use to
Toward	Towards
Anyway	Anyways
Couldn't care less	Could care less
For all intents and purposes	For all intensive purposes

Table continued on next page

CORRECT	INCORRECT
Come to see me	Come and see me
En route	In route
Regardless	Irregardless
Second, Third	Secondly, Thirdly

Other confusing words

Lie is an intransitive verb meaning to recline or rest on a surface. Its principal parts are *lie, lay,* and *lain.* **Lay** is a transitive verb meaning "to put or place." Its principal parts are *lay, laid,* and *laid.*

> *Birds lay eggs.*
>
> *I lie down for bed around 10 p.m.*

Set is a transitive verb meaning "to put or to place." Its principal parts are *set, set,* and *set.* **Sit** is an intransitive verb meaning "to be seated." Its principal parts are *sit, sat,* and *sat.*

> *I set my backpack down near the front door.*
>
> *They sat in the park until the sun went down.*

Among is a preposition to be used with three or more items. **Between** is to be used with two items.

> *Between you and me, I cannot tell the difference among those three Johnson sisters.*

As is a subordinating conjunction used to introduce a subordinating clause. **Like** is a preposition and is followed by a noun or a noun phrase.

> *As I walked to the lab, I realized that the recent experiment findings were much like those we found last year.*

Can is a verb that means "to be able." **May** is a verb that means "to have permission." "Can" and "may" are only interchangeable in cases of possibility.

> *I can lift 250 pounds.*
>
> *May I go to Alex's house?*

Sample Test Questions and Rationale

DIRECTIONS: Choose the most effective word within the context of the sentence.

(Average)

1. Many of the clubs in Boca Raton are noted for their _____ elegance.

    A. vulgar

    B. tasteful

    C. ordinary

    Answer: B. tasteful

    Tasteful means beautiful or charming, which would correspond to an elegant club. The words *vulgar* and *ordinary* have negative connotations.

(Average)

2. When a student is expelled from school, the parents are usually _____ in advance.

    A. rewarded

    B. congratulated

    C. notified

    Answer: C. notified

    Notified means informed or told, which fits into the logic of the sentence. The words *rewarded* and *congratulated* are positive actions, which do not make sense regarding someone being expelled from school.

(Average)

3. Before appearing in court, the witness was _____ the papers requiring her to show up.

    A. condemned

    B. served

    C. criticized

    Answer: B. served

    Served means given, which makes sense in the context of the sentence. *Condemned* and *criticized* do not make sense within the context of the sentence.

DIRECTIONS: Choose the underlined word or phrase that is unnecessary within the context of the passage.

(Easy)

4. The <u>expanding</u> number of television channels has <u>prompted</u> cable operators to raise their prices, <u>even though</u> many consumers do not want to pay a higher <u>increased</u> amount for their service.

    A. expanding

    B. prompted

    C. even though

    D. increased

    Answer: D. increased

    The word *increased* is redundant with *higher* and should be removed. All the other words are necessary within the context of the sentence.

Sample Test Questions and Rationale (cont.)

(Average)

5. <u>Considered by many to be</u> one of the worst <u>terrorist</u> incidents <u>on American soil</u> was the bombing of the Oklahoma City Federal Building, which will be remembered <u>for years to come</u>.

    A. Considered by many to be

    B. terrorist

    C. on American soil

    D. for years to come

Answer: A. Considered by many to be

Considered by many to be is a wordy phrase and unnecessary in the context of the sentence. All other words are necessary within the context of the sentence.

(Average)

6. The <u>flu</u> epidemic struck <u>most of</u> the <u>respected</u> faculty and students of the Woolbright School, forcing the Boynton Beach School Superintendent to close it down <u>for two weeks</u>.

    A. flu

    B. most of

    C. respected

    D. for two weeks

Answer: C. respected

The fact that the faculty might have been *respected* is not necessary to mention in the sentence. The other words and phrases are all necessary to complete the meaning of the sentence.

DIRECTIONS: Choose the most effective word or phrase within the context suggested by the sentence.

(Average)

7. Because George's _____ bothering him, he apologized for crashing his father's car.

    A. feelings were

    B. conscience was

    C. guiltiness was

Answer: B. conscience was

Option B shows the correct word choice because a *conscience* would motivate someone to confess. Option A is incorrect because *feelings* is not as accurate as *conscience*. Option C is incorrect because *guiltiness* is less descriptive of George's motive for confession than conscience.

(Rigorous)

8. The charity art auction _____ every year at Mizner Park has a wide selection of artists showcasing their work.

    A. attended

    B. presented

    C. displayed

Answer: B. presented

The word *presented* makes more sense in the context of the sentence than *attended* or *displayed*.

SKILL 7.3 Identify wrong word use

Practice Exercise: Word Choice I

Choose the most effective word or phrase within the context suggested by the sentences.

1. The defendant was accused of _____ money from his employer.

    A. stealing

    B. borrowing

    C. robbing

2. O.J. Simpson's angry disposition _____ his ex-wife Nicole.

    A. mortified

    B. intimidated

    C. frightened

3. Many tourists are attracted to the Paradise Island because of its _____ climate.

    A. friendly

    B. peaceful

    C. balmy

4. The woman was angry because the tomato juice left an _____ stain on her brand new carpet.

    A. unsightly

    B. ugly

    C. unpleasant

5. After disobeying orders, the army private was _____ by his superior officer.

    A. degraded

    B. attacked

    C. reprimanded

6. Sharon's critical evaluation of the student's book report left the student feeling _____, which caused him to want to quit school.

    A. surprised

    B. depressed

    C. discouraged

Practice Exercise: Word Choice I (cont.)

Choose the most effective word or phrase within the context suggested by the sentences.

7. The life-saving medication created by the scientist had a _____ impact on further developments in the treatment of cancer.

   A. beneficial

   B. fortunate

   C. miraculous

8. *The Phantom of the Opera* is one of Andrew Lloyd Webber's most successful musicals, largely because of its _____ themes.

   A. romantic

   B. melodramatic

   C. imaginary

9. The massive Fourth of July fireworks display _____ the partygoers with lots of colored lights and sound.

   A. disgusted

   B. captivated

   C. captured

10. Many of the residents of Grand Forks, North Dakota, were forced to _____ their homes because of the flood.

   A. escape

   B. evacuate

   C. exit

Answer Key

1. A
2. C
3. C
4. A
5. C

6. C
7. A
8. A
9. B
10. B

Practice Exercises: Word Choice II

Choose the sentence that expresses the thought most clearly and most effectively and that is structurally correct in grammar and syntax.

1. A. The movie was three hours in length, featuring interesting characters,and moved at a fast pace.

    B. The movie was three hours long, featured interesting characters, and moved at a fast pace.

    C. Moving at a fast pace, the movie was three hours long and featured interesting characters.

2. A. We were so offended by the waiter's demeanor that we left the restaurant without paying the check.

    B. The waiter's demeanor offended us so much that without paying the check, we left the restaurant.

    C. We left the restaurant without paying the check because we were offended by the waiter's demeanor.

3. A. In today's society, information about our lives is provided to us by computers.

    B. We rely on computers in today's society to provide us information about our lives.

    C. In today's society, we rely on computers to provide us with information about our lives.

4. A. Folding the sides of the tent carefully, Jack made sure to be quiet so none of the other campers would be woken up.

    B. So none of the other campers would be woken up, Jack made sure to be quiet by folding the sides of the tent carefully.

    C. Folding the sides of the tent carefully, so none of the other campers would wake up, Jack made sure to be quiet.

Answer Key

1. **B**
2. **A**
3. **C**
4. **A**

Practice Exercises: Word Choice III

Choose the most effective word or phrase within the context suggested by the sentence(s).

1. The six hundred employees of General Electric were _____ by the company due to budgetary cutbacks.

   A. released

   B. terminated

   C. downsized

2. The force of the tornado _____ the many residents of the town of Russell, Kansas.

   A. intimidated

   B. repulsed

   C. frightened

3. Even though his new car was easy to drive, Fred _____ to walk to work every day because he liked the exercise.

   A. needed

   B. preferred

   C. considered

4. June's parents were very upset over the school board's decision to suspend her from Adams High for a week. Before they filed a lawsuit against the board, they _____ with a lawyer to help them make a decision.

   A. consulted

   B. debated

   C. conversed

5. The race car driver's _____ in handling the automobile was a key factor in his victory.

   A. patience

   B. precision

   C. determination

6. After impressing the judges with her talent and charm, the beauty contestant _____ more popularity by singing an aria from *La Bohème*.

   A. captured

   B. scored

   C. gained

7. The stained-glass window was _____ when a large brick flew through it during the riot.

   A. damaged

   B. cracked

   C. shattered

Practice Exercises: Word Choice III (cont.)

Choose the most effective word or phrase within the context suggested by the sentence(s).

8. The class didn't know what happened to the professor until the principal _____ why the professor dropped out of school.

   A. informed

   B. discovered

   C. explained

9. The giant penthouse at the top of the building enables the billionaire industrialist _____ the citizens on the street.

   A. to view from above

   B. the chance to see

   C. to glance at

10. Sally's parents _____ her to attend the dance after she promised to return by midnight.

    A. prohibited

    B. permitted

    C. asked

Answer Key

1.	C	5.	B	9.	C
2.	C	6.	C	10.	B
3.	B	7.	C		
4.	A	8.	C		

Practice Exercises: Word Choice IV

The following passages contain irrelevant, repetitive, and/or wordy expressions. Select the underlined word or word group that is unnecessary to the context of the passage.

1. Some children decide to participate <u>actively</u> in <u>extracurricular</u> activities, such as after-school sports and <u>various</u> clubs. Many teachers and administrators <u>willingly</u> volunteer to supervise the activities during their <u>spare</u> time.

   A. actively

   B. extracurricular

   C. various

   D. willingly

   E. spare

2. Our high school reunion was held at the <u>swanky</u> Boca Hilton, which is known for its elegance and <u>glamour</u>. We arrived in a <u>rented</u> stretch limo and prepared to dance and have a good time, <u>reminiscing</u> with our <u>dear</u> friends.

   A. swanky

   B. glamour

   C. rented

   D. reminiscing

   E. dear

3. Once we reached <u>the top of</u> the mountain, a <u>powerful</u> storm came from <u>out of</u> nowhere, bringing rain and <u>large</u> hailstones from the dark <u>black</u> skies above.

   A. the top of

   B. powerful

   C. out of

   D. large

   E. black

4. Police officers often undergo a rigorous, <u>harsh</u> training period to prepare them <u>adequately</u> for the <u>intense</u> dangers and stresses of the job. <u>Only</u> the most physically fit candidates are capable of handling the challenges of dealing with the <u>criminal</u> elements of our society.

   A. harsh

   B. adequately

   C. intense

   D. Only

   E. criminal

Practice Exercises: Word Choice IV (cont.)

The following passages contain irrelevant, repetitive, and/or wordy expressions. Select the underlined word or word group that is unnecessary to the context of the passage.

5. The <u>early morning</u> hurricane struck at dawn, knocking out power lines and <u>ripping the roofs from</u> buildings <u>all</u> throughout Broward County. <u>Massive</u> winds and rain wreaked havoc, and terrified residents ran <u>madly</u> for shelter and safety.

   A. early morning

   B. ripping the roofs from

   C. all

   D. Massive

   E. madly

6. Alan's alcoholism affected the entire family <u>deeply</u>. When his father asked <u>him to</u> stop drinking, he <u>refused and</u> drove off in his sister's car, which he crashed into a utility pole. <u>Fortunately</u>, Alan miraculously survived and now is undergoing intensive treatment in a top-notch facility <u>that is well-regarded</u>.

   A. deeply

   B. him to

   C. refused and

   D. Fortunately

   E. that is well-regarded

7. Soap operas are popular among <u>many</u> television viewers because of their ability to <u>blend</u> real issues such as drug abuse, infidelity, and AIDS <u>with melodramatic plots</u> concerning lust, greed, vanity, and revenge. <u>These shows</u> often have very devoted followings among viewers who watch them <u>faithfully</u> every day.

   A. many

   B. blend

   C. with melodramatic plots

   D. These shows

   E. faithfully

8. Walt Disney World <u>is one of</u> the most visited tourist attractions in the United States. Its success <u>and prosperity</u> can be attributed to the <u>blend of</u> childhood fantasy and adult imagination. The park features rides and <u>attractions</u> that hold considerable appeal for <u>both</u> children and adults.

   A. is one of

   B. and prosperity

   C. blend of

   D. attractions

   E. both

Practice Exercises: Word Choice IV (cont.)

The following passages contain irrelevant, repetitive, and/or wordy expressions. Select the underlined word or word group that is unnecessary to the context of the passage.

9. Jason was the best <u>baseball</u> player on the Delray Beach High School baseball team; in fact, he was known as the star <u>of the team</u>. He could play several positions on the field <u>with enthusiasm and skill</u>, but his strength was hitting balls <u>out of the park</u>. When Jason was at the plate, the coach expected him to score a home run <u>every time</u>.

   A. baseball

   B. of the team

   C. with enthusiasm and skill

   D. out of the park

   E. every time

10. Many of the major cities in the United States are grappling with <u>a variety of</u> problems, such as crime, crumbling roadways, a shortage of <u>funding for</u> schools and healthcare, and a lack of jobs. There are <u>no easy</u> solutions to these problems, but mayors who have <u>strong</u> leadership abilities <u>work to</u> create good ideas to deal with them.

   A. a variety of

   B. funding for

   C. no easy

   D. strong

   E. work to

Answer Key

1.	D	5.	A	9.	A
2.	A	6.	E	10.	E
3.	E	7.	E		
4.	A	8.	B		

SKILL 7.4 Recognize and correct errors in redundancy

Syntactical redundancy occurs when a writer adds superfluous words to a sentence. Strong writing is lean; each word is necessary. Weak writing talks around points with a lot of unnecessary verbiage.

For example:

Incorrect: Joyce made sure that when her plane arrived that she retrieved all of her luggage.

Correct: Joyce made sure that when her plane arrived, she retrieved all her luggage.

Incorrect: He was a mere skeleton of his former self.

Correct: He was a skeleton of his former self.

Redundancy may also occur in a paragraph or in several paragraphs. Similar thoughts and information may appear more than once. Even if different phrasing is used, thoughts and information should not be repeated unless they lead to a new thought.

For example:

The Vietnam war was controversial. Traditional liberals opposed it, as did young radicals. Interestingly, the young radicals thought the traditional liberals were too "old school" in that they were not interested in revolution; they simply opposed a losing proposition in a faraway conflict of questionable goals and motivation. Because of all this, controversy dogged the war.

The final sentence of the paragraph is redundant; it has already been stated that the war was controversial.

COMPETENCY 8

LANGUAGE SKILLS FOR WRITING: CAPITALIZATION AND PUNCTUATION

SKILL 8.1 Identify errors in capitalization

Capitalize all proper names of persons (including specific organizations or agencies of government), places (countries, states, cities, parks, and specific geographical areas), things (political parties, structures, historical and cultural terms, and calendar and time designations), and religious terms (deities, revered persons or groups, and sacred writings).

> Percy Bysshe Shelley, Argentina, Mount Rainier National Park, Grand Canyon, League of Nations, the Sears Tower, Birmingham, Lyric Theater, Americans, Midwesterners, Democrats, Renaissance, Boy Scouts of America, Easter, God, Bible, Dead Sea Scrolls, Koran

Capitalize proper adjectives and titles used with proper names.

> California gold rush, President John Adams, French fries, Homeric epic, Romanesque architecture, Senator John Glenn

Note: Some words that represent titles and offices are not capitalized unless used with a proper name.

Capitalized	Not Capitalized
Congressman McKay	the congressman from Hawaii
Commander Alger	the commander of the Pacific Fleet
Queen Elizabeth	the queen of England

Capitalize all main words in titles of works of literature, art, and music.

Error: *Emma went to Dr. Peters for treatment because her own Doctor was on vacation.*

Problem: The use of capital letters with *Emma* and *Dr. Peters* is correct because they are specific (proper) names; the title *Dr.* is also capitalized. However, the word *doctor* is not a specific name and should not be capitalized.

Correction: *Emma went to Dr. Peters for treatment because her own doctor was on vacation.*

Error: *Our Winter Break does not start until next wednesday.*

Problem: Days of the week are capitalized, but seasons are not capitalized.

Correction: *Our winter break does not start until next Wednesday.*

Error: *The exchange student from Israel, who came to study biochemistry, spoke spanish very well.*

Problem: Languages and the names of countries are always capitalized. Courses are capitalized when one is referring to a specific course; courses in general are not capitalized.

Correction: *The exchange student from Israel, who came to study biochemistry, spoke Spanish very well.*

SKILL 8.2 Identify errors in punctuation

Commas

COMMAS are used to indicate a brief pause. They are used to set off dependent clauses and long introductory word groups, to separate words in a series, to set off unimportant material that interrupts the flow of the sentence, and to separate independent clauses joined by conjunctions.

COMMA: used to indicate a brief pause

Error: *After I finish my master's thesis I plan to work in Chicago.*

Problem: A comma is needed after an introductory dependent word group containing a subject and verb.

Correction: *After I finish my master's thesis, I plan to work in Chicago.*

Error: *I washed waxed and vacuumed my car today.*

Problem: Commas should separate nouns, phrases, or clauses in a list, as well as two or more coordinate adjectives that modify one word. Although the word and is sometimes considered optional, it is often necessary to clarify the meaning.

Correction: *I washed, waxed, and vacuumed my car today.*

Error: *She was a talented dancer but she is mostly remembered for her singing ability.*

Problem: A comma is needed before a conjunction that joins two independent clauses (complete sentences).

Correction: *She was a talented dancer, but she is mostly remembered for her singing ability.*

Error: *This incident is I think typical of what can happen when the community remains so divided.*

Problem: Commas are needed between nonessential words or words that interrupt the main clause.

Correction: *This incident is, I think, typical of what can happen when the community remains so divided.*

Semicolons and Colons

SEMICOLONS are needed to separate two or more closely related independent clauses when a transitional adverb introduces the second clause. (These clauses may also be written as separate sentences, preferably by placing the adverb within the second sentence.)

> **SEMICOLONS:** used to separate two or more closely related independent clauses when a transitional adverb introduces the second clause

Error: *I climbed to the top of the mountain, it took me three hours.*

Problem: A comma alone cannot separate two independent clauses. Instead, a semicolon is needed to separate two related sentences.

Correction: *I climbed to the top of the mountain; it took me three hours.*

Error: *In the movie, asteroids destroyed Dallas, Texas, Kansas City, Missouri, and Boston, Massachusetts.*

Problem: Semicolons are needed to separate items in a series that already contain internal punctuation.

Correction: *In the movie, asteroids destroyed Dallas, Texas; Kansas City, Missouri; and Boston, Massachusetts.*

COLONS are used to introduce lists and to emphasize what follows.

<table>
<tr><td>**Error:**</td><td>*Essays will receive the following grades, A for excellent, B for good, C for average, and D for unsatisfactory.*</td></tr>
<tr><td>**Problem:**</td><td>A colon is needed to emphasize the information or list that follows.</td></tr>
<tr><td>**Correction:**</td><td>*Essays will receive the following grades: A for excellent, B for good, C for average, and D for unsatisfactory.*</td></tr>
</table>

<table>
<tr><td>**Error:**</td><td>*The school carnival included: amusement rides, clowns, food booths, and a variety of games.*</td></tr>
<tr><td>**Problem:**</td><td>The material preceding the colon and the list that follows are not complete sentences. Do not separate a verb (or preposition) from the object.</td></tr>
<tr><td>**Correction:**</td><td>*The school carnival included amusement rides, clowns, food booths, and a variety of games.*</td></tr>
</table>

COLONS: used to introduce lists and to emphasize the text that follows

Apostrophes

APOSTROPHES are used to show contractions or possession.

<table>
<tr><td>**Error:**</td><td>*She shouldnt be permitted to smoke cigarettes in the building.*</td></tr>
<tr><td>**Problem:**</td><td>An apostrophe is needed in a contraction in place of the missing letter.</td></tr>
<tr><td>**Correction:**</td><td>*She shouldn't be permitted to smoke cigarettes in the building.*</td></tr>
</table>

<table>
<tr><td>**Error:**</td><td>*My cousins motorcycle was stolen from his driveway.*</td></tr>
<tr><td>**Problem:**</td><td>An apostrophe is needed to show possession.</td></tr>
<tr><td>**Correction:**</td><td>*My cousin's motorcycle was stolen from his driveway. (Note: The use of the apostrophe before the letter "s" means that there is just one cousin. The plural form would read as follows: My cousins' motorcycle was stolen from their driveway.)*</td></tr>
</table>

<table>
<tr><td>**Error:**</td><td>*The childrens new kindergarten teacher was also a singer.*</td></tr>
<tr><td>**Problem:**</td><td>An apostrophe is needed to show possession.</td></tr>
<tr><td>**Correction:**</td><td>*The children's new kindergarten teacher was also a singer.*</td></tr>
</table>

APOSTROPHES: used to show contractions or possession

Error: *Children screams could be heard for miles.*

Problem: An apostrophe and the letter *s* are needed in the sentence to show who is screaming.

Correction: *Children's screams could he heard for miles. (Note: Because the word children is already plural, the apostrophe and -s must be added afterward to show ownership.)*

Quotation Marks

In a quoted statement that is either declarative or imperative, place the period inside the closing quotation marks.

> *"The airplane crashed on the runway during takeoff."*

If other words, in the sentence follow the quotation, place a comma inside the closing quotations marks and a period at the end of the sentence.

> *"The airplane crashed on the runway during takeoff," said the announcer.*

Usually, when a quoted title or expression occurs at the end of a sentence, the period is placed before the single or double quotation marks.

> *"The middle school readers were unprepared to understand Bryant's poem 'Thanatopsis.'"*
>
> *Early book-length adventure stories such as Don Quixote and The Three Musketeers were known as "picaresque novels."*

The final quotation mark precedes the period if the content of the sentence is about a speech or quote.

> *The first thing out of his mouth was "Hi, I'm home."*
>
> *—BUT—*
>
> *The first line of his speech began: "I arrived home to an empty house".*

In interrogatory or exclamatory sentences, the question mark or exclamation point should be positioned outside the closing quotation marks if the quote itself is a statement, command, or cited title.

> Who decided to lead us in the recitation of the "Pledge of Allegiance"?
>
> Why was Tillie shaking as she began her recitation, "Once upon a midnight dreary..."?
>
> I was embarrassed when Mrs. White said, "Your slip is showing"!

In declarative sentences, where the quotation is a question or an exclamation, place the question mark or exclamation point inside the quotation marks.

> The hall monitor yelled, "Fire! Fire!"
>
> "Fire! Fire!" yelled the hall monitor.
>
> Cory shrieked, "Is there a mouse in the room?" (In this instance, the question supersedes the exclamation.)

Quotations—whether words, phrases, or clauses—should be punctuated according to the rules of the grammatical function they serve in the sentence.

> The works of Shakespeare, "the Bard of Avon," have been contested as originating with other authors.
>
> "You'll get my money," the old man warned, "when 'hell freezes over'."
>
> Sheila cited the passage that began "Four score and seven years ago . . . ." (Note the ellipsis followed by an enclosed period.)
>
> "Old Ironsides" inspired the preservation of the U.S.S. Constitution.

Use quotation marks to enclose the titles of shorter works: songs, short poems, short stories, essays, and chapters of books. (See "Dashes and Italics" for rules on punctuating longer titles.)

> "The Tell-Tale Heart" "Casey at the Bat" "America the Beautiful"

Practice Exercise: Capitalization and Punctuation (Commas, Colons, Semicolons, Apostrophes, and Quotation Marks)

Choose the option that corrects an error in the underlined portion(s). If no error exists, choose "No change is necessary."

1. **Greenpeace is an <u>Organization</u> that works to preserve the <u>world's</u> environment.**

    A. greenpeace

    B. organization

    C. worlds

    D. No change is necessary

2. **When our class travels to <u>France</u> next <u>year, we</u> will see the <u>country's</u> many famous landmarks.**

    A. france

    B. year; we

    C. countries

    D. No change is necessary

3. **<u>New York City</u>, the most heavily populated city <u>in America has</u> more than eight million people living there <u>every day</u>.**

    A. new york city

    B. in America, has

    C. Everyday

    D. No change is necessary

4. **The <u>television</u> show Lost gained a huge <u>following because</u> it focused on paranormal phenomena, time travel, and the frailties of <u>human existence</u>.**

    A. Television

    B. following, because

    C. Human existence

    D. No change is necessary

5. **Being a <u>Policeman</u> requires having many <u>qualities</u>: physical <u>agility</u>, good reflexes, and the ability to make quick decisions.**

    A. policeman

    B. qualities;

    C. agility:

    D. No change is necessary

Practice Exercise: Capitalization and Punctuation (Commas, Colons, Semicolons, Apostrophes, and Quotation Marks) (cont.)

Choose the option that corrects an error in the underlined portion(s). If no error exists, choose "No change is necessary."

6. "Tis <u>better to have loved and lost, than never to have loved at all</u>," <u>wrote Tennyson</u>, the poet <u>who</u> demonstrates the value of love in a <u>mans</u> life.

    A. Better to have loved and lost than never to have loved at all

    B. Tennyson who

    C. man's

    D. No change is necessary

7. The <u>Boston Americans</u> won the first <u>world series</u> championship by defeating the Pittsburgh Pirates in <u>October 1903</u>.

    A. Boston americans

    B. World Series

    C. October, 1903

    D. No change is necessary

Answer Key

1. **B**

   In the sentence, the word *organization* does not need to be capitalized because it is a general noun. In Option A, the name of the organization should be capitalized. In Option C, an apostrophe is needed to show that one world is being protected, not more than one.

2. **D**

   In Option A, *France* must be capitalized because it is the name of a country. In Option B, a comma, not a semicolon, should separate the dependent clause from the main clause. In Option C, an apostrophe and an -s are needed to indicate that only one country is being visited.

Answer Key (cont.)

3. **B**

   In Option A, New York City must be capitalized because it is the name of a place. In Option B, a comma is needed to separate the adjective clause ending with *America* from the verb *has*. In Option C, *every day* needs no capitalization and should not be joined as a compound word. (The word *everyday* is an adjective meaning *routine*.)

4. **D**

   In Option A, *television* does not need to be capitalized because it is a common noun. In Option B, a comma is only necessary to separate an independent clause from the main clause. In Option C, *human existence* is a general term that does not need capitalization.

5. **A**

   In Option A, *policeman* does not need capitalization because it is a common noun. In Option B, a colon, not a semicolon, is needed because the rest of the sentence is related to the main clause. In Option C, a comma, not a colon, is needed to separate the adjectives.

6. **C**

   In Option A, a comma is needed to break the quote into distinct parts that give it greater clarity. In Option B, a comma is needed to separate the subject of the sentence from the relative clause. In Option C, an apostrophe is needed to show possession.

7. **B**

   In Option A, *Americans* must be capitalized because it is the name of a team. In Option B, *World Series* is capitalized because it is the title of a sporting event. In Option C, no comma is needed because month and year need no distinction; they are general terms.

COMPETENCY 9
RESEARCH SKILLS

SKILL **Assess the credibility and relevance of sources**
9.1

Assessing Bias

BIAS is defined as an opinion, feeling, or influence that strongly favors one side in an argument. A statement or passage is biased if an author attempts to convince a reader of something.

Is there evidence of bias in the following statement?

Using a calculator cannot help a student understand the process of graphing, so its use is a waste of time.

Because the author makes it perfectly clear that he does not favor the use of the calculator in graphing problems, the answer is yes, there is evidence of bias. He has included his opinion in this statement.

Is there evidence of bias in the following statement?

There are teachers who feel that computer programs are quite helpful in helping students grasp certain math concepts. There are also those who disagree with this feeling. It is up to each individual math teacher to decide if computer programs benefit his or her particular group of students.

The author has presented two different points of view about the helpfulness of computer programs in helping students grasp math concepts. The author has also concluded that the usefulness of computer programs in helping students learn math is best observed by and decided on by the individual math teacher. It shows no bias.

Sources may be divided into two major categories: primary and secondary sources.

Primary sources are works, records, etc., that were created during the period being studied or immediately after it. *Secondary sources* are works written significantly after the period being studied and are based on primary sources. Primary sources are the basic materials that provide raw data and information. Secondary sources are the works that contain the explications of, and judgments on, this primary material.

Primary sources include the following kinds of materials:

- Documents that reflect the immediate, everyday concerns of people, such as memoranda, bills, deeds, charters, newspaper reports pamphlets, graffiti, popular writings, journals or diaries, records of decision-making bodies, letters, receipts, and photographs.

- Theoretical writings that reflect care and consideration in composition and an attempt to convince or persuade. The topic will generally be deeper and reflect more pervasive values than is the case with immediate documents; these may include newspaper or magazine editorials, sermons, political speeches, and philosophical writings.

- Narrative accounts of events ideas, trends, etc., written with intentionality by someone contemporary with the events described.

- Statistical data, although statistics can be misleading.

- Literature and nonverbal materials, novels, stories, poetry, and essays from the period, as well as coins, archaeological artifacts, and art produced during the period.

Examples and uses of secondary sources include:

- Books written based on primary materials about the period

- Books written based on primary materials about people who played a major role in the events under consideration

- Books and articles written based on primary materials about the culture, the social norms, the language, and the values of the period

- Quotations from primary sources

- Statistical data on the period

- The conclusions and inferences of other historians

- Multiple interpretations of the ethos of the time

Here are some guidelines for the use of secondary sources:

- Do not rely only upon a single secondary source

- Check facts and interpretations against primary sources whenever possible

- Accept the conclusions of other historians critically

- Place greatest reliance on the secondary sources created by the best and most respected scholars

- Do not use the inferences of other scholars as if they were facts

- Ensure that any bias the writer brings to his or her interpretation of history is recognized

- Understand the primary point of the book as a basis for evaluating the value of the material presented in it to one's questions

See Skill 2.7

SKILL 9.2 Recognize the different elements of a citation

There are three major styles of citation: the Modern Language Association (MLA) style, the American Psychological Association (APA) style for social science research, and the Chicago Manual of Style (CMA). The sample essays in Skills 4.1 and 4.2 are written in MLA style. In-text citations are used; that is, the author and the name of the work are referred to within the body of the essay with the understanding that the reader can refer back to the Source citation.

In in-text citations within an essay, the author is named in full, the article or book (even if accessed on the Internet) is named, and each time there is a direct quotation or a segment of paraphrased information, the author is cited. For example, both Luften and McGinty's names appear in parentheses after such a quotation or bloc of paraphrased information.

Usually in MLA style, a page number would appear after the author's name (McGinty, p. 564). However, since the sources were Internet ones (as indicated by the word "Web" in the citations) there were no page numbers available. Another reason for no page numbers being used is the brevity of the Source passage.

The Sources and sample written essay show examples of citations for book and magazine resources taken from the Web.

See Skill 4.1 and Skill 4.2

SKILL 9.3 Recognize effective research strategies

See Skill 9.4

SKILL 9.4 Recognize information relevant to a particular research task

We live in "The Information Age" where research and information has never been so abundant What's more, the wealth of human knowledge is increasing exponentially. In the past information and research were limited, with the sum of human knowledge advancing slowly rather than in quantum leaps.

Therefore, learning how to research effectively in order to cut through information that might not be relevant, useful, or even verified, is an important skill. One of the best research skills is to understand what sources are reliable.

The Internet, for example, is an invaluable research tool. At the same time, much of the information on the Internet is not verified or peer reviewed by experts. When doing Internet research, look for university affiliations of the author or at university websites themselves. Verify the name of the researcher as belonging to that university. A "Google scholar" search will allow you to type in the name of a scholar or researcher and will turn up articles, some of which are available on the Internet and some of which must be ordered through a subscription fee to the research site or a one-time payment for use of the particular journal article or research study. If you are researching a certain field, learn what journals, magazines, and publishers are respected in that field.

A good source of research is the references in a reputable research article. From one reputable research article on a topic, you can network a whole list of reliable sources from that article's references to references those authors use to support their articles

When performing a research task, the researcher has to discern whether or not a source is biased; whether the source is presenting only part of the picture or is selectively using statistics. A good way to do this is to compare one source with others; if there is not a tone of objectivity, if the figures used are substantially different from those in other sources, if some important points are conveniently ignored, it is possible that the source is not a reliable one.

See Skill 9.1

SAMPLE TEST
WRITING

DIRECTIONS: The passage below contains many errors. Read the passage. Then, answer each test item by choosing the option that corrects an error in the underlined portion(s). No more than one underlined error will appear in each item. If no error exists, choose "No change is necessary."

Climbing to the top of Mount Everest is an adventure. One that everyone—whether physically fit or not—seems eager to try. The trail stretches for miles, the cold temperatures are usually frigid and brutal.

Climbers must endure several barriers on the way including other hikers, steep jagged rocks, and lots of snow. Plus, climbers often find the most grueling part of the trip is their climb back down, just when they are feeling greatly exhausted. Climbers who take precautions are likely to find the ascent less arduous than the unprepared. By donning heavy flannel shirts, gloves, and hats, climbers prevented hypothermia, as well as simple frostbite. A pair of rugged boots are also one of the necessities. If climbers are to avoid becoming dehydrated, there is beverages available for them to transport as well.

Once climbers are completely ready to begin their lengthy journey, they can comfortable enjoy the wonderful scenery. Wide rock formations dazzle the observers eyes with shades of gray and white, while the peak forms a triangle that seems to touch the sky. Each of the climbers are reminded of the splendor and magnificence of God's great Earth.

1. Once climbers are completely prepared for <u>their</u> lengthy <u>journey, they</u> can <u>comfortable</u> enjoy the wonderful scenery.

   A. they're

   B. journey; they

   C. comfortably

   D. No change is necessary

2. Plus, climbers often find the most grueling part of the trip is <u>their</u> climb back <u>down, just</u> when they <u>are</u> feeling greatly exhausted.

   A. his

   B. down; just

   C. were

   D. No change is necessary

3. **A pair of rugged boots <u>are also one</u> of the <u>necessities</u>.**

   A. necesities

   B. also, one

   C. is

   D. No change is necessary

4. **By donning heavy flannel shirts, boots, and <u>hats, climbers prevented</u> hypothermia, as well as simple frostbite.**

   A. hats climbers

   B. can prevent

   C. hypothermia;

   D. No change is necessary

5. <u>Climbers who</u> take precautions are likely to find the ascent <u>less difficult than</u> the unprepared.

   A. Climbers, who

   B. least difficult

   C. then

   D. No change is necessary

6. If climbers are to avoid <u>becoming</u> dehydrated, there <u>is</u> beverages available for <u>them</u> to transport as well.

   A. becomming

   B. are

   C. him

   D. No change is necessary

7. Each of the climbers <u>are</u> reminded of the splendor and <u>magnificence</u> of <u>God's</u> great Earth.

   A. is

   B. magnifisence

   C. Gods

   D. No change is necessary

8. Climbers must endure <u>several</u> barriers <u>on the way including</u> other <u>hikers</u>, steep jagged rocks, and lots of snow.

   A. on the way, including

   B. severel

   C. hikers'

   D. No change is necessary

9. The <u>trail</u> stretches for <u>miles</u>, the cold temperatures are <u>usually</u> frigid and brutal.

   A. trails

   B. miles;

   C. usual

   D. No change is necessary

10. Wide rock formations dazzle the <u>observers eyes</u> with shades of gray and <u>white</u>, <u>while</u> the peak <u>forms</u> a triangle that seems to touch the sky.

    A. observers' eyes

    B. white; while

    C. formed

    D. No change is necessary

11. Climbing to the top of Mount Everest is an <u>adventure. One</u> that everyone—<u>whether</u> physically fit or not—<u>seems</u> eager to try.

    A. adventure, one

    B. people, whether

    C. seem

    D. No change is necessary

DIRECTIONS: The passage below contains several errors. Read the passage. Then, answer each test item by choosing the option that corrects an error in the underlined portion(s). No more than one underlined error will appear in each item. If no error exists, choose "No change is necessary."

Every job places different kinds of demands on their employees. For example, whereas such jobs as accounting and bookkeeping require mathematical ability; graphic design requires creative/artistic ability.

Doing good at one job does not usually guarantee success at another. However, one of the elements crucial to all jobs are especially notable—the chance to accomplish a goal.

The accomplishment of the employees vary according to the job. In many jobs, the employees become accustom to the accomplishments provided by the work they do every day.

In medicine, for example, every doctor tests him self or herself by treating badly injured or critically ill people. In the operating room, a team of Surgeons, is responsible for operating on many of these patients. In addition to the feeling of accomplishment that the workers achieve, some jobs also give a sense of identity to the employees'. Professions such as law, education, and sales offers huge financial and emotional rewards. Politicians are public servants: who work for the federal and state governments. President obama is basically employed by the American people to make laws and run the country.

Finally; the contributions that employees make to their companies and to the world cannot be taken for granted. Through their work, employees are performing a service for their employers and are contributing something to the world.

12. **Doing <u>good</u> at one job does not <u>usually</u> guarantee <u>success</u> at another.**

    A. well

    B. usualy

    C. succeeding

    D. No change is necessary

13. **In medicine, for example, every doctor <u>tests him self</u> or herself by treating badly injured and <u>critically</u> ill people.**

    A. test

    B. himself

    C. critical

    D. No change is necessary

14. **Every job <u>places</u> different kinds of demands on <u>their employees</u>.**

    A. place

    B. its

    C. employes

    D. No change is necessary

15. **The <u>accomplishment</u> of the <u>employees vary</u> according to the job.**

    A. accomplishments

    B. employee's

    C. varies

    D. No change is necessary

16. <u>However</u>, one of the elements crucial to all jobs <u>are</u> especially <u>notable</u>—the accomplishment of a goal.

    A. However

    B. is

    C. notable;

    D. No change is necessary

17. <u>Professions</u> such as law <u>education</u>, and sales <u>offers</u> huge financial and emotional rewards.

    A. A. offer

    B. B. education;

    C. C. Profesions

    D. D. No change is necessary

18. In many jobs, the employees <u>become accustom</u> to the accomplishments <u>provided</u> by the work they do every day.

    A. became

    B. accustomed

    C. provides

    D. No change is necessary

19. In the <u>operating room</u>, a team of <u>Surgeons, is</u> responsible for operating on many of <u>these</u> patients.

    A. operating room:

    B. surgeons is

    C. those

    D. No change is necessary

20. Politicians are public <u>servants: who work</u> for the federal and state governments.

    A. were

    B. servants who

    C. worked

    D. No change is necessary

21. <u>For example</u>, <u>whereas</u> such jobs as accounting and bookkeeping require mathematical <u>ability</u>; graphic design requires creative/artistic ability.

    A. For example

    B. whereas,

    C. ability,

    D. No change is necessary

22. In addition to the feeling of accomplishment that the workers <u>achieve</u>, some jobs also <u>give</u> a sense of self-identity to the <u>employees'</u>.

    A. acheive

    B. gave

    C. employees

    D. No change is necessary

23. <u>Finally</u>; the contributions that employees make to <u>their</u> companies and to the world cannot be <u>taken</u> for granted.

    A. Finally,

    B. thier

    C. took

    D. No change is necessary

24. President <u>obama</u> is basically employed <u>by</u> the American people to <u>make</u> laws and run the country.

    A. Obama

    B. to

    C. made

    D. No change is necessary

DIRECTIONS: The passage below contains several errors. Read the passage. Then, answer each test item by choosing the option that corrects an error in the underlined portion(s). No more than one underlined error will appear in each item. If no error exists, choose "No change is necessary."

The discovery of a body at Paris Point marina in Boca Raton shocked the residents of Palmetto Pines, a luxury condominium complex located next door to the marina.

The victim is a thirty-five-year-old woman who had been apparently bludgeoned to death and dumped in the ocean late last night. Many neighbors reported terrible screams, gunshots: as well as the sound of a car backfiring loudly to Boca Raton Police shortly after midnight. The woman had been spotted in the lobby of Palmetto Pines around ten thirty, along with an older man, estimated to be in his fifties, and a younger man, in his late twenties.

"Apparently, the victim had been driven to the complex by the older man and was seen arguing with him when the younger man intervened," said Sheriff Fred Adams, "all three of them left the building together and walked to the marina, where gunshots rang out an hour later." Deputies found five bullets on the sidewalk and some blood, along with

a steel pipe that is assumed to be the murder weapon. Two men were seen fleeing the scene in a red Mercedes short after, rushing toward the Interstate.

The Palm Beach County Coroner, Melvin Watts, said he concluded the victim's skull had been crushed by a blunt tool, which resulted in a brain hemorrhage. As of now, there is no clear motive for the murder.

25. Two men <u>were</u> seen fleeing the scene in a red Mercedes <u>short</u> after, <u>rushing</u> toward the Interstate.

    A. are

    B. shortly

    C. rushed

    D. No change is necessary

26. As of <u>now,</u> <u>there</u> <u>is</u> no clear motive for the murder.

    A. now;

    B. their

    C. was

    D. No change is necessary

27. Deputies found five bullets on the sidewalk and some <u>blood</u>, along with a steel pipe that is <u>assumed</u> <u>to be</u> the murder weapon.

    A. blood;

    B. assuming

    C. to have been

    D. No change is necessary

28. The victim is a thirty-five-year-old woman who <u>had been</u> apparently <u>bludgeoned</u> to death and dumped in the <u>ocean late</u> last night.

    A. was

    B. bludgoned

    C. ocean: late

    D. No change is necessary

29. Many <u>neighbors</u> reported terrible screams, <u>gunshots: as</u> well as the sound of a car backfiring <u>loudly</u> to Boca Raton Police shortly after midnight.

    A. nieghbors

    B. gunshots, as

    C. loud

    D. No change is necessary

30. "Apparently, the victim had been driven to the complex by the older man and was seen arguing with him when the younger man intervened," said <u>Sheriff Fred Adams, "all</u> three of them left the building together and walked to the marina, where gunshots rang out an hour later."

    A. sheriff Fred Adams, "all

    B. sheriff Fred Adams, "All

    C. Sheriff Fred Adams. "All

    D. No change is necessary

31. The woman <u>had</u> been spotted in the lobby of Palmetto Pines around ten <u>thirty</u>, along with an older <u>man, estimated</u> to be in his fifties, and a younger man in his late twenties.

    A. has

    B. thirty;

    C. man estimated

    D. No change is necessary

32. The discovery of a body at Paris Point marina in Boca Raton shocked the <u>residents</u> of Palmetto Pines, a luxury <u>condominium</u> complex located next door to the <u>marina</u>.

    A. Marina

    B. residence

    C. condominnium

    D. No change is necessary

33. The <u>Palm Beach</u> <u>county coroner</u>, Kelvin Watts, said he concluded the victim's skull had been crushed by a blunt tool, which resulted in a brain <u>hemorrhage</u>.

    A. hemorrage

    B. palm beach

    C. County Coroner

    D. No change is necessary

DIRECTIONS: Choose the sentence that logically and correctly expresses the comparison.

34. A. The Empire State Building in New York is taller than buildings in the city.

B. The Empire State Building in New York is taller than any other building in the city.

C. The Empire State Building in New York is tallest than other buildings in the city.

DIRECTIONS: For the underlined sentence(s), choose the option that expresses the meaning with the most fluency and the clearest logic within the context. If the underlined sentence should not be changed, choose Option A, which shows no change.

35. John wanted to join his friends on the mountain-climbing trip. <u>Seeing that the weather had become dark and stormy, John knew he would stay safe indoors.</u>

A. Seeing that the weather had become dark and stormy, John knew he would stay safe indoors.

B. The weather had become dark and stormy, and John knew he would stay indoors, and he would be safe.

C. Because the weather had become dark and stormy, John knew he would stay indoors, where he would be safe.

D. Because the weather had become dark, as well as stormy, John knew he would stay safe indoors.

36. A few hours later, the storm subsided, so John left the cabin to join his friends. <u>Even though he was tired from the four-mile hike the day before, he climbed the mountain in a few hours.</u>

A. Even though he was tired from the four-mile hike the day before, he climbed the mountain in a few hours.

B. He was tired from the four-mile the day before; he climbed the mountain in a few hours.

C. He climbed the mountain in a few hours, John was tired from the four-mile hike the day before.

D. Seeing as he was tired from the day before, when he went on a four-mile hike, John climbed the mountain in a few hours.

DIRECTIONS: Choose the most effective word within the context of the sentence.

37. Many of the clubs in Boca Raton are noted for their _____ elegance.

A. vulgar

B. tasteful

C. ordinary

38. When a student is expelled from school, the parents are usually _____ in advance.

A. rewarded

B. congratulated

C. notified

39. Before appearing in court, the witness was _____ the papers requiring her to show up.

   A. condemned

   B. served

   C. criticized

DIRECTIONS: Choose the underlined word or phrase that is unnecessary within the context of the passage.

40. The <u>expanding</u> number of television channels has <u>prompted</u> cable operators to raise their prices, <u>even though</u> many consumers do not want to pay a higher <u>increased</u> amount for their service.

   A. expanding

   B. prompted

   C. even though

   D. increased

Free Response Essay Sample Questions _____

Question 1.

Read the following poems about dreams by Edgar Allen Poe. Then write a well-organized essay in which you analyze the poems' literary elements such as figurative language, parallelism and tone to compare his two poems.

Poem one

Take this kiss upon the brow!
And, in parting from you now,
Thus much let me avow--
You are not wrong, who deem
That my days have been a dream;
Yet if hope has flown away
In a night, or in a day,
In a vision, or in none,
Is it therefore the less gone?
All that we see or seem
Is but a dream within a dream.

I stand amid the roar
Of a surf-tormented shore,
And I hold within my hand
Grains of the golden sand--
How few! yet how they creep
Through my fingers to the deep,
While I weep--while I weep!
O God! can I not grasp
Them with a tighter clasp?
O God! can I not save
One from the pitiless wave?
Is all that we see or seem
But a dream within a dream?

Poem two

In visions of the dark night
I have dreamed of joy departed-
But a waking dream of life and light
Hath left me broken-hearted.

Ah! what is not a dream by day
To him whose eyes are cast
On things around him with a ray
Turned back upon the past?

That holy dream- that holy dream,
While all the world were chiding,
Hath cheered me as a lovely beam
A lonely spirit guiding.

What though that light, thro' storm and night,
So trembled from afar-
What could there be more purely bright
In Truth's day-star?

Question 2.

Chose a literary work that describes a perception of utopia. In your analysis, describe impacts of that perception on a particular character and experiences or choices made because of that perception or devotion to a utopian ideal. In your essay, do not merely summarize the plot.

ANSWER KEY				
1. C	9. B	17. A	25. B	33. C
2. D	10. A	18. B	26. D	34. B
3. C	11. A	19. B	27. C	35. D
4. B	12. A	20. B	28. A	36. A
5. D	13. B	21. C	29. B	37. B
6. B	14. B	22. C	30. C	38. C
7. A	15. A	23. A	31. C	39. B
8. A	16. B	24. A	32. A	40. D

Sample Test Questions and Rationale

DIRECTIONS: The passage below contains many errors. Read the passage. Then, answer each test item by choosing the option that corrects an error in the underlined portion(s). No more than one underlined error will appear in each item. If no error exists, choose "No change is necessary."

Climbing to the top of Mount Everest is an adventure. One which everyone—whether physically fit or not—seems eager to try. The trail stretches for miles, the cold temperatures are usually frigid and brutal.

Climbers must endure several barriers on the way including other hikers, steep jagged rocks, and lots of snow. Plus, climbers often find the most grueling part of the trip is their climb back down, just when they are feeling greatly exhausted. Climbers who take precautions are likely to find the ascent less arduous than the unprepared. By donning heavy flannel shirts, gloves, and hats, climbers prevented hypothermia, as well as simple frostbite. A pair of rugged boots are also one of the necessities. If climbers are to avoid becoming dehydrated, there is beverages available for them to transport as well.

Once climbers are completely ready to begin their lengthy journey, they can comfortable enjoy the wonderful scenery. Wide rock formations dazzle the observers eyes with shades of gray and white, while the peak forms a triangle that seems to touch the sky. Each of the climbers are reminded of the splendor and magnificence of God's great Earth.

1. Once climbers are completely prepared for their lengthy journey, they can comfortable enjoy the wonderful scenery.

   A. they're

   B. journey; they

   C. comfortably

   D. No change is necessary

   Answer: C. comfortably

   The adverb form *comfortably* is needed to modify the verb phrase *can enjoy*. Option A is incorrect because the possessive plural pronoun is spelled *their*. Option B is incorrect because a semicolon would make the first half of the item seem like an independent clause when the subordinating conjunction once makes that clause dependent.

2. Plus, climbers often find the most grueling part of the trip is their climb back down, just when they are feeling greatly exhausted.

   A. his

   B. down; just

   C. were

   D. No change is necessary

   Answer: D. No change is necessary

   The present tense must be used consistently throughout; therefore, Option C is incorrect. Option A is incorrect because the singular pronoun *his* does not agree with the plural antecedent *climbers*. Option B is incorrect because a comma, not a semicolon, is needed to separate the dependent clause from the main clause.

Sample Test Questions and Rationale (cont.)

3. **A pair of rugged boots <u>are</u> <u>also</u> <u>one</u> of the necessities.**

   A. necesities

   B. also, one

   C. is

   D. No change is necessary

   Answer: C. is

   Option A is incorrect because the word *necessities* is spelled correctly in the text. Option B is incorrect because if *also* is set off with commas (potential correction), it should be set off on both sides. Option C is correct because the singular verb *is* must agree with the singular noun *pair* (a collective singular).

4. **By donning heavy flannel shirts, boots, and <u>hats, climbers</u> <u>prevented</u> hypothermia, as well as simple frostbite.**

   A. hats climbers

   B. can prevent

   C. hypothermia;

   D. No change is necessary

   Answer: B. can prevent

   The verb *prevented* is in the past tense and must be changed to the present *can prevent* to be consistent. Option A is incorrect because a comma is needed after a long introductory phrase. Option C is incorrect because the semicolon creates a fragment of the phrase *as well as simple frostbite.*

5. **<u>Climbers who</u> take precautions are likely to find the ascent less <u>difficult</u> <u>than</u> the unprepared.**

   A. Climbers, who

   B. least difficult

   C. then

   D. No change is necessary

   Answer: D. No change is necessary

   No change is needed. Option A is incorrect because a comma would make the phrase *who take precautions* seem less restrictive or less essential to the sentence. Option B is incorrect because *less* is appropriate when two items—the prepared and the unprepared—are compared. Option C is incorrect because the comparative adverb *than*, not *then*, is needed.

6. **If climbers are to avoid <u>becoming</u> dehydrated, there is beverages available for <u>them</u> to transport as well.**

   A. becomming

   B. are

   C. him

   D. No change is necessary

   Answer: B. are

   The plural verb *are* must be used with the plural subject *beverages*. Option A is incorrect because *becoming* is spelled correctly in the text. Option C is incorrect because the plural pronoun *them* is needed to agree with the referent *climbers*.

Sample Test Questions and Rationale (cont.)

7. Each of the climbers <u>are</u> reminded of the splendor and <u>magnificence</u> of <u>God's</u> great Earth.

   A. is

   B. magnifisence

   C. Gods

   D. No change is necessary

   Answer: A. is

   The singular verb *is* agrees with the singular subject *each*. Option B is incorrect because *magnificence* is spelled correctly in the text. Option C is incorrect because an apostrophe is needed to show possession.

8. Climbers must endure <u>several</u> barriers <u>on the way including</u> other <u>hikers</u>, steep jagged rocks, and lots of snow.

   A. on the way, including

   B. severel

   C. hikers'

   D. No change is necessary

   Answer: A. on the way, including

   Option B is incorrect because the word *several* is spelled correctly in the text. Option A is correct because a comma is needed to set off the modifying phrase. Option C is incorrect because no apostrophe is needed after *hikers* since possession is not involved.

9. The <u>trail</u> stretches for <u>miles</u>, the cold temperatures are <u>usually</u> frigid and brutal.

   A. trails

   B. miles;

   C. usual

   D. No change is necessary

   Answer: B. miles;

   A semicolon, not a comma, is needed to separate the first independent clause from the second independent clause. Option A is incorrect because the plural subject *trails* needs the singular verb *stretch*. Option C is incorrect because the adverb form *usually* is needed to modify the adjective *frigid*.

10. Wide rock formations dazzle the <u>observers eyes</u> with shades of gray and <u>white, while</u> the peak <u>forms</u> a triangle that seems to touch the sky.

    A. observers' eyes

    B. white; while

    C. formed

    D. No change is necessary

    Answer: A. observers' eyes

    An apostrophe is needed to show the plural possessive form *observers' eyes*. Option B is incorrect because the semicolon would make the second half of the item seem like an independent clause when the subordinating conjunction *while* makes that clause dependent. Option C is incorrect because *formed* is in the wrong tense.

Sample Test Questions and Rationale (cont.)

11. **Climbing to the top of Mount Everest is an <u>adventure. One</u> that everyone—<u>whether</u> physically fit or not—<u>seems</u> eager to try.**

    A. adventure, one

    B. people, whether

    C. seem

    D. No change is necessary

Answer: A. adventure, one

A comma is needed between adventure and one to avoid creating a fragment of the second part. In Option B, a comma after everyone would not be appropriate when the dash is used on the other side of not. In Option C, the singular verb seems is needed to agree with the singular subject everyone.

DIRECTIONS: The passage below contains several errors. Read the passage. Then, answer each test item by choosing the option that corrects an error in the underlined portion(s). No more than one underlined error will appear in each item. If no error exists, choose "No change is necessary."

Every job places different kinds of demands on their employees. For example, whereas such jobs as accounting and bookkeeping require mathematical ability; graphic design requires creative/artistic ability.

Doing good at one job does not usually guarantee success at another. However, one of the elements crucial to all jobs are especially notable—the chance to accomplish a goal.

The accomplishment of the employees vary according to the job. In many jobs, the employees become accustom to the accomplishments provided by the work they do every day.

In medicine, for example, every doctor tests him self or herself by treating badly injured or critically ill people. In the operating room, a team of Surgeons, is responsible for operating on many of these patients. In addition to the feeling of accomplishment that the workers achieve, some jobs also give a sense of identity to the employees'. Professions such as law, education, and sales offers huge financial and emotional rewards. Politicians are public servants: who work for the federal and state governments. President obama is basically employed by the American people to make laws and run the country.

Finally; the contributions that employees make to their companies and to the world cannot be taken for granted. Through their work, employees are performing a service for their employers and are contributing something to the world.

Sample Test Questions and Rationale (cont.)

12. Doing <u>good</u> at one job does not <u>usually</u> guarantee <u>success</u> at another.

    A. well

    B. usualy

    C. succeeding

    D. No change is necessary

    Answer: A. well

    The adverb well modifies the word *doing*. Option B is incorrect because *usually* is spelled correctly in the sentence. Option C is incorrect because *succeeding* is in the wrong tense.

13. In medicine, for example, every doctor <u>tests him self</u> or herself by treating badly injured and <u>critically</u> ill people.

    A. test

    B. himself

    C. critical

    D. No change is necessary

    Answer: B. himself

    The reflexive pronoun *himself* is needed. (*Him self* is nonstandard and never correct.) Option A is incorrect because the verb *test* is plural. Option C is incorrect because the adverb *critically* is needed to modify the verb *ill*.

14. Every job <u>places</u> different kinds of demands on <u>their</u> <u>employees</u>.

    A. place

    B. its

    C. employes

    D. No change is necessary

    Answer: B. its

    The singular possessive pronoun *its* must agree with its antecedent *job*, which is singular also. Option A is incorrect because *place* is a plural form and the subject, *job*, is singular. Option C is incorrect because the correct spelling of *employees* is given in the sentence.

15. The <u>accomplishment</u> of the <u>employees</u> <u>vary</u> according to the job.

    A. accomplishments

    B. employee's

    C. varies

    D. No change is necessary

    Answer: A. accomplishments

    The plural noun *accomplishments* is needed to agree with the plural noun *employees* and the plural verb *vary*. Option C is incorrect because vary is the correct form of the verb. Option B is incorrect because *employees* is not possessive.

Sample Test Questions and Rationale (cont.)

16. <u>However,</u> one of the elements crucial to all jobs <u>are</u> especially <u>notable</u>—the accomplishment of a goal.

   A. However

   B. is

   C. notable;

   D. No change is necessary

   Answer: B. is

   The singular verb *is* is needed to agree with the singular subject *one*. Option A is incorrect because a comma is needed to set off the transitional word *however*. Option C is incorrect because an em dash, not a semicolon, is needed to set off this item.

17. <u>Professions</u> such as law, <u>education,</u> and sales <u>offers</u> huge financial and emotional rewards.

   A. offer

   B. education;

   C. Profesions

   D. No change is necessary

   Answer: A. offer

   Option A is correct because it shows correct subject-verb agreement. Option B is incorrect because a comma, not a semicolon, is needed after *education*. In Option C, *Professions* is spelled correctly in the text.

18. In many jobs, the employees <u>become</u> <u>accustom</u> to the accomplishments <u>provided</u> by the work they do every day.

   A. became

   B. accustomed

   C. provides

   D. No change is necessary

   Answer: B. accustomed

   The past participle *accustomed* is needed with the verb *become*. Option A is incorrect because the verb tense does not need to change to the past *became*. Option C is incorrect because *provides* is the wrong tense.

19. In the <u>operating room,</u> a team of <u>Surgeons,</u> <u>is</u> responsible for operating on many of <u>these</u> patients.

   A. operating room:

   B. surgeons is

   C. those

   D. No change is necessary

   Answer: B. surgeons is

   Option B is correct because a comma is not needed to break up *a team of surgeons* from the rest of the sentence. Also, *surgeons* does not need to be capitalized. Option A is incorrect because a comma, not a colon, is needed to set off an item. Option C is incorrect because *those* is an incorrect pronoun.

Sample Test Questions and Rationale (cont.)

20. Politicians <u>are</u> public <u>servants: who</u> <u>work</u> for the federal and state governments.

    A. were

    B. servants who

    C. worked

    D. No change is necessary

    Answer: B. servants who

    Option B is correct because a colon is not needed to set off the introduction of the clause. In Option A, *were* is the incorrect tense of the verb. In Option C, *worked* is in the wrong tense.

21. <u>For example,</u> <u>whereas</u> such jobs as accounting and bookkeeping require mathematical <u>ability;</u> graphic design requires creative/artistic ability.

    A. For example

    B. whereas,

    C. ability,

    D. No change is necessary

    Answer: C. ability,

    An introductory dependent clause is set off with a comma, not a semicolon. Option A is incorrect because the transitional phrase *for example* should be set off with a comma. Option B is incorrect because the adverb *whereas* functions as *while* and does not take a comma after it.

22. In addition to the feeling of accomplishment that the workers <u>achieve</u>, some jobs also <u>give</u> a sense of self-identity to the <u>employees'.</u>

    A. acheive

    B. gave

    C. employees

    D. No change is necessary

    Answer: C. employees

    Option C is correct because *employees* is not possessive. Option A is incorrect because *achieve* is spelled correctly in the sentence. Option B is incorrect because *gave* is the wrong tense.

23. <u>Finally;</u> the contributions that employees make to <u>their</u> companies and to the world cannot be <u>taken</u> for granted.

    A. Finally,

    B. thier

    C. took

    D. No change is necessary

    Answer: A. Finally,

    A comma is needed to separate *Finally* from the rest of the sentence. *Finally* is a preposition that usually heads a dependent sentence, hence a comma is needed. Option B is incorrect because *their* is misspelled. Option C is incorrect because *took* is the wrong form of the verb.

Sample Test Questions and Rationale (cont.)

24. President <u>obama</u> is basically employed <u>by</u> the American people to <u>make</u> laws and run the country.

    A. Obama

    B. to

    C. made

    D. No change is necessary

Answer: A. Obama

Obama is a proper name and should be capitalized. In Option B, to does not fit with the verb employed. Option C uses the wrong form of the verb make.

DIRECTIONS: The passage below contains several errors. Read the passage. Then, answer each test item by choosing the option that corrects an error in the underlined portion(s). No more than one underlined error will appear in each item. If no error exists, choose "No change is necessary."

The discovery of a body at Paris Point marina in Boca Raton shocked the residents of Palmetto Pines, a luxury condominium complex located next door to the marina.

The victim is a thirty-five-year-old woman who had been apparently bludgeoned to death and dumped in the ocean late last night. Many neighbors reported terrible screams, gunshots: as well as the sound of a car backfiring loudly to Boca Raton Police shortly after midnight. The woman had been spotted in the lobby of Palmetto Pines around ten thirty, along with an older man, estimated to be in his fifties, and a younger man, in his late twenties.

"Apparently, the victim had been driven to the complex by the older man and was seen arguing with him when the younger man intervened," said Sheriff Fred Adams, "all three of them left the building together and walked to the marina, where gunshots rang out an hour later." Deputies found five bullets on the sidewalk and some blood, along with a steel pipe that is assumed to be the murder weapon. Two men were seen fleeing the scene in a red Mercedes short after, rushing toward the Interstate.

The Palm Beach County Coroner, Melvin Watts, said he concluded the victim's skull had been crushed by a blunt tool, which resulted in a brain hemorrhage. As of now, there is no clear motive for the murder.

25. Two men <u>were</u> seen fleeing the scene in a red Mercedes <u>short</u> after, <u>rushing</u> toward the Interstate.

    A. are

    B. shortly

    C. rushed

    D. No change is necessary

Answer: B. shortly

The adverb *shortly* is needed instead of the adjective *short*. Option A incorrectly uses the present tense *are* instead of the past tense *were*. Option C, *rushed*, is the wrong form of the verb.

Sample Test Questions and Rationale (cont.)

26. As of <u>now, there is</u> no clear motive for the murder.

    A. now;

    B. their

    C. was

    D. No change is necessary

Answer: D. No change is necessary

Option A is incorrect because a comma is needed to separate the independent clause from the dependent clause. Option B creates a misspelling. Option C uses the incorrect tense, *was*, which does not fit with the present tense phrase *as of now*.

27. Deputies found five bullets on the sidewalk and some <u>blood,</u> along with a steel pipe that is <u>assumed to be</u> the murder weapon.

    A. blood;

    B. assuming

    C. to have been

    D. No change is necessary

Answer: C. to have been

The past tense *to have been* is needed to maintain consistency. Option A incorrectly uses a semicolon instead of a comma. Option B uses the wrong form of the verb *assumed*.

28. The victim <u>is</u> a thirty-five-year-old woman who had been apparently <u>bludgeoned</u> to death and dumped in the <u>ocean late</u> last night.

    A. was

    B. bludgoned

    C. ocean: late

    D. No change is necessary

Answer: A. was

The past tense *was* is needed to maintain consistency. Option B creates a misspelling. Option C incorrectly uses a colon when none is needed.

29. Many <u>neighbors</u> reported terrible screams, <u>gunshots: as</u> well as the sound of a car backfiring <u>loudly</u> to Boca Raton Police shortly after midnight.

    A. nieghbors

    B. gunshots, as

    C. loud

    D. No change is necessary

Answer: B. gunshots, as

Option B correctly uses a comma, not a colon, to separate the items. Option A creates a misspelling. Option C incorrectly changes the adverb into an adjective.

Sample Test Questions and Rationale (cont.)

30. "Apparently, the victim had been driven to the complex by the older man and was seen arguing with him when the younger man intervened," said <u>Sheriff Fred Adams, "all</u> three of them left the building together and walked to the marina, where gunshots rang out an hour later."

    A. sheriff Fred Adams, "all

    B. sheriff Fred Adams, "All

    C. Sheriff Fred Adams. "All

    D. No change is necessary

Answer: C. Sheriff Fred Adams. "All

The quote's source comes in the middle of two independent clauses, so a period should follow *Adams*. Option A is incorrect because titles, when they come before a name, must be capitalized. Punctuation is also faulty. Option B is incorrect because the word *Adams* ends a sentence; a comma is not strong enough to support two sentences.

31. The woman <u>had</u> been spotted in the lobby of Palmetto Pines around ten <u>thirty,</u> along with an older <u>man, estimated</u> to be in his fifties, and a younger man in his late twenties.

    A. has

    B. thirty;

    C. man estimated

    D. No change is necessary

Answer: C. man estimated

A comma is not needed to separate the item because *an older man estimated to be in his fifties* is one complete fragment. Option A incorrectly uses the present tense *has* instead of the past tense *had*. Option B incorrectly uses a semicolon when a comma is needed.

32. The discovery of a body at Paris Point <u>marina</u> in Boca Raton shocked the <u>residents</u> of Palmetto Pines, a luxury <u>condominium</u> complex located next door to the marina.

    A. Marina

    B. residence

    C. condominnium

    D. No change is necessary

Answer: A. Marina

Marina is a name that needs to be capitalized. Options B and C create misspellings.

Sample Test Questions and Rationale (cont.)

33. The <u>Palm Beach</u> <u>county</u> <u>coroner,</u> Kelvin Watts, said he concluded the victim's skull had been crushed by a blunt tool, which resulted in a brain <u>hemorrhage</u>.

    A. hemorrage

    B. palm beach

    C. County Coroner

    D. No change is necessary

Answer: C. County Coroner

Option A is incorrect because *hemorrhage* is spelled correctly in the text. Option B is incorrect because *Palm Beach* is a proper name and needs to be capitalized, as it is in the text. Option C is correct because *County Coroner* is a job title and must be capitalized.

DIRECTIONS: Choose the sentence that logically and correctly expresses the comparison.

34. A. The Empire State Building in New York is taller than buildings in the city.

    B. The Empire State Building in New York is taller than any other building in the city.

    C. The Empire State Building in New York is tallest than other buildings in the city.

Answer: B.

Option B is the most specific and grammatically correct. Option A just says "buildings in the city", which is not specific enough. Option C is not grammatically correct. Therefore, option B, describing that the Empire State Building is taller than any other building, is the correct option.

DIRECTIONS: For the underlined sentence(s), choose the option that expresses the meaning with the most fluency and the clearest logic within the context. If the underlined sentence should not be changed, choose Option A, which shows no change.

35. John wanted to join his friends on the mountain-climbing trip. <u>Seeing that the weather had become dark and stormy, John knew he would stay safe indoors.</u>

    A. Seeing that the weather had become dark and stormy, John knew he would stay safe indoors.

    B. The weather had become dark and stormy, and John knew he would stay indoors, and he would be safe.

    C. Because the weather had become dark and stormy, John knew he would stay indoors, where he would be safe.

    D. Because the weather had become dark, as well as stormy, John knew he would stay safe indoors.

Answer: D.

The object of the sentence is the storm, and option D provides the most emphasis on John's feelings because the weather had become both dark and stormy. Option B also separates both descriptions, furthering why John wanted to stay home.

Sample Test Questions and Rationale (cont.)

36. A few hours later, the storm subsided, so John left the cabin to join his friends.
    <u>Even though he was tired from the four-mile hike the day before, he climbed the mountain in a few hours.</u>

    A. Even though he was tired from the four-mile hike the day before, he climbed the mountain in a few hours.

    B. He was tired from the four-mile the day before; he climbed the mountain in a few hours.

    C. He climbed the mountain in a few hours, John was tired from the four-mile hike the day before.

    D. Seeing as he was tired from the day before, when he went on a four-mile hike, John climbed the mountain in a few hours.

    Answer: A.

    There is no needed change because Option A makes the most sense with its order of information. With Option B, it removes "even though" and makes the previous day's activities seem like it does not affect his long hike. Option C has the information in the wrong order and it does not make sense. Option D also sounds like the previous day's activities were positive and would not affect his hike. Option D provides the best order of information, showing that John's previous activities were strenuous, but didn't completely affect him on his second hike.

DIRECTIONS: Choose the most effective word within the context of the sentence.

37. Many of the clubs in Boca Raton are noted for their _____ elegance.

    A. vulgar

    B. tasteful

    C. ordinary

    Answer: B.

    Option B is the best answer. The word "noted" has a positive connotation, and the option "vulgar" is negative. Option C of ordinary would not be something that would be recognized.

38. When a student is expelled from school, the parents are usually _____ in advance.

    A. rewarded

    B. congratulated

    C. notified

    Answer: C.

    Like question 37, the other two options have the wrong connotation. Both "rewarded" and "congratulated" are positive affirmations and would not apply to the expelling of a student.

Sample Test Questions and Rationale (cont.)

39. Before appearing in court, the witness was _____ the papers requiring her to show up.

    A. condemned

    B. served

    C. criticized

Answer: B.

Although all these words have the same negative connotation, the other two options are not in the right context. Option B, served, is the only word that fits this court context.

DIRECTIONS: Choose the underlined word or phrase that is unnecessary within the context of the passage.

40. The <u>expanding</u> number of television channels has <u>prompted</u> cable operators to raise their prices, <u>even though</u> many consumers do not want to pay a higher <u>increased</u> amount for their service.

    A. expanding

    B. prompted

    C. even though

    D. increased

Answer: D.

"Increased" is redundant in this passage. It already says the word "higher", which means the same thing. So "increased" would need to be removed to make sense of the sentence and the intended meaning.

DOMAIN III
MATHEMATICS

PERSONALIZED STUDY PLAN

✗
KNOWN MATERIAL/ SKIP IT

PAGE	COMPETENCY AND SKILL	
179	**10: Number and Quantity**	☐
	10.1: Understand ratio concepts and use ratio reasoning to solve problems	☐
	10.2: Analyze proportional relationships and use them to solve real-world and mathematical problems	☐
	10.3: Apply understanding of multiplication and division to divide fractions by fractions	☐
	10.4: Compute fluently with multi-digit numbers and find common factors and multiples	☐
	10.5: Apply understanding of operations with fractions to add, subtract, multiply, and divide rational number	☐
	10.6: Know that there are numbers that are not rational, and approximate them by rational numbers	☐
	10.7: Work with radicals and integer exponents	☐
	10.8: Reason quantitatively and use units to solve problem	☐
201	**11: Algebra and Functions**	☐
	11.1: Apply understanding of arithmetic to algebraic expressions	☐
	11.2: Solve real-life and mathematical problems using numerical and algebraic expressions	☐
	11.3: Use properties of operations to generate equivalent expressions	☐
	11.4: Understand the connections between proportional relationships, lines, and linear equations	☐
	11.5: Understand solving equations as a process of reasoning and explain the reasoning	☐
	11.6: Reason about and solve one-variable equations and inequalities	☐
	11.7: Solve equations and inequalities in one variable	☐
	11.8: Analyze and solve linear equations and pairs of simultaneous linear equations	☐
	11.9: Represent and solve equations and inequalities graphically	☐
	11.10: Interpreting functions	☐
	11.11: Building functions	☐

PERSONALIZED STUDY PLAN

✗

KNOWN MATERIAL/ SKIP IT

PAGE	COMPETENCY AND SKILL	
219	**12: Geometry**	☐
	12.1: Draw, construct, and describe geometrical figures and describe the relationships between them	☐
	12.2: Experiment with transformations in the plane	☐
	12.3: Understand and apply the Pythagorean theorem	☐
	12.4: Understand and apply theorems about circles	☐
	12.5: Solve real-life and mathematical problems involving angle measure, area, surface area, and volume	☐
	12.6: Explain volume formulas and use them to solve problems	☐
	12.7: Apply geometric concepts in modeling situations	☐
240	**13: Statistics and Probability**	☐
	13.1: Develop understanding of statistical variability	☐
	13.2: Summarize and describe distributions	☐
	13.3: Use random sampling to draw inferences about a population	☐
	13.4: Investigate chance processes and develop, use, and evaluate probability models	☐
	13.5: Investigate patterns of association in bivariate data	☐
	13.6: Summarize, represent, and interpret data on a single count or measurement variable	☐
	13.7: Interpret linear models	☐
	13.8: Understand and evaluate random processes underlying statistical experiments	☐
	13.9: Use probability to evaluate outcomes of decisions	☐

✗

COMPETENCY 10
NUMBER AND QUANTITY

Ratio

A **RATIO** is a comparison of two numbers. If a class had 11 boys and 14 girls, the ratio of boys to girls could be written in one of three ways:

- 11:14

- 11 to 14

- $\frac{11}{14}$

The ratio of girls to boys is:

- 14:11

- 14 to 11

- $\frac{14}{11}$

Ratios can be reduced when possible. A ratio of 12 cats to 18 dogs would reduce to 2:3, 2 to 3, or $\frac{2}{3}$.

Note: Read ratio questions carefully. Given a group of 6 adults and 5 children, the ratio of children to the entire group would be 5:11.

Example: A jar of candies contains 28 red candies and 21 green. Find the ratio of red to green in lowest terms.

Red: green starts out as 28:21 or $\frac{28}{21}$. If the ratio is to be expressed in lowest term, the fraction must be reduced. Since $\frac{28}{21} = \frac{4}{3}$, the ratio of red to green in lowest terms is 4 to 3.

RATIO: a comparison of two numbers

SKILL **Analyze proportional relationships and use them to solve real-world**
10.2 **and mathematical problems**

Proportion

> **PROPORTION:** an equation in which one fraction is set equal to another

A **PROPORTION** is an equation in which one fraction is set equal to another. To solve a proportion, multiply each numerator times the other fraction's denominator. Set these two products equal to each other and solve the resulting equation. This is called **cross-multiplying** the proportion.

Example:

$\frac{4}{15} \times \frac{x}{60}$ is a proportion.

To solve this, cross-multiply.

$15x = 240$

$x = 16$

Example:

$\frac{x+3}{3x+4} = \frac{2}{5}$ is a proportion.

To solve, cross-multiply.

$5(x + 3) = 2(3x + 4)$

$5x + 15 = 6x + 8$

$7 = x$

Proportions can be used to solve word problems whenever relationships are compared. Some applications of proportions include scale drawings and maps; similar polygons; speed, time, and distance; cost; and comparison shopping.

Example: Which is the better buy—6 apples for $1.29 or 8 apples for $1.69?

Find the unit price.

$\frac{6}{1.29} = \frac{1}{x}$ $\qquad$ $\frac{8}{1.69} = \frac{1}{x}$

$6x = 1.29$ $\qquad\quad$ $8x = 1.69$

$x = 0.215$ $\qquad\quad$ $x = 0.21125$

Thus, 8 apples for $1.69 is the better buy.

Example: A car travels 125 miles in 2.5 hours. How far will it go in 6 hours?

Write a proportion comparing the distance and time. . .

$\frac{miles}{hours} = \frac{125}{2.5} = \frac{x}{6}$

$2.5x = 750$

$x = 300$

Thus, the car can travel 300 miles in 6 hours.

Example: The scale on a map is $\frac{3}{4}$ inch = 6 miles. What is the actual distance between two cities if they are $1\frac{1}{2}$ inches apart on the map?

Write a proportion comparing the scale to the actual distance.

$$\frac{\frac{3}{4}}{\frac{3}{2}} = \frac{6}{x}$$

$$\frac{3}{4}\,x = \left[\frac{3}{2}\right](6)$$

$$\frac{3}{4}\,x = 9$$

$$3x = 36$$

Thus, the actual distance between the cities is 12 miles.

Operating with Percents

Example: 5 is what percent of 20?

This is the same as converting $\frac{5}{20}$ to percent form.

$$\frac{5}{20} \times \frac{100}{1} = \frac{5}{1} \times \frac{5}{1} = 25\%$$

Example: There are 64 dogs in a kennel, and 48 are collies. What percent are collies?

Restate the problem.   48 is what percent of 64?

Write an equation. $48 = n \times 64$

Solve. $\frac{48}{64} = n$

$n = \frac{3}{4} = 75\%$

75% of the dogs are collies.

Example: The auditorium was filled to 90% capacity. There were 558 seats occupied. What is the capacity of the auditorium?

Restate the problem.   90% of what number is 558?

Write an equation. $0.9n = 558$

Solve. $n = \frac{558}{.9}$

$n = 620$

The capacity of the auditorium is 620 people.

Example: A pair of shoes costs $42.00. Sales tax is 6%. What is the total cost of the shoes?

Restate the problem.   What is 6% of 42?

Write an equation. $n = 0.06 \times 42$

Solve. $n = 2.52$

Add the sales tax to the cost. $42.00 + \$2.52 = \$44.52$

Sample Test Questions and Rationale

(Rigorous)

1. It takes 5 equally skilled workers 9 hours to shingle Mr. Joe's roof. Let t be the time required for only 3 of these workers to do the same job. Select the correct statement of the given condition.

    A. $\frac{3}{5} = \frac{9}{t}$
    B. $\frac{9}{5} = \frac{3}{t}$
    C. $\frac{5}{9} = \frac{3}{t}$
    D. $\frac{14}{9} = \frac{t}{5}$

    Answer is A.

    $$\frac{3}{5} = \frac{9}{t}$$

    The answer is A.

(Easy)

2. **303 is what percent of 600?**

    A. 0.505%
    B. 5.05%
    C. 505%
    D. 50.5%

    Answer: D. 50.5%

    Use x for the percent. $600x = 303$. $\frac{600x}{600} = \frac{303}{600} \rightarrow x = 0.505 = 50.5\%$.

(Average)

3. A restaurant employs 465 people. There are 280 waiters and 185 cooks. If 168 waiters and 85 cooks receive pay raises, what percent of the waiters will receive a pay raise?

    A. 36.13%
    B. 60%
    C. 60.22%
    D. 40%

    Answer: B. 60%

    The total number of waiters is 280 and only 168 of them get a pay raise. Divide the number getting a raise by the total number of waiters to get the percent.

    $$\frac{168}{280} = 0.6 = 60\%$$

(Rigorous)

4. An item that sells for $375 is put on sale for $120. What is the percent of decrease?

    A. 25%
    B. 28%
    C. 68%
    D. 34%

    Answer: C. 68%

    Discount 5 375 2 120 5 225. $375x$ 5 255 $\rightarrow x$ 5 0.68 5 68%.

(Rigorous)

5. In a sample of 40 full-time employees at a particular company, 35 were also holding down a part-time job requiring at least 10 hours/ week. If this proportion holds for the entire company of 25,000 employees, how many full-time employees at this company are actually holding down a part-time job of at least 10 hours per week?

    A. 714
    B. 625
    C. 21,875
    D. 28,571

    Answer: C. 21,875

    $\frac{35}{40}$ full-time employees also have a part-time job. Out of 25,000 full-time employees, the number that also have a part-time job is $\frac{35}{40} = \frac{x}{2500}$ $\rightarrow 40x = 875000 \rightarrow x = 21875$, so 21,875 full-time employees also have a part time job.

SKILL 10.3 Apply understanding of multiplication and division to divide fractions by fractions

The operation of division is equivalent to multiplication by the reciprocal.

$a \div b = a \bullet \left(\dfrac{1}{b} \right)$ as long as $b \neq 0$.

Furthermore, according to the rules of fraction multiplication,

$a \bullet \left(\dfrac{1}{b} \right) = \left(\dfrac{a}{1} \right)\left(\dfrac{1}{b} \right) = \dfrac{a}{b}$

Therefore, $\dfrac{a}{b} = a \div b$. In other words, a fraction is just another way to rewrite a division problem. Transition between these equivalent operations is key to successfully navigating fraction computation.

Example: Express the relationship "half of 12" as both a division problem and a multiplication problem.

Since "of" represents multiplication, "half of 12" $= \left(\dfrac{1}{2} \right) \bullet 12$. Applying the Commutative Property and rewriting the reciprocal multiplication as division leads to $12 \bullet \left(\dfrac{1}{2} \right) = 12 \div 2$.

So "half of 12" is the same as $12 \div 2$ and $\left(\dfrac{1}{2} \right) \bullet 12$

Keeping a basic arithmetic notion like "half of 12" in mind can help to analyze more abstract situations.

Example: $\dfrac{30}{\frac{1}{3}} = 30 \div \left(\dfrac{1}{3} \right) = 30 \bullet 3 = 90$

Example: $\dfrac{\frac{2a}{7b}}{\frac{14a}{b}} = \left(\dfrac{2a}{7b} \right) \div \left(\dfrac{14a}{b} \right) = \left(\dfrac{2a}{7b} \right) \bullet \left(\dfrac{b}{14a} \right) = \dfrac{2ab}{7 \bullet 14ab} = \dfrac{1}{49}$

SKILL 10.4 Compute fluently with multi-digit numbers and find common factors and multiples

Whole Number Place Value

Consider the number 792. We can assign a place value to each digit.

Reading from left to right, the first digit (7) represents the hundreds place. The hundreds place tells us how many sets of 100 the number contains. Thus, there are seven sets of 100 in the number 792.

The second digit (9) represents the tens place. The tens place tells us how many sets of 10 the number contains. Thus, there are nine sets of 10 in the number 792.

The last digit (2) represents the ones place. The ones place tells us how many 1s the number contains. Thus, there are two sets of 1 in the number 792.

Therefore, there are seven sets of 100, plus nine sets of 10, plus two 1s in the number 792.

Decimal Place Value

More complex numbers have additional place values to both the left and right of the decimal point. Consider the number 374.8.

Reading from left to right, the first digit (3) is in the hundreds place and tells us the number contains three sets of 100.

The second digit (7) is in the tens place and tells us the number contains seven sets of 10.

The third digit (4) is in the ones place and tells us the number contains four 1s.

Finally, the number after the decimal (8) is in the tenths place and tells us the number contains eight tenths.

Addition of Whole Numbers

Example: At the end of a day of shopping, a shopper had $24 remaining in his wallet. He had spent $45 on various goods. How much money did the shopper have at the beginning of the day?

The total amount of money the shopper started with is the sum of the amount spent and the amount remaining at the end of the day.

$$
\begin{array}{r}
24 \\
+\ 45 \\
\hline
69
\end{array}
$$

The original total was $69.

Example: The winner of a race needed 1 hr, 58 min, 12 sec to complete the first half of the race and 2 hr, 9 min, 57 sec to complete the second half of the race. How much time did the entire race take?

1 hr 58 min 12 sec	
+ 2 hr 9 min 57 sec	Add these numbers.
3 hr 67 min 69 sec	
+ 1 min − 60 sec	Change 60 sec to 1 min.
3 hr 68 min 9 sec	
+ 1 hr − 60 min	Change 60 min to 1 hr.
4 hr 8 min 9 sec	Final answer.

Subtraction of Whole Numbers

Example: At the end of his shift, a cashier has $96 in the cash register. At the beginning of his shift, he had $15. How much money did the cashier collect during his shift?

The total collected is the difference between the ending amount and the starting amount.

96	
−15	
81	The total collected was $81.

Multiplication of Whole Numbers

Multiplication is one of the four basic number operations. In simple terms, multiplication is the addition of a number to itself a certain number of times. For example, 4 multiplied by 3 is equal to 4 + 4 + 4 or 3 + 3 + 3 + 3. Another way of conceptualizing multiplication is to think in terms of groups. For example, if we have 4 groups of 3 students, the total number of students is 4 multiplied by 3. We call the solution to a multiplication problem the PRODUCT.

> **PRODUCT:** the answer to a multiplication problem

The basic algorithm for whole number multiplication begins with aligning the numbers by place value, with the number containing more places on top.

172	
× 43	Note that we placed 172 on top because it has more places than 43 does.

Next, we multiply the ones place of the bottom number by each place value of the top number sequentially.

```
  (2)
  172        {3 × 2 = 6, 3 × 7 = 21, 3 × 1 = 3}
× 43         Note that we had to carry a 2 to the hundreds column
  516        because 3 × 7 = 21. Note also that we add carried numbers
             to the product.
```

Next, we multiply the number in the tens place of the bottom number by each place value of the top number sequentially. Because we are multiplying by a number in the tens place, we place a zero at the end of this product.

```
  (2)
  172
× 43         {4 × 2 = 8, 4 × 7 = 28, 4 = 1 = 4}
  516
 6880
```

Finally, to determine the final product, we add the two partial products.

```
   172
 × 43
   516
+ 6880
  7396      The product of 172 and 43 is 7396.
```

Example: A student buys 4 boxes of crayons. Each box contains 16 crayons. How many total crayons does the student have?

The total number of crayons is 16 × 4.

```
  16
× 4
  64         The total number of crayons equals 64.
```

Division of Whole Numbers

Division, the inverse of multiplication, is another of the four basic number operations. When we divide one number by another, we determine how many times we can multiply the **divisor** (number divided by) before we exceed the number we are dividing (**dividend**). For example, 8 divided by 2 equals 4 because we can multiply 2 four times to reach 8 (2 × 4 = 8 or 2 + 2 + 2 + 2 = 8). Using the grouping conceptualization we used with multiplication, we can divide 8 into 4 groups of 2 or 2 groups of 4. We call the answer to a division problem the **QUOTIENT**.

QUOTIENT: the answer to a division problem

If the divisor does not divide evenly into the dividend, we express the leftover amount either as a remainder or as a fraction with the divisor as the denominator. For example, 9 divided by 2 equals 4 with a remainder of 1, or $4\frac{1}{2}$.

The basic algorithm for division is long division. We start by representing the quotient as follows:

$$14\overline{)293}$$ 14 is the divisor and 293 is the dividend.

This represents $293 \div 14$.

Next, we divide the divisor into the dividend starting from the left.

$$14\overline{)293}^{\,2}$$ 14 divides into 29 two times with a remainder.

Next, we multiply the partial quotient by the divisor, subtract this value from the first digits of the dividend, and bring down the remaining dividend digits to complete the number.

$$\begin{array}{r} 2 \\ 14\overline{)293} \\ -28 \\ \hline 13 \end{array}$$ $2 \times 14 = 28$, $29 - 28 = 1$ and bringing down the 3 yields 13.

Finally, we divide again (the divisor into the remaining value) and repeat the preceding process. The number left after the subtraction represents the remainder.

$$\begin{array}{r} 2 \\ 14\overline{)293} \\ -28 \\ \hline 13 \\ -0 \\ \hline 13 \end{array}$$ The final quotient is 20 with a remainder of 13. We can also represent this quotient as 20.

Example: Each box of apples contains 24 apples. How many boxes must a grocer purchase to supply a group of 252 people with one apple each?

The grocer needs 252 apples. Because he must buy apples in groups of 24, we divide 252 by 24 to determine how many boxes he needs to buy.

$$\begin{array}{r} 10 \\ 24\overline{)252} \\ -24 \\ \hline 12 \\ -0 \\ \hline 12 \end{array}$$ The quotient is 10 with a remainder of 12.

Thus, the grocer needs 10 boxes plus 12 more apples. Therefore, the minimum number of boxes the grocer can purchase is 11.

Example: At his job, John gets paid $20 for every hour he works. If John made $940 in a week, how many hours did he work?

This is a division problem. To determine the number of hours John worked, we divide the total amount made ($940) by the hourly rate of pay ($20).

$$\begin{array}{r} 47 \\ 20\overline{)940} \\ -80 \\ \hline 140 \\ -140 \\ \hline 0 \end{array}$$

20 divides into 940, 47 times with no remainder.

John worked 47 hours.

Addition and Subtraction of Decimals

When adding and subtracting decimals, we align the numbers by place value as we do with whole numbers. After adding or subtracting each column, we bring the decimal down, placing it in the same location as in the numbers added or subtracted.

Example: Find the sum of 152.3 and 36.342.

$$\begin{array}{r} 152.300 \\ + \ 36.342 \\ \hline 188.642 \end{array}$$

Note that we placed two zeros after the final place value in 152.3 to clarify the column addition.

Example: Find the difference of 152.3 and 36.342.

$$\begin{array}{r} 2\ 9\ 10 \\ 152.\cancel{300} \\ -\ 36.342 \\ \hline 58 \end{array} \qquad \begin{array}{r} (4)11(12) \\ 1\cancel{52.300} \\ -\ 36.342 \\ \hline 115.958 \end{array}$$

Note how we borrowed to subtract from the zeros in the hundredths and thousandths places of 152.300.

Multiplication of Decimals

When multiplying decimal numbers, we multiply exactly as with whole numbers and place the decimal in from the right the total number of decimal places contained in the two numbers multiplied. For example, when multiplying 1.5 and 2.35, we place the decimal in the product 3 places in from the right (3.525).

Example: Find the product of 3.52 and 4.1.

$$
\begin{array}{r}
3.52 \\
\times\ \underline{4.1} \\
352 \\
+\ \underline{14080} \\
14.432
\end{array}
$$

3.52   Note that there are three decimal places in total in the two numbers.

14.432   We place the decimal three places in from the right.

Thus, the final product is 14.432.

Example: A shopper has 5 one-dollar bills, 6 quarters, 3 nickels, and 4 pennies in his pocket. How much money does he have?

$5 \times \$1.00 = \$5.00$

$$
\begin{array}{ccc}
1\ 3 & 1 & \\
\$0.25 & \$0.05 & \$0.01 \\
\times\ \underline{6} & \times\ \underline{3} & \times\ \underline{4} \\
\$1.50 & \$0.15 & \$0.04
\end{array}
$$

Note the placement of the decimals in the multiplication products. Thus, the total amount of money in the shopper's pocket is:

$$
\begin{array}{r}
\$5.00 \\
1.50 \\
0.15 \\
+\ \underline{0.04} \\
\$6.69
\end{array}
$$

Division of Decimals

When dividing decimal numbers, we first remove the decimal in the divisor so that the divisor is a whole number. We then move the decimal in the dividend the same number of spaces to the right. For example, when dividing 1.45 into 5.3, we convert the divisor to 145 (a whole number) and the dividend to 530, and then perform normal whole number division.

Example: Find the quotient of 5.3 divided by 1.45.

Convert to 145 and 530.

Divide.

$$
\begin{array}{r}
3 \\
145\overline{)530} \\
-\underline{435} \\
95
\end{array}
\qquad
\begin{array}{r}
3.65 \\
145\overline{)530} \\
-\underline{435} \\
950 \\
-\underline{870} \\
800
\end{array}
$$

Note that we insert the decimal to continue division.

Because one of the numbers being divided contained one decimal place, we round the quotient to one decimal place. Thus, the final quotient is 3.7.

Greatest Common Factor

GCF is the abbreviation for GREATEST COMMON FACTOR. The GCF is the largest number that is a factor of all the numbers given in a problem. The GCF can be no larger than the smallest number given in the problem. If no other number is a common factor, then the GCF will be the number 1.

> **GREATEST COMMON FACTOR:** the largest number that is a factor of all the numbers in a problem

To find the GCF, list all possible factors of the smallest number (include the number itself). Starting with the largest factor (which is the number itself), determine if that factor is also a factor of all the other given numbers. If so, that factor is the GCF. If that factor doesn't divide evenly into the other given numbers, try the same method on the next smaller factor. Continue until a common factor is found. That factor is the GCF. Note: There can be other common factors besides the GCF.

Example: Find the GCF of 12, 20, and 36.
The smallest number in the problem is 12. The factors of 12 are 1, 2, 3, 4, 6 and 12. 12 is the largest of these factors, but it does not divide evenly into 20. Neither does 6. However, 4 will divide into both 20 and 36 evenly.
Therefore, 4 is the GCF.

Example: Find the GCF of 14 and 15.
The factors of 14 are 1, 2, 7, and 14. 14 is the largest factor, but it does not divide evenly into 15. Neither does 7 or 2. Therefore, the only factor common to both 14 and 15 is the number 1, the GCF.

Least Common Multiple

LCM is the abbreviation for LEAST COMMON MULTIPLE. The least common multiple of a group of numbers is the smallest number that all of the given numbers will divide into. The LCM will always be the largest of the given numbers or a multiple of the largest number.

> **LEAST COMMON MULTIPLE:** the smallest number of a group of numbers that all the given numbers will divide into evenly

Example: Find the LCM of 20, 30, and 40.
The largest number given is 40, but 30 will not divide evenly into 40. The next multiple of 40 is 80 (2 × 40), but 30 will not divide evenly into 80 either. The next multiple of 40 is 120. 120 is divisible by both 20 and 30, so 120 is the LCM.

Example: Find the LCM of 96, 16, and 24.
The largest number is 96. 96 is divisible by both 16 and 24, so 96 is the LCM.

Example: Elly Mae can feed the animals in 15 minutes. Jethro can feed them in 10 minutes. How long will it take them to feed the animals if they work together?

If Elly Mae can feed the animals in 15 minutes, then she could feed $\frac{1}{15}$ of them in 1 minute, $\frac{2}{15}$ of them in 2 minutes, $\frac{x}{15}$ of them in x minutes. In the same fashion, Jethro could feed $\frac{x}{10}$ of them in x minutes. Together, they complete 1 job. The equation is:

$\frac{x}{15} + \frac{x}{10} = 1$

Multiply each term by the LCM of 30:

$2x + 3x = 30$

$x = 6$ minutes

SKILL 10.5 Apply understanding of operations with fractions to add, subtract, multiply, and divide rational number

Addition and Subtraction of Fractions

Key Points

1. You need a common denominator in order to add and subtract reduced and improper fractions

   Example:
   $$\frac{1}{3} + \frac{7}{3} = \frac{1+7}{3} = \frac{8}{3} = 2\frac{2}{3}$$

   Example:
   $$\frac{4}{12} + \frac{6}{12} - \frac{3}{12} = \frac{4+6-3}{3} = \frac{7}{12}$$

2. Adding an integer and a fraction of the same sign results directly in a mixed fraction

   Example:
   $$2 + \frac{2}{3} = 2\frac{2}{3}$$

   Example:
   $$-2 - \frac{3}{4} = -2\frac{3}{4}$$

1. Adding an integer and a fraction with different signs involves the following steps

   – Find a common denominator

   – Add or subtract as needed

   – Change to a mixed fraction if possible

Example:

$$2 - \frac{1}{3} = \frac{2 \times 3 - 1}{3} = \frac{6 - 1}{3} = \frac{5}{3} = 1\frac{2}{3}$$

Example: Add: $7\frac{3}{8} + 5\frac{2}{7}$

Add the whole numbers; add the fractions; combine the two results:

$$7\frac{3}{8} + 5\frac{2}{7} = (7 + 5) + (\frac{3}{8} + \frac{2}{7})$$

$$= 12 + \frac{(7 \times 3) + (8 \times 2)}{56} \quad (56 \text{ is the LCM of 8 and 7})$$

$$= 12 + \frac{21 + 16}{56} = 12 + \frac{37}{56} = 12\frac{37}{56}$$

Example: Perform the operation.

$$\frac{2}{3} - \frac{5}{6}$$

We first find the LCM of 3 and 6, which is 6.

$$\frac{2 \times 2}{3 \times 2} - \frac{5}{6} \rightarrow \frac{4 - 5}{6} = \frac{^-1}{6}$$

Example:

$$^-7\frac{1}{4} + 2\frac{7}{8}$$

$$^-7\frac{1}{4} + 2\frac{7}{8} = (^-7 + 2) + (\frac{^-1}{4} + \frac{7}{8})$$

$$= (^-5) + \frac{(^-2 + 7)}{8} = (^-5) + (\frac{5}{8})$$

$$= (^-5) + \frac{5}{8} = \frac{^-5 \times 8}{1 \times 8} + \frac{5}{8} = \frac{^-40 + 5}{8}$$

$$= \frac{^-35}{8} = ^-4\frac{3}{8}$$

Divide 35 by 8 to get 4, remainder 3.

Caution. A common error would be.

$$^-7\frac{1}{4} + 2\frac{7}{8} = ^-7\frac{2}{8} + 2\frac{7}{8} = ^-5\frac{9}{8} \qquad \text{Wrong.}$$

It is correct to add $^-7$ and 2 to get $^-5$, but adding $\frac{2}{8} + \frac{7}{8} = \frac{9}{8}$ is wrong. It should have been $\frac{^-2}{8} + \frac{7}{8} = \frac{5}{8}$. Then, $^-5 + \frac{5}{8} = ^-4\frac{3}{8}$ as before.

Multiplication of Fractions

Using the following example: $3\frac{1}{4} \times \frac{5}{6}$

1. Convert each number to an improper fraction

   $3\frac{1}{4} = \frac{(12+1)}{4} = \frac{13}{4}$. $\frac{5}{6}$ is already in reduced form.

2. Reduce (cancel) common factors of the numerator and denominator if they exist

   $\frac{13}{4} \times \frac{5}{6}$ No common factors exist.

3. Multiply the numerators by each other and the denominators by each other

   $\frac{13}{4} \times \frac{5}{6} = \frac{65}{24}$

4. If possible, reduce the fraction back to its lowest terms

   $\frac{65}{24}$ Cannot be reduced further.

5. Convert the improper fraction to a mixed fraction by using long division

   $$\frac{65}{24} = 24\overline{)65} = 2\frac{17}{24}$$
   $$\frac{48}{17}$$

Summary of sign changes for multiplication

A. $(+) \times (+) = (+)$

B. $(-) \times (+) = (-)$

C. $(+) \times (-) = (-)$

D. $(-) \times (-) = (+)$

Example: Reduce like terms

$7\frac{1}{3} \times \frac{5}{11} = \frac{22}{3} \times \frac{5}{11} = \frac{2}{3} \times \frac{5}{1} = \frac{10}{3} = 3\frac{1}{3}$

Example:

$-6\frac{1}{4} \times \frac{5}{9} = \frac{-25}{4} \times \frac{5}{9}$

$= \frac{-125}{36} = -3\frac{17}{36}$

Example:

$\frac{-1}{4} \times \frac{-3}{7}$ Negative times a negative equals positive.

$= \frac{1}{4} \times \frac{3}{7} = \frac{3}{28}$

Division of Fractions

1. Change mixed fractions to improper fractions

2. Change the division problem to a multiplication problem by using the reciprocal of the number after the division sign

3. Find the sign of the final product

4. Cancel if common factors exist between the numerator and the denominator

5. Multiply the numerators together and the denominators together

6. Change the improper fraction to a mixed number

Example:

$$3\frac{1}{5} \div 2\frac{1}{4} = \frac{16}{5} \div \frac{9}{4}$$

$$= \frac{16}{5} \times \frac{4}{9} \quad \text{Reciprocal of } \frac{9}{4} \text{ is } \frac{4}{9}.$$

$$= \frac{64}{45} = 1\frac{19}{45}$$

Example:

$$7\frac{3}{4} \div 11\frac{5}{8} = \frac{31}{4} \div \frac{93}{8}$$

$$= \frac{31}{4} \times \frac{8}{93} \quad \text{Reduce like terms.}$$

$$= \frac{1}{1} \times \frac{2}{3} = \frac{2}{3}$$

Example:

$$\left[-2\frac{1}{2}\right] \div 4\frac{1}{6} = \frac{-5}{2} \div \frac{25}{6}$$

$$= \frac{-5}{2} \times \frac{6}{25} \quad \text{Reduce like terms.}$$

$$= \frac{-1}{1} \times \frac{3}{5} = \frac{-3}{5}$$

Example:

$$\left[-5\frac{3}{8}\right] \div \left[\frac{-7}{16}\right] = \frac{-43}{8} \div \frac{-7}{16}$$

$$= \frac{-43}{8} \times \frac{-16}{7} \quad \text{Reduce like terms.}$$

$$= \frac{-43}{8} \times \frac{2}{7} \quad \text{Negative times a negative equals a positive.}$$

$$= \frac{86}{7} = 12\frac{3}{5}$$

Sample Test Questions and Rationale

(Easy)

1. What is the greatest. common factor of 16, 28, and 36?

   A. 2

   B. 4

   C. 8

   D. 16

   Answer: B. 4

   The smallest number in this set is 16; its factors are 1, 2, 4, 8, and 16. Sixteen is the largest factor, but it does not divide into 28 or 36. Neither does 8. Four does divide into both 28 and 36.

(Average)

2. $\left(\frac{-4}{9}\right) + \left(\frac{-7}{10}\right) =$

   A. $\frac{23}{90}$

   B. $\frac{-23}{90}$

   C. $\frac{103}{90}$

   D. $\frac{-103}{90}$

   Answer: D. $\frac{-103}{90}$

   Find the LCD of $\frac{-4}{9}$. and $\frac{-7}{10}$. The LCD is 90, so you get $\frac{-40}{90} + \frac{-63}{90} = \frac{-103}{90}$.

(Average)

3. $(5.6) \times (-0.11) =$

   A. -0.616

   B. 0.616

   C. -6.110

   D. 6.110

   Answer: A. -0.616

   Simple multiplication. The answer will be negative because a positive number multiplied by a negative number is a negative number.

(Easy)

4. $\frac{7}{9} + \frac{1}{3} \div \frac{2}{3}$

   A. $\frac{5}{3}$

   B. $\frac{3}{2}$

   C. 2

   D. $\frac{23}{18}$

   Answer: D. $\frac{23}{18}$

   First, do the division.
   $\frac{1}{3} \div \frac{2}{3} = \frac{1}{3} \times \frac{3}{2} = \frac{1}{2}$

   Next, add the fractions.
   $\frac{7}{9} + \frac{1}{2} = \frac{14}{18} + \frac{9}{18} = \frac{23}{18}$,
   which is answer D.

(Rigorous)

5. $4\frac{2}{9} \times \frac{7}{10}$

   A. $4\frac{9}{10}$

   B. $\frac{266}{90}$

   C. $2\frac{43}{45}$

   D. $2\frac{6}{20}$

   Answer: C. $2\frac{43}{45}$

   Convert any mixed number to an improper fraction: $\frac{38}{9} \times \frac{7}{10}$. Since no common factors of numerators or denominators exist, multiply the numerators and the denominators by each other $= \frac{266}{90}$. Convert back to a mixed number and reduce: $2\frac{86}{90} = 2\frac{43}{45}$.

RATIONAL NUMBERS: numbers that can be expressed as the ratio of two integers, $\frac{a}{b}$, where b ≠ 0

RATIONAL NUMBERS are numbers that can be expressed as the ratio of two integers, $\frac{a}{b}$, where b ≠ 0. For example, $\frac{2}{3}, -\frac{4}{5}$, and $5 = \frac{5}{1}$ are all rational numbers.

The rational numbers include integers, fractions and mixed numbers, and terminating and repeating decimals. Every rational number can be expressed as a repeating or terminating decimal and can be shown on a number line.

INTEGERS: the positive and negative whole numbers and zero

INTEGERS are the positive and negative whole numbers and zero.

...-6, -5, -4, -3, -2, -1, 0, 1, 2, 3, 4, 5, 6,...

WHOLE NUMBERS: the natural numbers and zero

WHOLE NUMBERS are the natural numbers and zero.

0, 1, 2, 3, 4, 5, 6...

NATURAL NUMBERS: the counting numbers

NATURAL NUMBERS are the counting numbers.

1, 2, 3, 4, 5, 6...

IRRATIONAL NUMBERS: real numbers that cannot be written as the ratio of two integers; they are infinite, nonrepeating decimals

IRRATIONAL NUMBERS are real numbers that cannot be written as the ratio of two integers. They are infinite, non-repeating decimals.

$\sqrt{5} = 2.2360$, pi $= \pi = 3.1415927...$

FRACTION: an expression of numbers in the form of $\frac{x}{y}$, where x is the numerator and y is the denominator; the denominator cannot be zero

A **FRACTION** is an expression of numbers in the form of $\frac{x}{y}$, where x is the numerator and y is the denominator. The denominator cannot be zero.

$\frac{3}{7}$ 3 is the numerator; 7 is the denominator

If the fraction has common factors in the numerator and denominator, divide both by the common factors to reduce the fraction to its simplest form.

$\frac{13}{39} = \frac{1 \times 13}{3 \times 13} = \frac{1}{3}$ Divide by the common factor 13.

A **MIXED NUMBER** has an integer part and a fractional part.

$2\frac{1}{4}, -5\frac{1}{6}, 7\frac{1}{3}$

MIXED NUMBER: has an integer part and a fractional part

PERCENT = per 100 (written with the symbol %). Thus, 10%.$= \frac{10}{100} = \frac{1}{10}$

DECIMALS = deci = part of ten. To find the decimal equivalent of a fraction, use the denominator to divide the numerator, as shown in the following example:

Find the decimal equivalent of $\frac{7}{10}$.

Since 10 cannot divide into 7 evenly,

$\frac{7}{10} = 0.7$

PERCENT: means "per 100;" ten percent is 10 parts out of 100

An **IRRATIONAL NUMBER** is <u>not rational</u>, and therefore cannot be expressed as the ratio of two integers.

Some examples of irrational numbers are mathematical constants like π and e, as well as square roots of imperfect squares, like $\sqrt{26}$. In many cases, these numbers are best left in their exact, irrational form. However, there are applications when an estimate, in the form of a rational number, is needed. The geometry constant π is acceptably estimated as 3.14 or $\frac{22}{7}$. A radical expression, like $\sqrt{26}$ can be estimated to the nearest tenth, for example, on a calculator. It is helpful to know that $\sqrt{26}$ will be slightly bigger than its closest perfect square neighbor: $\sqrt{25} = 5$. Using a calculator shows $\sqrt{26} \approx 5.099$ when carried to the nearest thousandth.

> **DECIMAL:** a number written with a whole-number part, a decimal point, and a decimal part

---

SKILL 10.7 **Work with radicals and integer exponents**

Calculating With Exponents

An exponential expression represents repeated multiplication: $x^6 = x \bullet x \bullet x \bullet x \bullet x \bullet x$ where, in this case, x is the base and 6 is the exponent, or power.

Following this expansion pattern leads to a series of calculation rules for exponents.

I) $x^3 \bullet x^5 = xxx(xxxxx) = x^8$ "When multiplying like bases, add exponents."

II) $\dfrac{x^9}{x^2} = \dfrac{xxxxxxxxx}{xx} = x^7$ "When dividing like bases, subtract exponents."

III) $(x^3)^2 = (xxx)(xxx) = x^6$ "When raising a power to another power, multiply exponents"

Example: Simplify $\dfrac{a^3 b^5}{b} \bullet 7a^4$

$$\dfrac{a^3 b^5}{b} \bullet 7a^4 = 7a^3 a^4 \left(\dfrac{b^5}{b^1} \right) = 7a^{3+4}b^{5-1} = 7a^7 b^4$$

Additionally, an exponent can be negative. The following division problem demonstrates this concept: $\dfrac{x^3}{x^5} = \dfrac{xxx}{xxxxx} = \dfrac{1}{x^2}$. But applying the division of like bases rule suggests $\dfrac{x^3}{x^5} = x^{3-5} = x^{-2}$. Therefore $x^{-2} = \dfrac{1}{x^2}$ or $x^{-n} = \dfrac{1}{x^n}$.

Example: Simplify $\left(\dfrac{2x^7 y^5}{x^5 y^9}\right)^3$ *and answer with positive exponents*

$$\left(\frac{2x^7 y^5}{x^5 y^9}\right)^3 = \left(2x^2 y^{-4}\right)^3 = 8x^6 y^{-12} = \frac{8x^6}{y^{12}}$$

Example: Simplify $\dfrac{\left(m^3\right)^4}{m^{12}}$

$\dfrac{\left(m^3\right)^4}{m^{12}} = \dfrac{m^{12}}{m^{12}} = m^0$ Subtraction of exponents gives the answer m^0, but anytime a numerator and denominator are equal, the fraction simplifies to 1. $\left(\dfrac{m^{12}}{m^{12}} = 1\right)$.

This relationship suggests that any base raised to the power of zero equals one, or $x^0 = 1$.

Simplifying Radicals

First, know that a square root is the inverse operation of raising to a power of two, a cube root is the inverse of raising to the third power, or, in other words $\sqrt[n]{x^n} = x$ for all values of $x > 0$.

Example: $\sqrt[3]{125} = \sqrt[3]{5^3} = 5$

Additionally, the relationship $\sqrt[n]{ab} = \sqrt[n]{a} \cdot \sqrt[n]{b}$ states that radicals can be expanded under multiplication (but not addition: $\sqrt[n]{a+b} \neq \sqrt[n]{a} + \sqrt[n]{b}$). This directs the simplification of more complex radical expressions.

Example: $\sqrt{98} = \sqrt{49} \cdot \sqrt{2} = \sqrt{7^2} \cdot \sqrt{2} = 7\sqrt{2}$

Example: $\sqrt{45a^2 b^3} = \sqrt{5 \cdot 3^2 \cdot a^2 b^2 b} = 3ab\sqrt{5b}$ *(where a > 0 and b > 0)*

SKILL 10.8 Reason quantitatively and use units to solve problem

---

Rounding numbers is a form of estimation that is very useful in many mathematical operations. For example, when estimating the sum of two three-digit numbers, it is helpful to round the two numbers to the nearest hundred prior to addition. We can round numbers to any place value.

Rounding Whole Numbers

To round whole numbers, first find the place value you want to round to (the rounding digit). Look at the digit directly to the right. If the digit is less than 5, do not change the rounding digit and replace all numbers after the rounding digit with zeros. If the digit is greater than or equal to 5, increase the rounding digit by 1, and replace all numbers after the rounding digit with zeros.

Example: Round 517 to the nearest ten.

1 is the rounding digit because it occupies the tens place. 517 rounded to the nearest ten = 520; because $7 > 5$, we add 1 to the rounding digit.

Example: Round 15,449 to the nearest hundred.

The first 4 is the rounding digit because it occupies the hundreds place. 15,449 rounded to the nearest hundred = 15,400; because $4 < 5$, we do not add to the rounding digit.

Sample Test Question and Rationale

(Easy)

1. **Round $1\frac{13}{16}$ of an inch to the nearest quarter of an inch.**

   A. $1\frac{1}{4}$ inch

   B. $1\frac{5}{8}$ inch

   C. $1\frac{3}{4}$ inch

   D. 2 inches

Answer: C. inch

$1\frac{13}{16}$ inches is approximately $1\frac{12}{16}$, which is also $1\frac{3}{4}$, which is the nearest $\frac{1}{4}$ of an inch, so the answer is C.

Rounding Decimals

Rounding decimals is identical to rounding whole numbers except that you simply drop all the digits to the right of the rounding digit.

Example: Round 417.3621 to the nearest tenth.

3 is the rounding digit because it occupies the tenths place. 417.3621 rounded to the nearest tenth = 417.4; because $6 > 5$, we add 1 to the rounding digit.

Length

Example: A car skidded 170 yards on an icy road before coming to a stop. How long is the skid distance in kilometers?

Since 1 yard $\approx$ 0.9 meter, multiply 170 yards by 0.9.

    $170 \times 0.9 = 153$ meters

    Since 1000 meters = 1 kilometer, divide 153 by 1000.

    $\frac{153}{1000} = 0.153$ kilometers

Example: The distance around a race course is exactly 1 mile, 17 feet, and $9\frac{1}{4}$ inches. Approximate this distance to the nearest tenth of a foot.

    Convert the distance to feet.

    1 mile = 1760 yards = 1760×3 feet = 5280 feet.

    $9\frac{1}{4}$ inches = $\frac{37}{4} \times \frac{1}{12} = \frac{37}{4}$ 0.77083 feet

    So 1 mile, 17 feet, and $9\frac{1}{4}$ inches = $5280 + 17 + 0.77083$ feet

    = 5297.$\underline{7}$7083 feet.

Now, we need to round to the nearest tenth. The underlined 7 is in the tenths place. The digit in the hundredths place, also a 7, is greater than 5, so the 7 in the tenths place needs to be rounded up to 8 to get a final answer of 5297.8 feet.

Weight

Example: Zachary weighs 150 pounds. Tom weighs 153 pounds. What is the difference in their weights in grams?

    153 pounds $-$ 150 pounds = 3 pound.

    1 pound = 454 grams

    3(454 grams) = 1362 grams

Capacity

Example: Students in a fourth grade class want to fill a 3-gallon jug using cups of water. How many cups of water are needed?

    1 gallon = 16 cups of water

    3 gallons $\times$ 16 cups = 48 cups of water are needed.

Time

Example: It takes Cynthia 45 minutes to get ready each morning. How many hours does she spend getting ready each week?

    45 minutes $\times$ 7 days = 315 minutes

    $\frac{315 \text{ minutes}}{60 \text{ minutes in an hour}}$ = 5.25 hours

COMPETENCY 11
ALGEBRA AND FUNCTIONS

> **SKILL 11.1** **Apply understanding of arithmetic to algebraic expressions**

See Skill 11.2.

> **SKILL 11.2** **Solve real-life and mathematical problems using numerical and algebraic expressions**

When a variable is used in place of a number in a mathematical calculation, the representation becomes "an algebraic expression." Consider, for example, the variable y, where y represents any real number. Then "twice y" is represented by $2y$. "Seven more than y" can be written as $7 + y$. Virtually any mathematical calculation can be represented by an algebraic expression.

Furthermore, the basic properties of arithmetic (*see Skill 11.3*), apply to variables as well.

Example: Write an expression for three times the sum of a number and 10.

- Let n = a number
- The sum of a number and 10 is $n + 10$.
- Three times the sum would be $3(n + 10)$.
- Applying the distributive property would yield an equivalent expression $3n + 30$

Example: Write an expression representing the sum of 5 consecutive integers.

- Let n equal the first integer. Then the next consecutive is one away and can be represented by $n + 1$. The pattern continues and builds a sum as follows: $n + (n + 1) + (n + 2) + (n + 3) + (n + 4)$
- This sum can be simplified to the algebraic expression 5n + 10

Example: If the sides of a rectangular picture frame are tripled, what is the effect on the area?

- Let x and y be the dimensions of the frame. The original area then is the product of the two dimensions, or xy.

- Tripling the sides gives dimensions of $3x$ and $3y$. The new area, then will be $(3x)(3y) = 9xy$. One can see that this area is 9 times the area of the original frame.

SKILL 11.3   **Use properties of operations to generate equivalent expressions**

Properties are rules that apply to the addition, subtraction, multiplication, or division of real numbers.

PROPERTIES OF BASIC OPERATIONS	
Property	**Rules**
Commutative	You can change the order of the terms or factors as follows: For addition: $a + b = b + a$ For multiplication: $ab = ba$ Since addition is the inverse operation of subtraction and multiplication is the inverse operation of division, subtraction and division do not need separate laws. Example: $5 + (-8) = -8 + 5 = -3$ Example: $-2 \times 6 = 6 \times (-2) = -12$
Associative	You can regroup the terms as you like. For addition: $a + (b + c) = (a + b) + c$ For multiplication: $a(bc) = (ab)c$ This rule does not apply for division and subtraction. Example: $(-2 + 7) + 5 = -2 + (7 + 5)$ $\qquad 5 + 5 = -2 + 12 = 10$ Example: $[3 + (-7)] \times 5 = 3 \times (-7 \times 5)$ $\qquad -21 \times 5 = 3 \times (-35) = -105$

Table continued on next page

Property	Rules
Identity	An **additive identity** is a number that when added to a term results in that term. A **multiplicative identity** is a number that when multiplied by a term results in that term. For addition: $a + 0 = a$ (0 is additive identity) For multiplication: $a \times 1 = a$ (1 is multiplicative identity) Example: $17 + 0 = 17$ Example: $-34 \times 1 = -34$ The product of any number and 1 is that number.
Inverse	A number that when added to another number results in zero, or that when multiplied by another number results in 1. For addition: $a + (-a) = 0$ For multiplication: $a\,(1/a) = 1$ $(-a)$ is the additive inverse of a. $1/a$, also called the reciprocal, is the multiplicative inverse of a. Example: $25 + (-25) = 0$ Example: $5 \times \dfrac{1}{5} = 1$ The product of any number and its reciprocal is 1.
Distributive	This property allows us to operate on terms applied to parentheses without first performing operations within the parentheses. This is especially helpful when we cannot combine terms within the parentheses. $a\,(b + c) = ab + ac$ Example: $6 \times (-4 + 9) = (6 \times -4) + (6 \times 9)$ $\qquad\quad 6 \times 5 = -24 + 54 = 30$ To multiply a sum by a number, multiply each addend by the number, and then add the products.

Order of Operations

Follow the ORDER OF OPERATIONS when evaluating algebraic expressions. Follow these steps in order:

ORDER OF OPERATIONS: a set of rules that tell in what order to evaluate the operations of a mathematical expressions

Order of operations

1. Simplify inside grouping characters such as parentheses, brackets, square roots, fraction bars, etc.

2. Multiply out expressions with exponents

3. Do multiplication and division from left to right

4. Do addition and subtraction from left to right

Example:

$3^3 - 5(b + 2)$

$= 3^3 - 5b - 10$

$= 27 - 5b - 10 = 17 - 5b$

Example:

$2 - 4 \times 2^3 - 2(4 - 2 \times 3)$

$= 2 - 4 \times 2^3 - 2(4 - 6) = 2 - 4 \times 2^3 + -2(-2)$

$= 2 - 4 \times 2^3 + 4 = 2 - 4 \times 8 + 4$

$= 2 - 32 + 4 = -30 + 4 = -26$

Sample Test Questions and Rationale

(Average)

1. **Choose the expression that is not equivalent to $5x + 3y + 15z$.**

   A. $5(x + 3z) + 3y$

   B. $3(x + y + 5z)$

   C. $3y + 5(x + 3z)$

   D. $5x + 3(y + 5z)$

   Answer: B. $3(x + y + 5z)$

   $5x + 3y + 15z = (5x + 15z) + 3y = 5(x + 3z) + 3y$. A is true.

   $= 5x + (3y + 15z) = 5x + 3(y + 5z)$. D is true.

   $= 3y + (5x + 15z) = 3y + 5(x + 3z)$. C is true.

   We can solve all of these by using the associative property and then factoring. However, in B, by the distributive property, $3(x + y + 5z) = 3x + 3y + 15z$ does not equal $5x + 3y + 15z$.

(Rigorous)

2. **Choose the statement that is true for all real numbers.**

   A. $a = 0, b \ 0$, then $\frac{a}{b} =$ undefined.

   B. $-(a + (-a)) = 2a$

   C. $2(ab) = -2(a)b$

   D. $-a(b + 1) = ab - a$

   Answer: A. then $=$ undefined.

   Any number divided by 0 is undefined.

1. For a set of values, (a, b), to be proportional, the ratio of a to b must be constant. For instance, the table below displays a set of proportional data.

a	−2	1	2	5	11
b	−10	5	10	25	55

   $a{:}b = \dfrac{a}{b} = \dfrac{1}{5} = \dfrac{2}{10} = \dfrac{11}{55}$

2. Another way to quantify this proportional relationship, is by identifying the common factor, or constant of direct variation, within the data set. Continue to consider the data given above. Since $\dfrac{a}{b} = \dfrac{1}{5}$, cross multiplication shows that $b = 5a$. This statement serves as an **equation** to represent the data. The equation can be evaluated to find any b, given an input for a.

Example: Given the equation b = 5a, find b if a = 11.

Evaluate $b = 5a$ for $a = 11$: $b = 5(11) = 55$. (note that this value confirms the last entry in the table)

Find b if a = 100: $b = 5(100) = 500$.

Observe that these values for (a, b) still share the constant ratio: $\dfrac{a}{b} = \dfrac{100}{500} = \dfrac{1}{5}$

This type of equation representing proportional data is often referred to as a **direct variation equation**.

3. Any set of proportional data, when graphed, will create a straight line containing the origin, (0, 0). The data from part 1 demonstrates this.

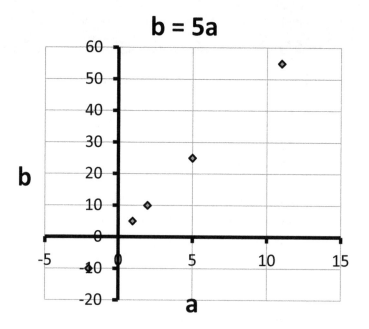

This linear relationship directly correlates to the basic algebraic equation for a line: y = mx + b, where m is the slope, or steepness, of the line and (0, b) is the y intercept, or the point where the graph crosses the y axis.

In the case of direct variation, y = kx, the "b" portion is simply zero, which is why the graph of y = kx will always pass through the origin. The constant, or k, represents the slope of the line.

Example: Use the direct variation equation y = $\frac{3}{7}$ x, to create a table of proportional values and the graph of a straight line.

Any values for x can be chosen to create a table, but given the nature of the constant, choosing multiples of 7 will keep the numbers easy to work with. For instance, if x = 14, then y = $\frac{3}{7}$ (14) = $\frac{3}{7} \cdot \frac{14}{1}$ = $\frac{3}{1} \cdot \frac{2}{1}$ = 6.

x	−7	0	7	14	21
y	−3	0	3	6	9

Confirm the constant ratio and its connection to the given equation:

$\frac{x}{y} = \frac{-7}{-3} = \frac{14}{6} = \frac{7}{3}$

$\frac{x}{y} = \frac{7}{3}$

$7y = 3x$

$y = \frac{3}{7}x$

Graph the data:

$$y = \frac{3}{7}x$$

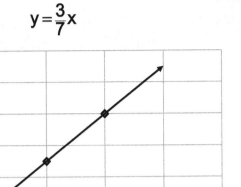

See Skill 11.7.

See Skill 11.7.

SKILL Solve equations and inequalities in one variable
11.7

EQUATION: two statements linked by an equal sign

An **EQUATION** consists of two statements linked by an equal sign.

Left Hand Side (LHS) = Right Hand Side (RHS)
Example:

$2x = 6$

(LHS) (RHS)

This statement is only true if we substitute 3 for x.

$2x = 6$ (True)

Therefore, 3 is a solution of the equation.

Example: Is 2 a solution of $2x - 6 = 6x + 1$?

Substituting 2 for x:

$2(2) - 6 = 6(2) + 1 \rightarrow 4 - 6 = 12 + 1 \rightarrow -2 = 13$ (False)

2 is not a solution.

Procedure for Solving Algebraic Equations

Example: Solve for x.

$3(x + 3) = -2x + 4$

1. Expand to eliminate all parentheses

2. Multiply each term by the LCD to eliminate all denominators

3. Combine like terms on each side when possible

4. Use the properties to put all variables on one side and all constants on the other side

   $3x + 9 - 9 = -2x + 4 - 9$ Subtract 9 from both sides.

   $3x = -2x - 5$

   $3x + 2x = -2x + 2x - 5$ Add 2x to both sides.

   $5x = -5$

   $\frac{5x}{5} = \frac{-5}{5}$ Divide both sides by 5.

   $x = -1$

Example: Solve:

$$3(2x + 5) - 4x = 5(x + 9)$$
$$6x + 15 - 4x = 5x + 45$$
$$2x + 15 = 5x + 45$$
$$-3x + 15 = 45$$
$$-3x = 30$$
$$x = -10$$

Solving and Graphing Inequalities

We use the same procedure to solve and graph inequalities that we used for solving linear equations, but we represent the answer in graphical form on the number line or in interval form.

Example: Solve the inequality, show its solution using interval form, and graph the solution on the number line.

$$\frac{5x}{8} + 3 \geq 2x - 5$$
$$8\left(\frac{5x}{8}\right) + 8\,(3) \geq 8(2x) - 5(8) \qquad \text{Multiply by LCD = 8.}$$
$$5x + 24 \geq 16x - 40$$
$$5x + 24 - 24 - 16x \geq 16x - 16x - 40 - 24 \qquad \text{Subtract } 16x \text{ and } 24 \text{ from}$$
$$-11x \geq -64 \qquad\qquad\qquad\qquad\qquad\qquad \text{both sides of the equation.}$$
$$\frac{-11x}{-11} \leq \frac{-64}{-11}$$
$$x \leq \frac{64}{11}; \qquad x \leq 5\frac{9}{11}$$

Solution in interval form: $\left(-\infty, 5\frac{9}{11}\right]$

Note: "$\,]\,$" means $5\frac{9}{11}$ is included in the solution.

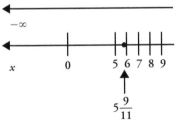

Example: Solve the following inequality and express your answer in both interval and graphical form.

$$3x - 8 < 2(3x - 1)$$
$$3x - 8 < 6x - 2 \qquad\qquad \text{Distributive property}$$
$$3x - 6x - 8 + 8 < 6x - 6x - 2 + 8$$

Add 8 and subtract 6x from both sides of the equation.

$$-3x < 6$$
$$\frac{-3x}{-3} > \frac{6}{-3} \qquad\qquad \text{Note the change in direction of the inequality.}$$
$$x > -2$$

Graphical form: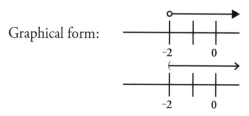

Interval form: $(-2, \infty)$

Recall that a parenthesis or an open circle implies that the point is not included in the answer, and a bracket or a closed circle implies that the point is included in the answer.

> Recall that a parenthesis or an open circle implies that the point is not included in the answer, and a bracket or a closed circle implies that the point is included in the answer.

Example: Solve:

$6x + 21 < 8x + 31$

$-2x + 21 < 31$

$-2x < 10$

$x > -5$

Note that the inequality sign has changed.

SKILL 11.8 Analyze and solve linear equations and pairs of simultaneous linear equations

Solving Systems of Equations

SYSTEM OF LINEAR EQUATIONS: two or more linear equations taken together

The solution set of a **SYSTEM OF LINEAR EQUATIONS** is all the ordered pairs of real numbers that satisfy both equations. Thus the solution is the intersection of the lines. There are two methods for solving linear equations: linear combinations and substitution.

In the substitution method, we solve an equation for either variable. Then, we substitute that solution into the other equation to find the remaining variable.

Example:

1. $2x + 8y = 4$
2. $x - 3y = 5$
2a. $x = 3y + 5$ \qquad Solve equation (2) for x.
1a. $2(3y + 5) + 8y = 4$ \qquad Substitute for x in equation (1).
\qquad $6y + 10 + 8y = 4$ \qquad Solve.
\qquad $14y = -6$

$$y = \tfrac{-3}{7}$$ Solution.

2. $x - 3y = 5$

$x - 3(\tfrac{-3}{7}) = 5$ Substitute the value of y.

$x = \tfrac{26}{7} = 3\tfrac{5}{7}$ Solution.

Thus, the solution set of the system of equations is $(3\tfrac{5}{7}, \tfrac{-3}{7})$.

In the **linear combinations method**, we replace one or both of the equations with an equivalent equation so that we can combine (add or subtract) the two equations to eliminate one variable.

Example:

1. $4x + 3y = -2$

2. $5x - y = 7$

1. $4x + 3y = -2$

2a. $15x - 3y = 2$ Multiply equation (2) by 3.

$\quad\quad + 9x = 19$ Combining (1) and (2a).

$\quad\quad\quad x = 1$ Solve.

To find y, substitute the value of x in equation 1 (or 2).

1. $4x + 3y = -2$

$4(1) + 3y = -2$

$4 + 3y = -2$

$3y = -6$

$y = -2$

Thus, the solution is $x = 1$ and $y = -2$ or the ordered pair $(1, -2)$.

Example: Solve for x and y.

$4x + 6y = 340$

$3x + 8y = 360$

To solve by linear combinations:

Multiply the first equation by 4: $4(4x + 6y = 340)$

Multiply the second equation by: -3: $-3(3x + 8y = 360)$

After doing this, the equations can be added to each other to eliminate one variable and solve for the other variable.

$16x + 24y = 1360$

$\underline{-9x - 24y = -1080}$

$7x = 280$

$x = 40$

Solving for y, $y = 30$

SKILL 11.9 Represent and solve equations and inequalities graphically

Graphing an inequality on a number line

An inequality in one variable can be graphed on a number line. Consider, for instance, the inequality $x \leq 5$. Some possible solutions of this statement are $\{5, 4, 3.2, 1, -1.8, -100\}$. If these individual values were graphed on a number line they would each be represented by a dot. But the list of all numbers less than or equal to 5 plots an infinite number of dots on the number line. All of these dots blur together to form a solid region traced over the number line.

The closed dot represents an inequality where the bound is inclusive ("or equal to") while an open circle is used when the bound does not include the endpoint. If the previous example were changed to $x > 5$, the shaded arrow would point to the right, to represent greater than, and would have an open circle on the 5, to indicate that the endpoint is not included.

Graphing a linear equation

The graph of a linear equation represents a straight line. It takes two points to define a unique straight line.

1. Choose 3 values of x.

2. Substitute each chosen value of x in the equation to find the corresponding y-value.

3. Plot the 3 points and join them with a straight line.

Note: It is typically helpful to choose the x-intercept and the y-intercept as the two key points (when possible).

The **x-intercept** is the point where the line intersects the x-axis. To find this point we substitute 0 for y and solve for x.

The **y-intercept** is the point where the line intersects the *y*-axis. To find this point we substitute 0 for *x* and solve for *y*.

Example: sketch the graph of the line represented by 2x + 3y = 6

Let $x = 0 \rightarrow 2(0) + 3y = 6$
$\rightarrow 3y = 6$
$\rightarrow y = 2$
$\rightarrow (0, 2)$ is the *y*-intercept.

Let $y = 0 \rightarrow 2x + 3(0) = 6$
$\rightarrow 2x = 6$
$\rightarrow x = 3$
$\rightarrow (3, 0)$ is the *x*-intercept.

Let $x = -3 \rightarrow 2(-3) + 3y = 6$
$\rightarrow -6 + 3y = 6$ (add 6 to both sides)
$\rightarrow 3y = 12$ (Divide both sides by 3)
$\rightarrow y = 4$
$\rightarrow (-3, 4)$ is the third point.

Plotting the 3 points or the coordinate system, we get the following graph:

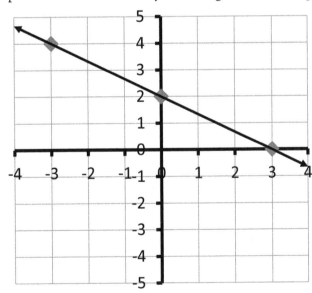

Note: Two points are sufficient to graph the line; the third point is for checking purposes.

Example: Use the graph below of the equation $y = -\frac{1}{2}x + 2$ to solve the equation $1 = -\frac{1}{2}x + 2$

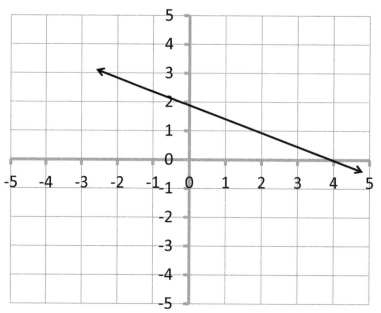

To solve the requested equation is the same as to find which quantity of x will make y have a value of 1. The provided graph can be used to search for the point on the line $(x, 1)$. It appears as if the graphed line contains the point $(2, 1)$ so x would be 2. However, graphing, especially when done by hand can be inaccurate, so checking the solution is advised.

Use substitution to verify that the line $y = -\frac{1}{2}x + 2$ contains the point $(2, 1)$.

$1? -\frac{1}{2}(2) + 2$

$1? - 1 + 2$ Therefore, the solution is verified.

$1 = 1$

Graphing a linear inequality in two dimensions

A linear inequality in two variables is similar in form to a linear equation <u>except</u> that the = sign is replaced by an inequality sign of >, <, ≥, or ≤. The procedure to graph it is as follows:

1. Graph the equivalent equation with the inequality sign replaced by an equals sign. Use a solid line for this line if the inequality contains the equals sign (≤ or ≥); use a dashed line if the inequality contains no equals sign (< or >).

2. Pick a point on either side of the line and test whether its x- and y-values satisfy the inequality. If so, mark that region as a solution set with shading or slanted lines. If not, shade the opposite region.

Example: Identify the region that satisfies 5x – 3y ≥ -15.

1. Graph the equivalent equation of $5x - 3y = -15$ using a solid line. Substituting $y = 0$ produces an x-intercept of $(-3, 0)$; substituting $x = 0$ produces a y-intercept of $(0, 5)$.

2. Pick a test point on either side of this line. Pick the origin for simplicity $(0, 0)$. Substitute $x = 0$ and $y = 0$ into the inequality and test:

$0 \geq -15$ is true, so accept the region containing $(0, 0)$ and shade it.

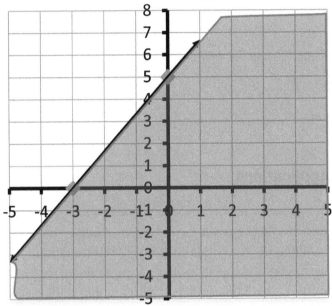

Example: Is (–4, 6) a solution to 5x – 3y ≥ –15?

Substitution of -4 for x and 6 for would normally be implemented to identify whether or not the point in question is a solution of the inequality, but since a graph of the inequality already exists, it is clear to note that the point $(-4, 6)$ is outside of the shaded region so it is NOT a solution to the inequality.

SKILL 11.10 Interpreting functions

In mathematics, an equation is a statement of equality relating numbers and variables, such as $2x + 7 = 11$ or $x^2 + y^2 = 49$. An equation becomes a function with a change in notation and/or application of the equation.

Function Notation

Function notation names an equation with a function letter and its input value, or independent variable. For instance, f(x) = 3x − 2 represents a function of x, or "f of x." A function can be written with any letters: p(n) = n³ − 2n + 8. The independent variable represents the **domain**, or input, of the function while the output shows the **range**. An output value is calculated from the function rule and an input. For instance, if f(x) = 3x − 2 and the input is 10, then f(10 = 3(10) − 2 = 28. The input, 10, resulted in an output of 28. This process is known as **evaluating** a function.

Example: Evaluate the function h(x) = $\frac{3x-2}{x^2}$ for x = 3.

h(3) = $\frac{3(3)-2}{3^2}$ = $\frac{9-2}{9}$ = $\frac{7}{9}$

h(3) = $\frac{7}{9}$, or "h of 3 equals seven ninths."

Function Applications

A function can represent a mathematical relationship or application. Suppose, for example, that the shipping costs on an item are calculated at $0.45 per pound plus a $1.25 handling fee. A function that models this relationship is c(s) = 0.45x + 1.25. To find the cost of shipping a 4lb. package, **evaluate** the function for x = 4: c(4) = 0.45(4) + 1.25 = 3.05. It will cost $3.05 to ship a 4lb. package.

A list of inputs for the function represents the domain of the function, and the corresponding outputs represents the range.

Domain	x	2	4	6	8	10
Range	c(x)	2.15	3.05	3.95	4.85	5.75

SKILL 11.11 Building functions

As seen in the previous section, a function can be built in response to a real world situation, and its corresponding table of values displays the domain and range of the function. Sometimes a table or a graph of ordered pairs can come first, and the function can be written to represent the data.

f(x)

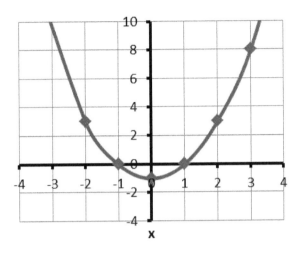

x	f(x)
–2	3
–1	0
0	–1
1	0
2	3
3	8

Every output value is 1 less than the square of its input. Therefore the function representing this data is $f(x) = x^2 - 1$.

A function can also be created from other existing funcions. Mathematical operations can combine functions. For instance, given $f(x) = 6x$ and $g(x) = 10x + 2$, observe the following:

$h(x) = f(x) + g(x)$	$w(x) = g(x) - f(x)$	$p(x) = f(x)(g(x))$
$h(x) = 6x + 10x + 2$	$w(x) = 10x + 2 - 6$	$p(x) = 6x(10x + 2)$
$h(x) = 16x + 2$	$w(x) = 4x + 2$	$p(x) = 60x^2 + 12x$

Function compostion also builds a new function out of existing functions. Using functions f and g above, f ∘ g(x) represents "f composed with g." To write the new function, use g(x) as the input for f(x).

f ∘ g(x) = f(g(x)) = f(10x + 2) = 6(10x + 2) = 60x + 12

Note that this is not the same operation (or result) as f(x)·g(x). Also take notice that compostion is not commutative (except in the case of inverse functions)

g ∘ f(x) = g(f(x)) = g(6x) = 10(6x) + 2 = 60x + 2

COMPETENCY 12
GEOMETRY

SKILL **Draw, construct, and describe geometrical figures and describe the**
12.1 **relationships between them**

Two-Dimensional Figures

We name **POLYGONS**—simple, closed, two-dimensional figures composed of line segments—according to the number of sides they have.

A **QUADRILATERAL** is a polygon with four sides.

The sum of the measures of the angles of a quadrilateral is 360°.

A **TRAPEZOID** is a quadrilateral with exactly one pair of parallel sides.

In an **ISOSCELES TRAPEZOID**, the nonparallel sides are congruent.

A **PARALLELOGRAM** is a quadrilateral with two pairs of parallel sides.

> **POLYGON:** a simple, closed, two-dimensional figure composed of line segments

> **QUADRILATERAL:** a polygon with four sides

> **TRAPEZOID:** a quadrilateral with exactly *one* pair of parallel sides

> **ISOSCELES TRAPEZOID:** a quadrilateral in which the nonparallel sides are congruent

> **PARALLELOGRAM:** a quadrilateral with two pairs of parallel sides

In a parallelogram:

- The diagonals bisect each other

- Each diagonal divides the parallelogram into two congruent triangles

- Both pairs of opposite sides are congruent

- Both pairs of opposite angles are congruent

- Two adjacent angles are supplementary

RECTANGLE: a parallelogram with a right angle

A **RECTANGLE** is a parallelogram with a right angle.

RHOMBUS: a parallelogram with all sides equal in length

A **RHOMBUS** is a parallelogram with all sides equal in length.

SQUARE: a rectangle with all sides equal in length

A **SQUARE** is a rectangle with all sides equal in length.

Example: True or false?

All squares are rhombuses.	True
All parallelograms are rectangles.	False—<u>some</u> parallelograms are rectangles
All rectangles are parallelograms.	True
Some rhombuses are squares.	True
Some rectangles are trapezoids.	False—trapezoids have only <u>one</u> pair of parallel sides
All quadrilaterals are parallelograms.	False—some quadrilaterals are parallelograms
Some squares are rectangles.	False—all squares are rectangles
Some parallelograms are rhombuses.	True

A **TRIANGLE** is a polygon with three sides. We can classify triangles by the types of angles or the lengths of their sides.

An **ACUTE TRIANGLE** has exactly three *acute* angles. An **ACUTE ANGLE** is an angle that measures less than 90 degrees.

A **RIGHT TRIANGLE** has one *right* angle. A **RIGHT ANGLE** is an angle that measures 90 degrees.

An **OBTUSE TRIANGLE** has one *obtuse* angle. An **OBTUSE ANGLE** measures between 90 degrees and 180 degrees.

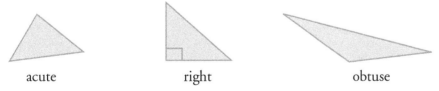

acute   right   obtuse

All three sides of an **EQUILATERAL TRIANGLE** are the same length.

Two sides of an **ISOSCELES TRIANGLE** are the same length.

TRIANGLE: a polygon with three sides

ACUTE TRIANGLE: has exactly three *acute* angles

ACUTE ANGLE: an angle that measures less than 90 degrees

RIGHT TRIANGLE: has one *right* angle

RIGHT ANGLE: an angle that measures 90 degrees

OBTUSE TRIANGLE: has one *obtuse* angle

OBTUSE ANGLE: measures between 90 degrees and 180 degrees

EQUILATERAL TRIANGLE: all sides are the same length

ISOSCELES TRIANGLE: two sides are the same length

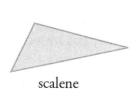

SCALENE TRIANGLE: no sides are the same length

None of the sides of a **SCALENE TRIANGLE** is the same length.

equilateral

isosceles

scalene

Example: Can a triangle have two right angles?
No. A right angle measures 90°; therefore, the sum of two right angles would be 180°, and there could not be a third angle.

Example: Can a triangle have two obtuse angles?
No. Since an obtuse angle measures more than 90°, the sum of two obtuse angles would be greater than 180°.

Three-dimensional figures

CYLINDER: a space figure that has two parallel, congruent circular bases

A **CYLINDER** is a space figure that has two parallel, congruent circular bases.

SPHERE: a space figure having all its points the same distance from the center

A **SPHERE** is a space figure having all its points the same distance from the center.

CONE: a space figure having a circular base and a single vertex

A **CONE** is a space figure having a circular base and a single vertex.

PYRAMID: a space figure with a square base and four triangle-shaped sides

A **PYRAMID** is a space figure with a square base and four triangle-shaped sides.

A **TETRAHEDRON** is a four-sided space triangle. Each face is a triangle.

A **PRISM** is a space figure with two congruent, parallel bases that are polygons.

Finding Perimeter and Area

The **PERIMETER** of a polygon is the sum of the lengths of the sides.

The **AREA** of a polygon is the number of square units covered by the figure.

FIGURE	AREA FORMULA	PERIMETER FORMULA
Rectangle	LW	$2(L + W)$
Triangle	$\frac{1}{2}bh$	$a + b + c$
Parallelogram	bh	sum of lengths of sides
Trapezoid	$\frac{1}{2}h(a + b)$	sum of lengths of sides

Perimeter

Example: A farmer has a piece of land shaped as shown below. He wishes to fence this land at an estimated cost of $25 per linear foot. What is the total cost of fencing this property, to the nearest foot?

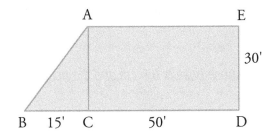

For the right triangle ABC, $AC = 30$ and $BC = 15$.
Since $(AB)^2 = (AC)^2 + (BC)^2$, we have
$(AB)^2 = (30)^2 + (15)^2$

So $\sqrt{(AB)^2} = AB = \sqrt{1125} = 33.5410$ feet

To the nearest foot, $AB = 34$ feet.

Perimeter of the piece of land =

$= 34 + 15 + 50 + 30 + 50 = 179$ feet

Cost of fencing = $\$25 \times 179 = \$4,475.00$

Area

Area is the space that a figure occupies.

Example: What will be the cost of carpeting a rectangular office that measures 12 feet by 15 feet if the carpet costs $12.50 per square yard?

12 ft.

15 ft.

The problem is asking you to determine the area of the office. The area of a rectangle is *length $\times$ width = A.*

Substitute the given values in the equation $A = lw$.

$A = (12\ \text{ft}) (15\ \text{ft})$

$A = 180\ \text{ft}^2$

The problem asks you to determine the cost of the carpet at $12.50 per square yard.

First, you need to convert 180 ft² into yd².

1 yd = 3 ft

(1 yd)(1 yd) = (3 ft)(3 ft)

1 yd² = 9 ft ²

Hence, $\frac{180\ \text{ft}^2}{1} = \frac{1\ \text{yd}^2}{9\ \text{ft}^2} = \frac{20}{1} = 20$ yd²

The carpet costs $12.50 per square yard; thus, the cost of carpeting the office is $12.50 $\times$ 20 = $250.00.

Example: Find the area of a parallelogram whose base is 6.5 cm and the height of the altitude to that base is 3.7 cm.

6.5 cm

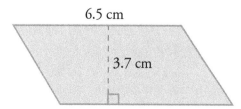

3.7 cm

$$A_{\text{parallelogram}} = bh$$
$$A_{\text{parallelogram}} = (3.7)(6.5)$$
$$A_{\text{parallelogram}} = 24.05 \text{ cm}^2$$

Example: Find the area of this triangle.

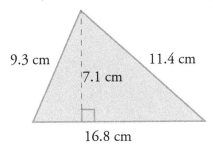

9.3 cm   11.4 cm

7.1 cm

16.8 cm

$$A_{\text{triangle}} = \frac{1}{2}bh$$
$$= 0.5\,(16.8)\,(7.1)$$
$$= 59.64 \text{ cm}^2$$

Example: Find the area of this trapezoid.

17.5 cm

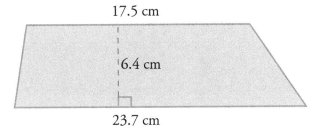

6.4 cm

23.7 cm

The area of a trapezoid equals one-half the sum of the bases times the altitude.

$$A_{\text{trapezoid}} = \frac{1}{2}h(b_1 + b_2)$$
$$= 0.5\,(6.4)\,(17.5 + 23.7)$$
$$= 131.84 \text{ cm}^2$$

The distance around a circle is called the **CIRCUMFERENCE**. The Greek letter pi represents the ratio of the circumference to the diameter.

$$\pi \approx 3.14 \approx \frac{22}{7}.$$

The circumference of a circle is found by the formula $C = 2\pi r$ or $C = \pi d$, where r is the radius of the circle and d is the diameter.

The **area of a circle** is found by the formula $A = \pi r^2$.

> **CIRCUMFERENCE:**
> distance around a circle

Example: Find the circumference and area of a circle whose radius is 7 meters.

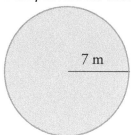

7 m

$C = 2\pi r$ $A = \pi r^2$
   $= 2(3.14)(7)$ $= 3.14(7)(7)$
   $= 43.96$ m $= 153.86$ m^2

Volume and Surface Area

We use the following formulas to compute **volume** and **surface area**:

FIGURE	VOLUME TOTAL	SURFACE AREA
Right Cylinder	$\pi r^2 h$	$2\pi rh + \pi r^2$
Right Cone	$\dfrac{\pi r^2 h}{3}$	$\pi r \sqrt{r^2 + h^2} + \pi r^2$
Sphere	$\dfrac{4}{3}\pi r^2 h$	$4\pi r^2$
Rectangular Solid	LWH	$2LW + 2WH + 2LH$

FIGURE	LATERAL AREA	TOTAL AREA	VOLUME
Regular Pyramid	$\dfrac{1}{2}Pl$	$\dfrac{1}{2}Pl + B$	$\dfrac{1}{3}Bh$

P = Perimeter   h = height   B = Area of base   l = slant height

Example: What is the volume of a shoebox with a length of 35 cm, a width of 20 cm, and a height of 15 cm?

Volume of a rectangular solid

   $=$ Length $\times$ Width $\times$ Height
   $= 35 \times 20 \times 15$
   $= 10,500$ cm^3

Example: A water company is trying to decide whether to use traditional cylindrical paper cups or to offer conical paper cups, since both cost the same. The traditional cups are 8 cm wide and 14 cm high. The conical cups are 12 cm wide and 19 cm high. The company will use the cup that holds the most water.

Draw and label a sketch of each.

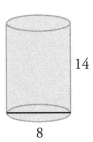

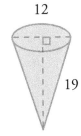

$V = \pi\, r^2 h$	$V = \dfrac{\pi\, r^2 h}{3}$	1. Write formula.
$V = \pi\, (4)^2\, (14)$	$V = \dfrac{1}{3}\pi\, (6)^2\, (19)$	2. Substitute.
$V = 703.717$ cm³	$V = 716.283$ cm³	3. Solve.

The choice should be the conical cup, since its volume is greater.

Example: How much material do we need to make a basketball that has a diameter of 15 inches? How much air do we need to fill the basketball?

Draw and label a sketch:

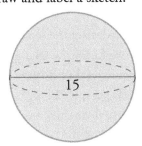

Total surface area	Volume	
$TSA = 4\,\pi\, r^2$	$V = \dfrac{4}{3}\,\pi\, r^3$	1. Write formula.
$= 4\,\pi\, (7.5)^2$	$= \dfrac{4}{3}\,\pi\, (7.5)^3$	2. Substitute.
$= 706.858$ in²	$= 1767.1459$ in³	3. Solve.

Sample Test Questions and Rationale

(Average)

1. For the following statements:
   I. All parallelograms are rectangles.
   II. Some rhombuses are squares.
   III. All parallelograms are rhombuses.

   A. All statements are correct.

   B. All statements are incorrect.

   C. Only II and III are correct.

   D. Only II is correct.

   Answer: D. Only II is correct.

   I is false because only some parallelograms are rectangles. II is true. III is false because only some parallelograms are rhombuses. Only II is correct.

(Average)

2. What type of triangle is $\triangle ABC$?

   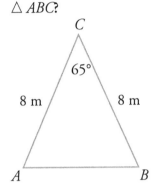

   A. Right

   B. Equilateral

   C. Scalene

   D. Isosceles

   Answer: D. isosceles

   Two of the sides are the same length, so we know the triangle is either equilateral or isosceles. $\angle CAB$ and $\angle CBA$ are equal because their sides are. Therefore, $180° = 65° - 2x = \frac{115°}{2} = 57.5°$. Because not all three angles are equal, the triangle is isosceles.

Sample Test Questions and Rationale (cont.)

(Easy)

1. What is the area of a square whose side is 13 feet?

   A. 169 feet

   B. 169 square feet

   C. 52 feet

   D. 52 square feet

   Answer: B. 169 square feet

   Area = length times width (*lw*)
   Length = 13 feet
   Width = 13 feet (square, so length and width are the same).
   Area = square feet
   We measure area in square feet, so the answer is B.

(Rigorous)

2. The trunk of a tree has a 2.1 meter radius. What is the trunk's circumference?

   A. 2.1π square meters

   B. 4.2π meters

   C. 2.1π meters

   D. 4.2π square meters

   Answer: B. 4.2 π meters

   Circumference is 2π*r*, where *r* is the radius. The circumference is 2π(2.1) = 4.2π meters (not square meters because we are not measuring area).

(Rigorous)

3. The figure below shows a running track in the shape of a rectangle with semicircles at each end.

   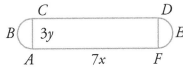

   Calculate the distance around the track.

   A. 6π*y* + 14*x*

   B. 3π*y* + 7*x*

   C. 6π*y* + 7*x*

   D. 3π*y* + 14*x*

   Answer: D. 3π*y* + 14*x*

   The two semicircles of the track create one circle with a diameter 3*y*. The circumference of a circle is C = π*d* so C = 3π*y*. The length of the track is 7*x* on each side, so the total circumference around the track is 3π*y* + 7*x* + 7*x* = 3π*y* + 14*x*.

(Rigorous)

4. What is the area of this triangle?

   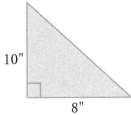

   A. 80 square inches

   B. 20 square inches

   C. 40 square inches

   D. 30 square inches

   Answer: C. 40 square inches

   The area of a triangle is
   $\frac{1}{2} bh$. $\frac{1}{2} \times 8 \times 10 = 40$
   square inches.

Congruence

CONGRUENT FIGURES have the same size and shape. If one is placed atop the other, it will fit exactly. Congruent lines have the same length. Congruent angles have equal measures.

The symbol for congruent is $\cong$.

Polygons (pentagons) *ABCDE* and *VWXYZ* are congruent. They are exactly the same size and shape.

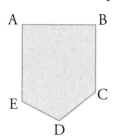
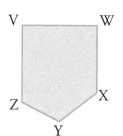

Corresponding parts are corresponding angles and sides. That is:

Corresponding angles	Corresponding sides
$\angle A \leftrightarrow \angle V$	$AB \leftrightarrow VW$
$\angle B \leftrightarrow \angle W$	$BC \leftrightarrow WX$
$\angle C \leftrightarrow \angle X$	$CD \leftrightarrow XY$
$\angle D \leftrightarrow \angle Y$	$DE \leftrightarrow YZ$
$\angle E \leftrightarrow \angle Z$	$AE \leftrightarrow VZ$

Example: Given two similar quadrilaterals, find the lengths of sides x, y, and z.

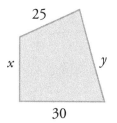
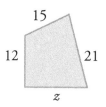

Corresponding sides are proportional, so the scale is:

$$\frac{12}{x} = \frac{3}{5} \qquad\qquad \frac{21}{y} = \frac{3}{5} \qquad\qquad \frac{z}{30} = \frac{3}{5}$$

$$3x = 60 \qquad\qquad 3y = 105 \qquad\qquad 5z = 90$$

$$x = 20 \qquad\qquad y = 35 \qquad\qquad z = 18$$

Similarity

Two figures that have the same shape are **SIMILAR**. Polygons are similar if and only if corresponding angles are congruent and corresponding sides are in proportion. Corresponding parts of similar polygons are proportional.

> **SIMILAR:** two figures that have the same shape

Example: Given the rectangles below, compare their areas and perimeters.

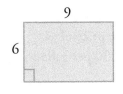 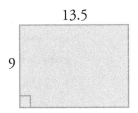

A = LW	A = LW	1. Write formula.
A = (6)(9)	A (9)(13.5)	2. Substitute known values.
A = 54 sq. units	A = 121.5 sq. units	3. Compute.

P = 2(L + W)	P = 2(L + W)	1. Write formula.
P = 2(6 + 9)	P = 2(9 + 13.5)	2. Substitute known values.
P = 30 units	P = 45 units	3. Compute.

Notice that the areas relate to each other in the following manner:

Ratio of sides $9/13.5 = 2/3$

Multiply the first area by the square of the reciprocal $(2/3)^2$ to get the second area.

$54 \times (2/3)^2 = 121.5$

The perimeters relate to each other in the following manner:

Ratio of sides $9/13.5 = 2/3$

Multiply the first perimeter by the reciprocal of the ratio $(3/2)$ to get the second perimeter.

$30 \times 3/2 = 45$

Example: Tommy draws and cuts out two triangles for a school project. One of them has sides of 3, 6, and 9 inches. The other triangle has sides of 2, 4, and 6 inches. Is there a relationship between the two triangles?

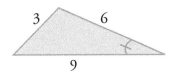 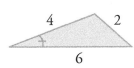

Find the ratios of the corresponding sides.

$\frac{2}{3}$ $\frac{4}{6} = \frac{2}{3}$ $\frac{6}{9} = \frac{2}{3}$

The smaller triangle is 2/3 the size of the large triangle.

Sample Test Questions and Rationale

(Average)

1. Given the formula $d = rt$, (where d = distance, r = rate, and t = time), calculate the time required for a vehicle to travel 585 miles at a rate of 65 miles per hour.

   A. 8.5 hours

   B. 6.5 hours

   C. 9.5 hours

   D. 9 hours

   Answer: D. 9 hours

   We are given d = 585 miles and r = 65 miles per hour. Since $d = rt$, solve for t. $585 = 65t \rightarrow t = 9$ hours.

(Average)

2. The price of gas is $3.27 per gallon. Your tank holds 15 gallons of gas. You are using two tanks a week. How much will you save weekly if the price of gas goes down to $2.30 per gallon?

   A. $26.00

   B. $29.00

   C. $15.00

   D. $17.00

   Answer: B. $29.00

   15 gallons $\times$ 2 tanks = 30 gallons a week
   30 gallons $\times$ $3.27 = $98.10
   30 gallons $\times$ $2.30 = $69.00
   $98.10 $-$ $69.00 = $29.10 is approximately $29.00.

Sample Test Questions and Rationale (cont.)

(Rigorous)

1. Study figures A, B, C, and D. Select the letter for which all triangles are similar.

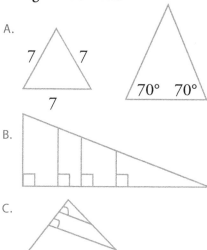

A.

B.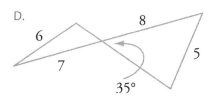

C.

D.

(Average)

2. A car gets 25.36 miles per gallon. The car has been driven 83,310 miles. What is a reasonable estimate for the number of gallons of gas used?

A. 2,087 gallons

B. 3,000 gallons

C. 1,800 gallons

D. 164 gallons

Answer: B. 3,000 gallons

Divide the number of miles by the miles per gallon to determine the approximate number of gallons of gas used.

$$\frac{83310 \text{ miles}}{25.36 \text{ miles per gallon}} = 3285 \text{ gallons}$$

This is approximately 3000 gallons.

Answer: B.

Choice A is not correct because one triangle is equilateral and the other is isosceles. Choice C is not correct because the two smaller triangles are similar, but the large triangle is not. Choice D is not correct because the lengths and angles are not proportional to each other. Therefore, the correct answer is B because all the triangles have the same angles.

SKILL **Experiment with transformations in the plane**
12.2

Transformational Symmetries

> **IMAGE:** the transformation of an object

There are four basic **transformational symmetries** that can be used: translation, rotation, reflection, and **glide reflection**. The transformation of an object is called its **IMAGE**. If the original object was labeled with letters, such as *ABCD*, the image may be labeled with the same letters followed by prime symbols, *A'B'C'D'*.

> **TRANSLATION:** a transformation that "slides" an object a fixed distance in a given direction

A **TRANSLATION** is a transformation that "slides" an object a fixed distance in a given direction. The original object and its translation have the same shape and size, and they face in the same direction.

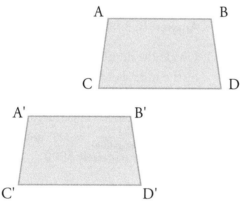

An example of a translation in architecture would be stadium seating. The seats are the same size and the same shape and face the same direction.

> **ROTATION:** a transformation that turns a figure about a fixed point called the center of rotation

A **ROTATION** is a transformation that turns a figure about a fixed point called the **center of rotation**. An object and its rotation are the same shape and size, but the figures may be turned in different directions. Rotations can occur in either a clockwise or a counterclockwise direction.

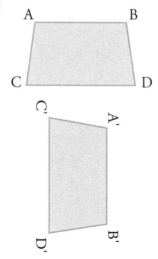

Rotations can be seen in wallpaper and art. A Ferris wheel is an example of rotation.

An object and its **REFLECTION** have the same shape and size, but the figures face in opposite directions.

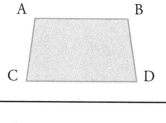

The line between the figures (where a mirror may be placed) is called the **line of reflection.** The distance from a point to the line of reflection is the same as the distance from the point's image to the line of reflection.

A **GLIDE REFLECTION** is a combination of a reflection and a translation.

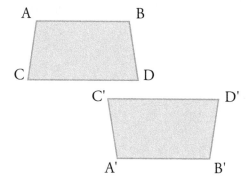

The Pythagorean Theorem

Given any right triangle *ABC* the square of the hypotenuse is equal to the sum of the squares of the other two sides.

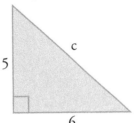

Hypotenuse (side opposite the 90° angle)

The Pythagorean Theorem states that $c^2 = a^2 + b^2$.

Example: Find the area and perimeter of a rectangle if its length is 12 inches and its diagonal is 15 inches.

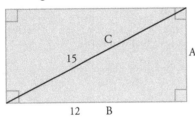

1. Draw and label sketch.
2. Since the height is still needed, use Pythagorean formula to find missing leg of the triangle.

$$A^2 + B^2 = C^2$$
$$A^2 + 12^2 = 15^2$$
$$A^2 = 15^2 - 12^2$$
$$A^2 = 81$$
$$A = 9$$

Now use this information to find the area and perimeter.

A = LW	P = 2(L + W)	1. Write formula.
A = (12)(9)	P = 2(12 + 9)	2. Substitute.
A = 108 in²	P = 42 inches	3. Solve.

Sample Test Question and Rationale

(Rigorous)

1. The owner of a rectangular piece of land 40 yards in length and 30 yards in width wants to divide it into two parts. She plans to join two opposite corners with a fence, as shown in the diagram below. The cost of the fence will be approximately $25 per linear foot. What is the estimated cost of the fence?

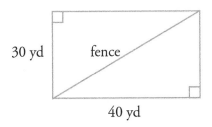

30 yd   fence

40 yd

A. $1,250

B. $62,500

C. $5,250

D. $3,750

Answer: D. $3,750

Find the length of the diagonal by using the Pythagorean Theorem. Let x be the length of the diagonal.

$$30^2 + 40^2 = x^2 \rightarrow$$
$$900 + 1600 = x^2$$

$$2500 = x^2 \rightarrow$$
$$\sqrt{2500} = \sqrt{x^2}$$

$$x = 50 \text{ yards}$$

Convert to feet.
$$\frac{50 \text{ yards}}{x \text{ feet}} = \frac{1 \text{ yard}}{3 \text{ feet}} \rightarrow 150 \text{ feet}$$

The fence costs $25.00 per linear foot, so the cost is (150 ft)($25) = $3750.

SKILL 12.4 Understand and apply theorems about circles

See Skill 12.1.

SKILL 12.5 Solve real-life and mathematical problems involving angle measure, area, surface area, and volume

See Skill 12.1.

Length is a measure of one dimension. Area is a measurement in two dimensions, represented by some form of the product of the two dimensions. Volume, as a three dimensional measurement, has its basis in the product of 3 dimensions. However, another way to compare these properties is to compare volume with area. A notion connecting area and volume is often referred to as "cross sectioning" or using "slices" to analyze the volume of a 3 dimensional solid.

Imagine that a right cylinder is cut into 1 inch slices.

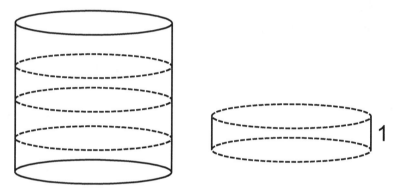

If the radius of the cylinder is r, then the area of the base, a circle, is $A = \pi r^2$. The volume of one slice is $A \bullet 1 = A$. If the cylinder is stacked with 4 cross sections, as shown in the example diagram, then the total volume equals the sum of the volume of each slice: $A + A + A + A = 4A$. This parallels the actual formula for the volume of a cylinder which is known to be $V = \pi r^2 h = Ah$ where A is the area of the base.

Example: Suppose a wedding cake is made with 3 square layers that are 9 inches on a side, 2 layers that are 6 inches on a side, and 1 layer that is 4 inches square. Each layer is 2 inches tall. Find the total volume of cake.

The area of the top slice is $4^2 = 16$, so its volume is $16(2) = 32$.
The area of one middle slice is $6^2 = 36$, so its volume is $36(2) = 72$.
The area of one lower slice is $9^2 = 81$, so its volume is $81(2) = 162$.

3 large layers represent a volume of $3(162) = 486$ in^2.
2 middle layers represent a volume of $2(72) = 144$ in^2.

The total volume, then, is $486 + 144 + 32 = 662$ in^2.

SKILL 12.7 Apply geometric concepts in modeling situations

See Skill 12.1.

COMPETENCY 13
STATISTICS AND PROBABILITY

SKILL Develop understanding of statistical variability
13.1

Quite often, the study of mathematics focuses intently on "getting the right answer" to a problem, whether it be an independent arithmetic problem like 8 – 15 = -7 or a word problem like "how much flour will be needed if the given recipe is doubled?" But the world of mathematics goes beyond the exactness of one solution for each problem. Instead, there are circumstances where numbers and patterns represent possibilities and trends. Statistics is the chapter of math that communicates this variability and representation.

When the question "how far is it from Chicago to Columbus?" is altered to "how far away does the average first grader think Chicago is from Columbus?" the answer changes from a specifically requested measurement to a representation of a child's abstract view of distance. The latter question provides opportunity for selection of participants, collection of data, and analysis of a variety of answers. The inquiry and its findings represent a statistical experiment.

SKILL Summarize and describe distributions
13.2

MEAN: the sum of a set of numbers divided by the number of items being averaged; also called the average

The arithmetic **MEAN** (or average) of a set of numbers is the *sum* of the numbers *divided by* the number of items being averaged.

Example: Find the mean. Round to the nearest tenth.
24.6, 57.3, 44.1, 39.8, 64.5
   The sum is 230.3 ÷ 5 = 46.06, rounded to 46.1

MEDIAN: the middle number when a set of numbers is arranged in order

The **MEDIAN** of a set of numbers is the middle number when the numbers are arranged in order. To calculate the median, we must arrange the terms in order. If there is an even number of terms, the median is the mean of the two middle terms.

Example: Find the median.

12, 14, 27, 3, 13, 7, 17, 12, 22, 6, 16

    Rearrange the terms from least to greatest.

    3, 6, 7, 12, 12, 13,14,16,17, 22, 27

    Since there are eleven numbers, the middle would be the sixth number, or 13.

The **MODE** of a set of numbers is the number that occurs with the greatest frequency. A set can have no mode if each term appears exactly one time. Similarly, there can also be more than one mode.

> **MODE** the number that occurs with the greatest frequency in a set of numbers

Example: Find the mode.

26, 15, 37, **26**, 35, **26**, 15

    15 appears twice, but 26 appears three times. Therefore, the mode is 26.

The **RANGE** of a set of numbers is the difference between the highest and lowest data value.

> **RANGE:** the difference between the highest and lowest data value in a set of numbers

Example: Given the ungrouped data below, calculate the mean and range.

15	22	28	25	34	38
18	25	30	33	19	23

Mean($\overline{x}$) = 25.8333333
Range: $38 - 15 = 23$

Mean, median and mode are measurements of central tendency, that is, their values show how evenly spread a set of data may or may not be. Often, the value for mean and median in a set of data can be very close, but that can be changed when a set of data contains outliers. Outliers are data values that are a noticeable extreme compared to most other values. Consider a set of data: 1, 2, 3, 4, 5, 98. Most of the data lies between 1 and 5 and 98 is an outlier. The median, at 3.5, represents most of the data, but the mean of 18.8 is significantly higher due to the outlier. Therefore a look at how the data is **distributed** can help many statistical interpretations.

A histogram (*see section IV B1*) is an example of a **discrete frequency distribution**. It can be used to represent discrete (data that falls within a set, finite sample space) as well as continuous data (data that can take on a continuous range of values, e.g. height) sorted in bins. A large data set of continuous data may also be represented using a **continuous frequency distribution**, which is essentially a histogram with very narrow bars. Below, a trend line has been added to the example histogram above. Notice that this approximates the most common continuous distribution, a normal or bell curve.

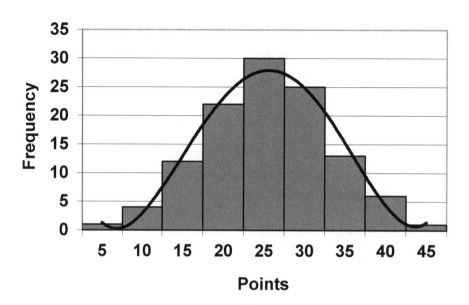

A **normal distribution** is symmetric with the mean equal to the median. The tails of the curve in both directions fall off rapidly. The spread of data is measured by the standard deviation.

Example: In the graph above, suppose the mean is 23 with a standard deviation of ☒4. What values are 3 standard deviations away from the mean?

The standard deviations are measured to the right and left. So 3 standard deviations to the right is $23 + 3(4) = 35$ while 3 standard deviations to the left is at $23 + 3(-4) = 11$

When the maximum of the curve appears closer to the left, the data is said to be "skewed right," or "positively skewed."

PERCENTILES: divide a set of data into 100 equal parts

PERCENTILES divide data into 100 equal parts. A person whose score falls in the 65th percentile has outperformed 65 percent of all those who took the test. This does not mean that the score was 65 out of 100, nor does it mean that 65 percent of the questions were answered correctly. It means that the person's grade was higher than 65 percent of all the other grades.

STANINES: divide the bell curve into nine sections

STANINES, or "standard nines," scores combine the understandability of percentages with the properties of the normal probability curve. Stanines divide the bell curve into nine sections, the largest of which stretches from the 40th to the 60th percentile and is the "Fifth Stanine" (the average of taking into account error possibilities).

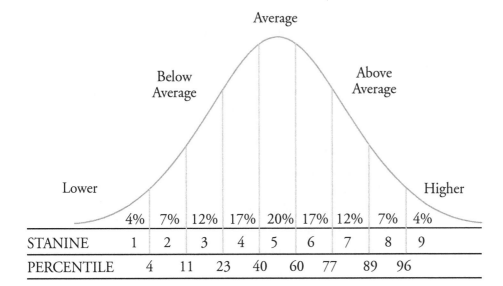

QUARTILES divide the data into four parts. First, find the median of the data set (Q2), then find the median of the upper (Q3) and lower (Q1) halves of the data set. If there are an odd number of values in the data set, include the median value in both halves when finding quartile values. For example, given the data set {1, 4, 9, 16, 25, 36, 49, 64, 81}, first find the median value, which is 25. This is the second quartile (Q2). Since there are an odd number of values in the data set (9), we include the median in both halves.

> **QUARTILES:** divide the data into four parts

To find the quartile values, we must find the medians of {1, 4, 9, 16, 25} and {25, 36, 49, 64, 81}. Since each of these subsets has an odd number of elements (5), we use the middle value. Thus, the first quartile value is 9 and the third quartile value is 49. If the data set has an even number of elements, average the middle two values. The quartile values are always either one of the data points or exactly halfway between two data points.

Example: Given the following set of data, find the percentile of the score 104.
70, 72, 82, 83, 84, 87, 100, 104, 108, 109, 110, 115

Find the percentage of scores below 104.

7/12 of the scores are less than 104. This is 58.333%; therefore, the score of 104 is in the 58th percentile.

Example: Find the first, second and third quartile for the data listed.
6, 7, 8, 9, 10, 12, 13, 14, 15, 16, 18, 23, 24, 25, 27, 29, 30, 33, 34, 37

Quartile 1: The first quartile is the median of the lower half of the data set, which is 11.

Quartile 2: The median of the data set is the second quartile, which is 17.

Quartile 3: The third quartile is the median of the upper half of the data set, which is 28.

Sample Test Questions and Rationale

(Average)

1. What is the mode of the data in the following sample?
   9, 10, 11, 9, 10, 11, 9, 13

   A. 9

   B. 9.5

   C. 10

   D. 11

   Answer: A. 9

   The mode is the number that occurs most frequently. Nine occurs three times, which is more times than the other numbers.

(Rigorous)

2. Mary did comparison shopping on her favorite brand of coffee. Over half of the stores priced the coffee at $1.70. Most of the remaining stores priced the coffee at $1.80, except for a few who charged $1.90. Which of the following statements is true about the distribution of prices?

   A. The mean and the mode are the same

   B. The mean is greater than the mode

   C. The mean is less than the mode

   D. The mean is less than the median

Answer: B. The mean is greater than the mode.

Over half the stores priced the coffee at $1.70, so this means that $1.70 is the mode. The mean would be slightly over $1.70 because other stores priced the coffee at over $1.70.

SKILL 13.3 Use random sampling to draw inferences about a population

A **TREND** line on a line graph shows the correlation between two sets of data. A trend may show positive correlation (both sets of data get bigger together), negative correlation (one set of data gets bigger while the other gets smaller), or no correlation.

An **INFERENCE** is a statement that is derived from reasoning. When reading a graph, inferences help us interpret the data that is being presented. From this information, a conclusion and even predictions about what the data actually mean are possible.

> **TREND:** line on a line graph that shows the correlation between two sets of data

> **INFERENCE:** a statement that is derived from reasoning

Example: Katherine and Tom were both doing poorly in math class. Their teacher had a conference with each of them in November. The following graph shows their math test scores during the school year.

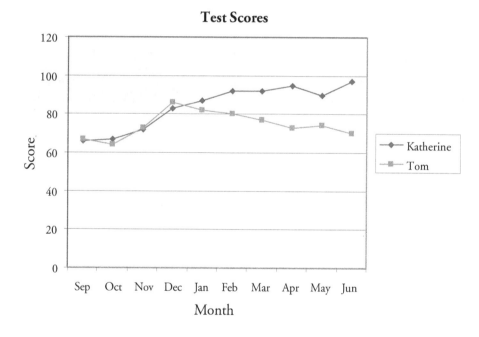

Test Scores

What kind of trend does this graph show?

This graph shows that there is a positive trend in Katherine's test scores and a negative trend in Tom's test scores.

What inferences can you make from this graph?

We can infer that Katherine's test scores rose steadily after November. Tom's test scores spiked in December but then began to fall again and became negatively trended.

What conclusion can you draw based upon this graph?

> We can conclude that Katherine took her teacher's meeting seriously and began to study in order to do better on the exams. It seems as though Tom tried harder for a bit, but his test scores eventually slipped back down to the level at which he began.

The analysis above focuses on just one year's worth of data for two people, but many studies encompass far more participants and values. When selecting data to represent a large population, it is unreasonable to use all values available. There would simply be too much data to collect and to work with. Instead, a carefully built, random sample space will assure the most reasonable representation without a glut of data. For instance, if a study is to measure the amount of money a high school student spends on entertainment each month, participants can be randomly selected but should still fairly represent each grade and gender.

SKILL 13.4 Investigate chance processes and develop, use, and evaluate probability models

SAMPLE SPACE: a list of all possible outcomes of an experiment

PROBABILITY: measures the chance of an event occurring

In probability, a **SAMPLE SPACE** is a list of all possible outcomes of an experiment. For example, the sample space of tossing two coins is the set {HH, HT, TT, TH}; the sample space of rolling a six-sided die is the set {1, 2, 3, 4, 5, 6}; and the sample space of measuring the height of students in a class is the set of all real numbers {R}. **PROBABILITY** measures the chance of an event occurring. The probability of an event that *must* occur, a certain event, is **1**. When no outcome is favorable, the probability of an impossible event is **0**.

$$P(\text{event}) = \frac{\text{number of favorable outcomes}}{\text{number of possible outcomes}}$$

Example: Given one die with faces numbered 1–6, the probability of tossing an even number on one throw of the die is $\frac{3}{6}$ or $\frac{1}{2}$, since there are three favorable outcomes (even faces) and six possible outcomes (faces).

Example: If we roll a fair die:
- A. Find the probability of rolling an even number.
- B. Find the probability of rolling a number less than 3.

A. The sample space is

S ={1, 2, 3, 4, 5, 6}, and the event representing even numbers is

E ={2, 4, 6}.

Hence, the probability of rolling an even number is

$$p(E) = \frac{n(E)}{n(S)} = \frac{3}{6} = \frac{1}{2} \text{ or } 0.5$$

B. We represent the event of rolling a number less than 3 by

A = {1, 2}

Hence, the probability of rolling a number less than 3 is

$$p(A) = \frac{n(A)}{n(S)} = \frac{2}{6} = \frac{1}{3} \text{ or } 0.33$$

Example: A class has thirty students. Out of the thirty students, twenty-four are males. Assuming all the students have the same chance of being selected, find the probability of selecting a female. (Only one person is selected.)

The number of females in the class is

30 − 24 = 6

Hence, the probability of selecting a female is

$$p(female) = \frac{6}{30} = \frac{1}{5} \text{ or } 0.2$$

Independent Events

If A and B are **INDEPENDENT EVENTS**, then the outcome of event A does not affect the outcome of event B, and vice versa. We use the multiplication rule to find joint probability.

P(A and B) = P(A) × P(B)

INDEPENDENT EVENTS: when the outcome of event A does not affect the outcome of event B, and vice versa

Example: The probability that a patient is allergic to aspirin is 0.30. If the probability of a patient having a window in his or her room is 0.40, find the probability that the patient is allergic to aspirin and has a window in his or her room.

Defining the events:

A = the patient is allergic to aspirin

B = the patient has a window in his or her room

Events A and B are independent; hence

p(A and B) = p(A) × p(B)

= (0.30) (0.40)

= 0.12 or 12%

Example: Given a jar containing 10 marbles—3 red, 5 black, and 2 white— what is the probability of drawing a red marble and then a white marble if the marble is returned to the jar after choosing?

$3/10 \times 2/10 = 6/100 = 3/50$

Dependent Events

DEPENDENT EVENTS:
when the outcome of event A affects the outcome of event B

When the outcome of the first event affects the outcome of the second event, the events are **DEPENDENT EVENTS**. Any two events that are not independent are dependent. This is also known as conditional probability.

Probability of (A and B) = P(A) × P(B given A)

Example: Two cards are drawn from a deck of 52 cards without replacement; that is, the first card is not returned to the deck before the second card is drawn. What is the probability of drawing a diamond?

A = drawing a diamond first
B = drawing a diamond second
P(A) = drawing a diamond first
P(B) = drawing a diamond second
P(A) = 13/52 = ¼   P(B) = 12/52 = 4/17
P(A and B) = ¼ × 4/17 = 1/17

Example: A class of ten students consists of six males and four females. If two students are selected to represent the class, find the probability that:

A. The first is a male and the second is a female
B. The first is a female and the second is a male
C. Both are females
D. Both are males

Define the events:

F = a female is selected to represent the class
M = a male is selected to represent the class
F/M = a female is selected after a male has been selected
M/F = a male is selected after a female has been selected

A. Since F and M are dependent events, it follows that
P(M and F) = P(M) · P(F/M)
$= \frac{6}{10} \times \frac{4}{9} = \frac{3}{5} \times \frac{4}{9} = \frac{12}{45}$
P(F/M) = instead of because the selection of a male first changed the sample space from ten to nine students.

B. P(F and M) = P(F) · P(M/F)
$= \frac{4}{10} \times \frac{6}{9} = \frac{2}{5} \times \frac{2}{3} = \frac{4}{15}$

C. P(both are females) = P(F and F) = P(F) · P(F/F)

$$= \frac{4}{10} \times \frac{3}{9} = \frac{2}{5} \times \frac{1}{3} = \frac{2}{15}$$

D. $P(\text{both are males}) = P(M \text{ and } M) = P(M) \cdot P(M/M)$

$$= \frac{6}{10} \times \frac{5}{9} = \frac{30}{90} = \frac{1}{3}$$

Sample Test Question and Rationale

(Rigorous)

1. The table below shows the distribution of majors for a group of college students.

Major	Proportion of students
Mathematics	0.32
Photography	0.26
Journalism	0.19
Engineering	0.21
Criminal Law	0.02

If it is known that a student chosen at random is not majoring in mathematics or engineering, what is the probability that the student is majoring in journalism?

A. 0.19

B. 0.36

C. 0.40

D. 0.81

Answer: C. 0.40

The proportion of students majoring in math or engineering is $0.32 + 0.21 = 0.53$. This means that the proportion of students NOT majoring in math or engineering is $1.00 - 0.53 = 0.47$. The proportion of students majoring in journalism out of those not majoring in math or engineering is $\frac{0.19}{0.47} = 0.404$.

We can use a table, graph, or rule to show a relationship between two quantities. In this example, the rule $y = 9x$ describes the relationship between the total amount earned, y, and the total number of $9 sunglasses sold, x.

A table using these data would appear as:

number of sunglasses sold	1	5	10	15
total dollars earned	9	45	90	135

Each (x, y) relationship between a pair of values is called a **coordinate pair** and can be plotted on a graph. The coordinate pairs (1, 9), (5, 45), (10, 90), and (15,135), are plotted on the graph below.

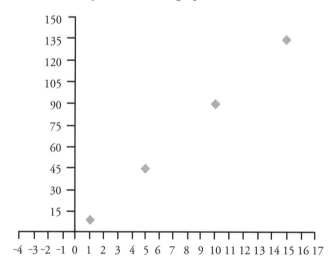

LINEAR RELATIONSHIP: is one in which two quantities are proportional to each other

The graph shows a linear relationship. A **LINEAR RELATIONSHIP** is one in which two quantities are proportional to each other. Doubling x also doubles y. On a graph, a straight line depicts a linear relationship.

We can analyze the function or relationship between two quantities to determine how one quantity depends on the other. For example, the function below shows a relationship between y and x:

$$y = 2x + 1$$

The function, $y = 2x + 1$, is written as a symbolic rule. The table below shows the same relationship:

x	0	2	3	6	9
y	1	5	7	13	19

We can write this relationship in words by saying "the value of y is equal to 2 times the value of x, plus 1." We can show this relationship on a graph by plotting given points such as the ones shown in the table above.

Functions

One way to describe a function is as a process in which one or more numbers are input into an imaginary machine that produces another number as the output. If 5 is the input, x, into a machine with a process of $x + 1$, then the output, y, will equal 6.

In real-life situations, we can describe such relationships mathematically. The function $y = x + 1$ can be used to describe the idea that people age 1 year on each birthday. To describe the relationship in which a person's monthly medical costs are six times a person's age, we could write $y = 6x$. We can use this function to predict the monthly cost of medical care. A 20-year-old person would spend $120 per month ($120 = 20 \cdot 6$). An 80-year-old person would spend $480 per month ($480 = 80 \cdot 6$). Therefore, we could analyze the relationship and say, "As a person gets older, medical costs increase $6.00 each year."

Example: What is the equation that expresses the relationship between x and y in the table below?

x	y
0	3
1	5
2	7
3	9
4	11
5	13

A. $y = x + 2$

B. $y = \frac{1}{3}x + 3$

C. $y = 2x + 3$

D. $y = 2x - 3$

Solve by plugging in the values of x and y into the equations to see if they work. The answer is C because it is the only equation for which the values of x and y are correct.

Example: For the following set of test scores, what kind of graph would be most appropriate?

	Test 1	Test 2	Test 3	Test 4	Test 5
Evans, Tim	75	66	80	85	97
Miller, Julie	94	93	88	97	98
Thomas, Randy	81	86	88	87	90

A **bar graph** would be most appropriate because the data is quantitative—each student has taken five tests. A bar graph will show the comparison of each student's own test scores, as well as the comparison among the students' test scores.

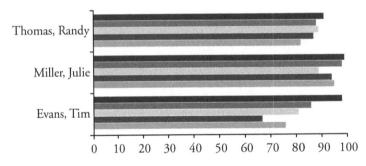

Circle graphs show the relationships of various parts to each other and to the whole. Percents are used to create circle graphs.

Example: Julie spends 8 hours each day in school, 2 hours doing homework, 1 hour eating dinner, 2 hours watching television, 10 hours sleeping, and the rest of the time doing other things.

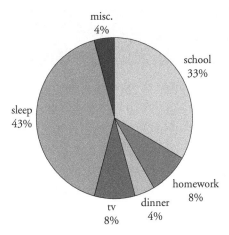

Line graphs show trends in two variables, often over a period.

Example: For the following information about average temperature, what is the most appropriate type of graph?

Month	Jan	Feb	Mar	Apr	May	Jun	Jul	Aug	Sep	Oct	Nov	Dec
Temp (°F)	29	30	39	48	58	68	74	72	65	55	45	34

Sample Test Question and Rationale

(Rigorous)

1. What is the equation that expresses the relationship between x and y in the table below?

x	y
−2	4
−1	2
0	−2
1	−5

2	−8

A. $y = -x - 2$

B. $y = -3x - 2$

C. $y = 3x - 2$

D. $y = x - 1$

Answer: B. $y = -3x - 2$

Solve by plugging the values of x and y into the equations to see if they work. The answer is B because it is the only equation for which the values of x and y are correct.

To make a **bar graph** or a **pictograph**, we determine the scale for the graph. Then we determine the length of each bar on the graph or determine the number of pictures needed to represent each item of information. We need to be sure to include an explanation of the scale in the legend.

Pictographs can be misleading, especially if drawn to represent 3-dimensional objects. If two or more dimensions are changed in reflecting ratio, the overall visual effect can be misinterpreted. Bar and line graphs can be misleading if the scales are changed. For example, using relatively small scale increments for large numbers will make the comparison differencesseem much greater than if larger-scale increments are used. Circle graphs, or pie charts, are excellent for comparing relative amounts; however, they cannot be used to represent absolute amounts, and if interpreted as such, they are misleading.

Example: A class had the following grades: 4 As, 9 Bs, 8 Cs, 1 D, 3 Fs. Graph these on a pictograph and a bar graph.

Grade	Number of Students
A	☺☺☺☺
B	☺☺☺☺☺☺☺☺☺
C	☺☺☺☺☺☺☺☺
D	☺
F	☺☺☺

Bar graph

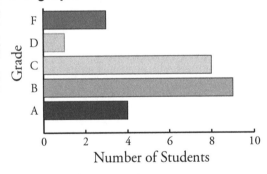

To make a **line graph**, we determine appropriate scales for both the vertical and horizontal axes (based on the information we are graphing). Describe what each axis represents and mark the scale periodically on each axis. Graph the individual points of the graph and connect the points on the graph from left to right.

Example: Graph the following information using a line graph.

THE NUMBER OF NATIONAL MERIT FINALISTS PER SCHOOL YEAR						
YEAR	**90–91**	**91–92**	**92–93**	**93–94**	**94–95**	**95–96**
Central	3	5	1	4	6	8
Wilson	4	2	3	2	3	2

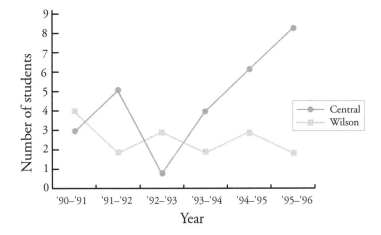

To make a **circle graph,** we total all the information that is to be included on the graph. We then determine the central angle to be used for each sector of the graph using the following formula:

$$\frac{\text{information}}{\text{total information}} \times 360° = \text{degrees in central} \sphericalangle$$

We lay out the central angles to these sizes, label each section, and include its percent.

Example: Graph the following information on a circle graph

Monthly expenses:
Rent, $400
Food, $150
Utilities, $75
Clothes, $75
Church, $100
Misc., $200

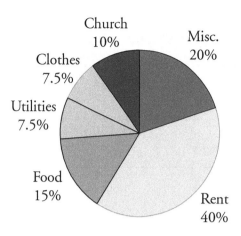

Scatter plots compare two characteristics of the same group of things or people and usually consist of a large body of data. They show how much one variable affects another. The relationship between the two variables is their CORRELATION. The closer the data points come to forming a straight line when plotted, the closer the correlation.

CORRELATION: the relationship between the two variables in a scatter plot

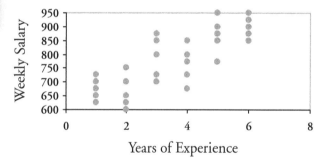

Stem-and-leaf plots are visually similar to line plots. The stems are the digits in the greatest place value of the data values, and the leaves are the digits in the next greatest place value. Stem-and-leaf plots are best suited for small sets of data and are especially useful for comparing two sets of data. The following is an example using test scores:

4	9
5	4 9
6	1 2 3 4 6 7 8 8
7	0 3 4 6 6 6 7 7 7 8 8 8 8
8	3 5 5 7 8
9	0 0 3 4 5
10	0 0

FREQUENCY OF THE INTERVAL.

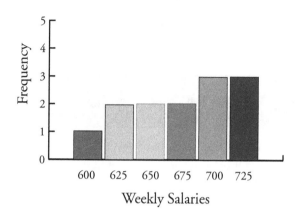

Weekly Salaries

> **FREQUENCY OF THE INTERVAL:** the number of data values in any interval

---

Sample Test Questions and Rationale

(Easy)

1. **The following chart shows the yearly average number of international tourists visiting Palm Beach for 1990–1994. How many more international tourists visited Palm Beach in 1994 than in 1991?**

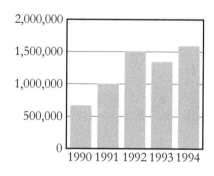

A. 100,000

B. 600,000

C. 1,600,000

D. 8,000,000

Answer: B. 600,000

The number of tourists in 1991 was 1,000,000 and the number in 1994 was 1,600,000. Subtract to get a difference of 600,000.

(Easy)

2. **Consider the graph of the distribution of the length of time it took individuals to complete an employment form.**

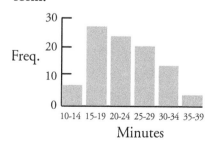

Minutes

Approximately how many individuals took less than 15 minutes to complete the employment form?

A. 35

B. 28

C. 7

D. 4

Answer: C. 7

According to the chart, the number of people who took under 15 minutes is 7.

SKILL
13.7
Interpret linear models

See Skill 13.5.

SKILL
13.8
Understand and evaluate random processes underlying statistical experiments

We use histograms to summarize information from large sets of data that we can naturally group into intervals. The vertical axis indicates FREQUENCY (the number of times any particular data value occurs), and the horizontal axis indicates data values or ranges of data values. The number of data values in any interval is the experiment's result.

FREQUENCY : the number of times any particular data value occurs

Sample size and **randomization** are two important characteristics of a data set. If only a small quantity of data is collected, the results may not fully represent a situation. Usually, a larger sample size better characterizes a situation; trends in the data will more reliably predict future data results. It is also important that the data has been collected randomly. For instance, if people are to be polled for their opinion on a topic, it is best to randomly choose participants from a population rather than letting the candidates decide on their own to participate.

Once a set of data has been collected, it should be inspected for trends and variations. A set of numbers, for example, can be clustered around a common point, but a few values may be quantitatively distanced from the majority. These remote values can be considered **outliers** and can sometimes be excluded from the data analysis. If the outliers are kept in the data set, their influence on trends and predictions should be acknowledged.

Example: The following data represents prices, in dollars, for a gallon of milk at local grocery stores: 2.99, 3.75, 2.50, 2.75, 3.50, 1.50. Find the average price of a gallon of milk.

The average price of milk, based on this set of data is $\frac{16.99}{6}$ = \$2.83. However, if the outlier \$1.50 is excluded, the mean rises to $\frac{15.49}{5}$ = \$3.10. If that low outlier is a temporary sale price, then its influence on the data set may not be fair and exclusion from the calculation gives a truer representation of the average price of a gallon of milk.

When displaying or interpreting data in a graph or table, attention should be given to the spread of the data, as certain presentation conditions can affect the interpretation of results.

Compare the two graphs below. Graph (1) shows two trials having seemingly similar results. But Graph (2), with a different scale on the y axis, shows more clearly how these two trials differ.

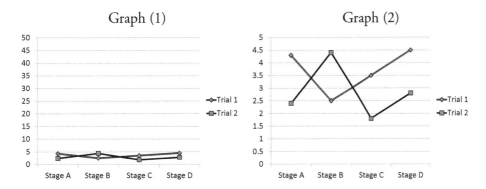

Conclusions should be drawn appropriately, based on the nature of the data.

SKILL **Use probability to evaluate outcomes of decisions**
13.9

See Skill 13.4.

SAMPLE TEST

MATHEMATICS

1. $-9\frac{1}{4} \;\square\; -8\frac{2}{3}$

   A. $=$

   B. $<$

   C. $>$

   D. $\leq$

2. $0.74 =$

   A. $\frac{74}{100}$

   B. 7.4%

   C. $\frac{33}{50}$

   D. $\frac{74}{10}$

3. $(3 \times 9)^4$

   A. $(3 \times 9)(3 \times 9)(27 \times 27)$

   B. $(3 \times 9) + (3 \times 9)$

   C. (12×36)

   D. $(3 \times 9) + (3 \times 9) + (3 \times 9) + (3 \times 9)$

4. $(-2.1 \times 10^4)(4.2 \times 10^{-5}) =$

   A. 8.82

   B. -8.82

   C. -0.882

   D. 0.882

5. $\frac{2^{10}}{2^5} =$

   A. 2^2

   B. 2^5

   C. 2^{50}

   D. 2

6. Choose the expression that is not equivalent to $5x + 3y + 15z$.

   A. $5(x + 3z) + 3y$

   B. $3(x + y + 5z)$

   C. $3y + 5(x + 3z)$

   D. $5x + 3(y + 5z)$

7. Choose the statement that is true for all real numbers.

   A. $a = 0, b \; 0$, then $\frac{a}{b} =$ undefined.

   B. $-(a + (-a)) = 2a$

   C. $2(ab) = -2(a)b$

   D. $-a(b + 1) = ab - a$

8. What is the greatest. common factor of 16, 28, and 36?

   A. 2

   B. 4

   C. 8

   D. 16

9. $\left(\frac{-4}{9}\right) + \left(\frac{-7}{10}\right) =$

   A. $\frac{23}{90}$

   B. $\frac{-23}{90}$

   C. $\frac{103}{90}$

   D. $\frac{-103}{90}$

10. $(5.6) \times (-0.11) =$

    A. -0.616

    B. 0.616

    C. -6.110

    D. 6.110

1. $\dfrac{7}{9} + \dfrac{1}{3} \div \dfrac{2}{3} =$

    A. $\dfrac{5}{3}$

    B. $\dfrac{3}{2}$

    C. 2

    D. $\dfrac{23}{18}$

2. $4\dfrac{2}{9} \times \dfrac{7}{10}$

    A. $4\dfrac{9}{10}$

    B. $\dfrac{266}{90}$

    C. $2\dfrac{43}{45}$

    D. $2\dfrac{6}{20}$

3. Round $1\dfrac{13}{16}$ of an inch to the nearest quarter of an inch.

    A. $1\dfrac{1}{4}$ inch

    B. $1\dfrac{5}{8}$ inch

    C. $1\dfrac{3}{4}$. inch

    D. 2 inches

4. It takes 5 equally skilled workers 9 hours to shingle Mr. Joe's roof. Let t be the time required for only 3 of these workers to do the same job. Select the correct statement of the given condition.

    A. $\dfrac{3}{5} = \dfrac{9}{t}$

    B. $\dfrac{9}{5} = \dfrac{3}{t}$

    C. $\dfrac{5}{9} = \dfrac{3}{t}$

    D. $\dfrac{14}{9} = \dfrac{t}{5}$

5. 303 is what percent of 600?

    A. 0.505%

    B. 5.05%

    C. 505%

    D. 50.5%

6. A restaurant employs 465 people. There are 280 waiters and 185 cooks. If 168 waiters and 85 cooks receive pay raises, what percent of the waiters will receive a pay raise?

    A. 36.13%

    B. 60%

    C. 60.22%

    D. 40%

7. In a sample of 40 full-time employees at a particular company, 35 were also holding down a part-time job requiring at least 10 hours/week. If this proportion holds for the entire company of 25,000 employees, how many full-time employees at this company are actually holding down a part-time job of at least 10 hours per week?

    A. 714

    B. 625

    C. 21,875

    D. 28,571

8. An item that sells for $375 is put on sale for $120. What is the percent of decrease?

    A. 25%

    B. 28%

    C. 68%

    D. 34%

1. **Sets A, B, C, and U are related as shown in the diagram.**

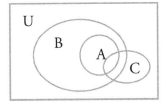

Which of the following is true, assuming not one of the six regions is empty?

A. Any element that is a member of set B is also a member of set A

B. No element is a member of all three sets A, B, and C

C. Any element that is a member of set U is also a member of set B

D. None of the above statements is true

2. **Select the statement that is the negation of the statement "If the weather is cold, then the soccer game will be played."**

A. If the weather is not cold, then the soccer game will be played

B. The weather is cold and the soccer game was not played

C. If the soccer game is played, then the weather is not cold

D. The weather is cold and the soccer game will be played

3. **Select the statement below that is NOT logically equivalent to "If Mary works late, then Bill will prepare lunch."**

A. Bill prepares lunch or Mary does not work late

B. If Bill does not prepare lunch, then Mary did not work late

C. If Bill prepares lunch, then Mary works late

D. Mary does not work late or Bill prepares lunch

4. **Given that:**
I. No athletes are weak.
II. All football players are athletes.
Determine which conclusion can be logically deduced.

A. Some football players are weak

B. All football players are weak

C. No football player is weak

D. None of the above is true

5. **Study the information given below. If a logical conclusion is given, select that conclusion.**
Bob eats donuts, or he eats yogurt. If Bob eats yogurt, then he is healthy. If Bob is healthy, then he can run the marathon. Bob does not eat yogurt.

A. Bob does not eat donuts

B. Bob is healthy

C. If Bob runs the Marathon, then he eats yogurt

D. None of the above is warranted

1. Select the rule of logical equivalence that directly (in one step) transforms statement (I) into statement (II).
   I. Not all the students have books.
   II. Some students do not have books.

   A. "If p, then q" is equivalent to "if not q, then p"

   B. "Not all are p" is equivalent to "some are not p"

   C. "Not q" is equivalent to "p"

   D. "All are not p" is equivalent to "none is p"

2. **All of the following arguments have true conclusions, but one of the arguments is not valid. Select the argument that is not valid.**

   A. All sea stars are Echinoderms, and all echinoderms are marine; therefore, all sea stars are marine.

   B. All spiders are dangerous. The black widow is dangerous. Therefore, the black widow is a spider.

   C. All crocodiles are amphibians, and all amphibians breathe by lungs, gill, or skin; therefore, all crocodiles breathe by lungs, gill, or skin.

   D. All kids have hats, and all boys are kids; therefore, all boys have hats.

3. **If $4x - (3 - x) = 7(x - 3) + 10$, then**

   A. $x = 8$

   B. $x = -8$

   C. $x = 4$

   D. $x = -4$

4. For each of the statements below, determine whether $x = \frac{1}{6}$ is a solution.
   I. $6x \le 4x^2 + 2$
   II. $10x + 1 = 3(4x - 3)$
   III. $|x - 1| = x$

   A. I, II, and III

   B. I and III only

   C. I only

   D. III only

5. **Given $f(x) = (x)^3 - 3(x)^2 + 5$, find $f(-2)$.**

   A. 15

   B. –15

   C. 25

   D. –25

6. **Choose the equation that is equivalent to the following: $\frac{3x}{5} - 5 = 5x$**

   A. $3x - 25 = 25x$

   B. $x - \frac{25}{3} = 25x$

   C. $6x - 50 = 75x$

   D. $x + 25 = 25x$

7. **Solve for $3x - \frac{2}{3} = \frac{5x}{2} + 2$**

   A. $5\frac{1}{3}$

   B. $\frac{17}{3}$

   C. 2

   D. $\frac{16}{2}$

1. Two mathematics classes have a total of 410 students. The 8:00 a.m. class has 40 more than the 10:00 a.m. class. How many students are in the 10:00 a.m. class?

    A. 123.3

    B. 370

    C. 185

    D. 330

2. For the following statements:
    I. All parallelograms are rectangles.
    II. Some rhombuses are squares.
    III. All parallelograms are rhombuses.

    A. All statements are correct

    B. All statements are incorrect

    C. Only II and III are correct

    D. Only II is correct

3. What type of triangle is △ ABC?

    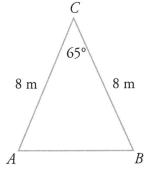

    A. Right

    B. Equilateral

    C. Scalene

    D. Isosceles

4. What is the area of a square whose side is 13 feet?

    A. 169 feet

    B. 169 square feet

    C. 52 feet

    D. 52 square feet

5. The trunk of a tree has a 2.1 meter radius. What is the trunk's circumference?

    A. 2.1 π square meters

    B. 4.2 π meters

    C. 2.1 π meters

    D. 4.2 π square meters

6. The figure below shows a running track in the shape of a rectangle with semicircles at each end.

    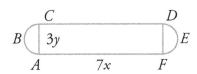

    Calculate the distance around the track.

    A. 6πy + 14x

    B. 3πy + 7x

    C. 6πy + 7x

    D. 3πy + 14x

1. What is the area of this triangle?

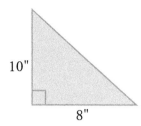

10"

8"

A. 80 square inches

B. 20 square inches

C. 40 square inches

D. 30 square inches

2. Given the formula $d = rt$, (where $d =$ distance, $r =$ rate, and $t =$ time), calculate the time required for a vehicle to travel 585 miles at a rate of 65 miles per hour.

A. 8.5 hours

B. 6.5 hours

C. 9.5 hours

D. 9 hours

3. The price of gas is $3.27 per gallon. Your tank holds 15 gallons of gas. You are using two tanks a week. How much will you save weekly if the price of gas goes down to $2.30 per gallon?

A. $26.00

B. $29.00

C. $15.00

D. $17.00

4. A car gets 25.36 miles per gallon. The car has been driven 83,310 miles. What is a reasonable estimate for the number of gallons of gas used?

A. 2,087 gallons

B. 3,000 gallons

C. 1,800 gallons

D. 164 gallons

5. Study figures A, B, C, and D. Select the letter for which all triangles are similar.

A.

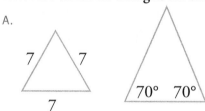

7   7

7

70° 70°

B.

C.

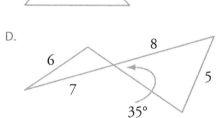

D.

8

6

5

7

35°

1. The owner of a rectangular piece of land 40 yards in length and 30 yards in width wants to divide it into two parts. She plans to join two opposite corners with a fence, as shown in the diagram below. The cost of the fence will be approximately $25 per linear foot. What is the estimated cost of the fence?

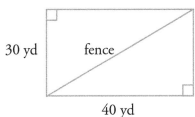

30 yd   fence

40 yd

A. $1,250

B. $62,500

C. $5,250

D. $3,750

2. What measure could be used to report the distance traveled in walking around a track?

A. Degrees

B. Square meters

C. Kilometers

D. Cubic feet

3. What unit of measurement would describe the spread of a forest fire in a unit time?

A. 10 square yards per second

B. 10 yards per minute

C. 10 feet per hour

D. 10 cubic feet per hour

4. The following chart shows the yearly average number of international tourists visiting Palm Beach for 1990–1994. How many more international tourists visited Palm Beach in 1994 than in 1991?

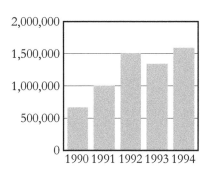

A. 100,000

B. 600,000

C. 1,600,000

D. 8,000,000

5. Consider the graph of the distribution of the length of time it took individuals to complete an employment form.

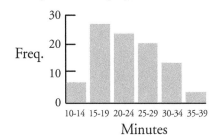

Minutes

Approximately how many individuals took less than 15 minutes to complete the employment form?

A. 35

B. 28

C. 7

D. 4

ANSWER KEY				
1. B	13. C	24. B	35. B	46. C
2. A	14. A	25. B	36. D	47. B
3. A	15. D	26. C	37. C	48. A
4. C	16. B	27. C	38. D	49. B
5. B	17. C	28. B	39. B	50. C
6. B	18. C	29. A	40. B	51. B
7. A	19. D	30. A	41. B	52. D
8. B	20. A	31. C	42. D	53. A
9. D	21. C	32. D	43. C	54. A
10. A	22. C	33. D	44. A	55. B
11. D	23. D	34. B	45. B	56. C
12. C				

Interested in dual certification?

XAMonline offers over 30 Praxis study guides which are aligned to current standards and provide a comprehensive review of the core test content. Want certification success on your first exam? Trust XAMonline's study guides to help you succeed!

Praxis Series:

- **Middle School English Language Arts**
  9781607873457
- **English to Speakers of Other Languages**
  9781607876267
- **Principles of Learning and Teaching 7-12**
  9781607876250
- **Principles of Learning and Teaching K-6**
  9781607876243
- **School Guidance and Counseling**
  9781607870678
- **Social Studies: Content Knowledge**
  9781607874652
- **Special Education 0354/5354, 5383, 0543/5543 [Book and Online]**
  9781607874157
- **Special Education: Core Knowledge and Applications**
  9781607876281
- **Educational Leadership: Administration and Supervision**
  9781607873297
- **Elementary Education: Multiple Subjects**
  9781607874607

- **English Arts: Content Knowledge**
  9781607876274
- **Mathematics: Content Knowledge**
  9781607876298
- **Middle School Mathematics**
  9781607876304
- **Middle School Social Studies**
  9781607873440
- **Middle School Science**
  9781607873433
- **ParaPro Assessment**
  9781607870524
- **Physical Education**
  9781607870715
- **Chemistry**
  9781581976915
- **General Science**
  9781607873495
- **Social Studies**
  9781607873426
- **Biology**
  9781607873464
- **Spanish**
  9781607870869

Don't see your test? Visit our website: www.xamonline.com

XAMonline.com

9 781607 874584